THE TRAILBLAZERS

No. 2.

Great Falls of Columbia River
laid down by a scale of 200 yards to the inch

E. nee. sher Nation

River

Sand bar

Portage of 1200 yards

37 feet 8 in fall

THE OLD WEST

THE TRAILBLAZERS

By the Editors of

TIME-LIFE BOOKS

with text by

Bil Gilbert

TIME-LIFE BOOKS / ALEXANDRIA, VIRGINIA

Time-Life Books Inc.
is a wholly owned subsidiary of
TIME INCORPORATED

Founder: Henry R. Luce 1898-1967

Editor-in-Chief: Hedley Donovan
Chairman of the Board: Andrew Heiskell
President: James R. Shepley
Vice Chairmen: Roy E. Larsen, Arthur Temple
Corporate Editors: Ralph Graves,
Henry Anatole Grunwald

TIME-LIFE BOOKS INC.

Managing Editor: Jerry Korn
Executive Editor: David Maness
Assistant Managing Editors: Dale M. Brown,
Martin Mann, John Paul Porter
Art Director: Tom Suzuki
Chief of Research: David L. Harrison
Director of Photography: Robert G. Mason
Planning Director: Thomas Flaherty (acting)
Senior Text Editor: Diana Hirsh
Assistant Art Director: Arnold C. Holeywell
Assistant Chief of Research: Carolyn L. Sackett
Assistant Director of Photography: Dolores A. Littles

Chairman: Joan D. Manley
President: John D. McSweeney
Executive Vice Presidents: Carl G. Jaeger,
John Steven Maxwell, David J. Walsh
Vice Presidents: Peter G. Barnes (Comptroller),
Nicholas Benton (Public Relations),
John L. Canova (Sales), Herbert Sorkin
(Production), Paul R. Stewart (Promotion)
Personnel Director: Beatrice T. Dobie
Consumer Affairs Director: Carol Flaumenhaft

THE OLD WEST

EDITORIAL STAFF FOR "THE TRAILBLAZERS"
Editor: George Constable
Picture Editors: Adrian Allen, Carole Kismaric
Text Editors: Jay Brennan, William Frankel
Designer: Herbert H. Quarmby
Staff Writers: Erik Amfitheatrof, Michael Drons,
Sam Halper, Suzanne Seixas,
Timberlake Wertenbaker, Peter Wood
Chief Researcher: Joan Mebane
Researchers: Elizabeth Dagenhardt, Angela Dews,
Diana Edkins, Mary Leverty, Mary Kay Moran,
Ann Morrison, Wendy Rieder, Kathy Slate,
Jane Sugden, John Conrad Weiser

EDITORIAL PRODUCTION
Production Editor: Douglas B. Graham
Operations Manager: Gennaro C. Esposito
Assistant Production Editor: Feliciano Madrid
Quality Control: Robert L. Young (director),
James J. Cox (assistant),
Michael G. Wight (associate)
Art Coordinator: Anne B. Landry
Copy Staff: Susan B. Galloway (chief),
Ricki Tarlow, Florence Keith, Celia Beattie
Picture Department: Barbara S. Simon
Traffic: Jeanne Potter

THE AUTHOR: Bil Gilbert has spent much of his adult life roaming the land across which early Western explorers carved their trails. He has run white-water rapids and backpacked in Arizona, Idaho and the High Sierra country, and he interrupted the writing of *The Trailblazers* to round up wild horses with the Sioux in South Dakota. A freelance writer specializing in natural history and the American past, Gilbert has published four books and contributed to such magazines as SPORTS ILLUSTRATED and *Esquire*.

THE COVER: The exploration of the Old West was partly haphazard, partly achieved through careful planning. Thus, the famous mountain men, exemplified in the 1844 cover portrait of *The Trapper* by Charles Deas, thought of themselves as beaver hunters, not explorers — although in their search for beaver water in the Rockies, they accumulated a remarkable body of geographic lore. By contrast, the meticulous frontispiece map of a part of the Columbia River basin, drawn in 1805 by William Clark as one of the records of the Lewis and Clark expedition, marks the beginning of seven decades of systematic topographic and scientific work in the lands beyond the Mississippi.

CORRESPONDENTS: Elisabeth Kraemer (Bonn); Margot Hapgood, Dorothy Bacon (London); Susan Jonas, Lucy T. Voulgaris (New York); Maria Vincenza Aloisi, Josephine du Brusle (Paris); Ann Natanson (Rome). Valuable assistance was also provided by: Bernard Diederich, James Budd (Mexico City); Carolyn T. Chubet, Miriam Hsia (New York); Traudl Lessing (Vienna).

Other Publications:

THE SEAFARERS
THE ENCYCLOPEDIA OF COLLECTIBLES
THE GREAT CITIES
WORLD WAR II
HOME REPAIR AND IMPROVEMENT
THE WORLD'S WILD PLACES
THE TIME-LIFE LIBRARY OF BOATING
HUMAN BEHAVIOR
THE ART OF SEWING
THE EMERGENCE OF MAN
THE AMERICAN WILDERNESS
THE TIME-LIFE ENCYCLOPEDIA OF GARDENING
LIFE LIBRARY OF PHOTOGRAPHY
THIS FABULOUS CENTURY
FOODS OF THE WORLD
TIME-LIFE LIBRARY OF AMERICA
TIME-LIFE LIBRARY OF ART
GREAT AGES OF MAN
LIFE SCIENCE LIBRARY
THE LIFE HISTORY OF THE UNITED STATES
TIME READING PROGRAM
LIFE NATURE LIBRARY
LIFE WORLD LIBRARY
FAMILY LIBRARY:
    HOW THINGS WORK IN YOUR HOME
    THE TIME-LIFE BOOK OF THE FAMILY CAR
    THE TIME-LIFE FAMILY LEGAL GUIDE
    THE TIME-LIFE BOOK OF FAMILY FINANCE

CONTENTS

A thunderstorm sweeps through the Grand Canyon in Thomas Moran's *The Chasm of the Colorado.*

1|The lure of the wild country

As the 19th Century began, the vast area west of the Mississippi was a mysterious void to most Americans. But then in 1803 President Thomas Jefferson completed the Louisiana Purchase—and opened the West to anyone with the curiosity and courage to probe it. Over the next 75 years more than two million square miles revealed their secrets to an army of hunters, soldiers, naturalists and other adventurers.

Not until mid-century, however, did most citizens get their first look at this wild land, and then it was through the eyes—and canvases—of a few bold painters, some of them Europeans. The landscapes they painted, shown here and on the following pages, fired their imaginations, prompting them at times to add all sorts of embellishments.

Yet such was the dramatic variety of the West that as each region opened, explorers found actual scenes surpassing the artists' wildest imaginings.

On an exploration of what is now Montana and the Da-
kotas, German artist Charles Wimar painted this eerie
impression of a buffalo herd plunging across a river to escape
a prairie fire. Wimar's imagination re-created the riverbank
in the form of a southwestern pueblo lit by the fire's glow.

For his romanticized landscape of the Wind River country in Wyoming, German-born Albert Bierstadt made a series of sketches of this spectacular region of the Rocky Mountains during a trip to the area in 1859. Returning to the East, he created a dramatic vision from the sketches, adding a waterfall and a different perspective to the actual scene.

Karl Bodmer painted Montana's Citadel Rock (since re-
named Cathedral Rock) with the look of a castle on the
Rhine. Bodmer's Swiss hand gave the Rockies the darker,
more forbidding aspect of mountains in his native Europe.

13

An epochal thrust to the Pacific

On January 18, 1803, President Thomas Jefferson sent a confidential message to Congress. "The river Missouri," it stated, "& the Indians inhabiting it, are not as well known as is rendered desireable by their connection with the Missisipi, & consequently with us.... An intelligent officer with ten or twelve chosen men ... might explore the whole line, even to the Western Ocean...." This group, variously known as the Lewis and Clark expedition or the Corps of Discovery, turned out to be the most carefully conceived, brilliantly led, and probably the most profitable piece of trailblazing in history up to that time.

This first announcement of Jefferson's, only 1,300 words long, was deliberately sketchy about the nature of the mission — and understandably so. For in his artful fashion, Jefferson was asking Congress to authorize a military reconnaissance into vast and virtually unknown lands that were claimed by the two most powerful nations in the world, France and Britain, with a third, Spain, clinging to a hold in the South and Far West. Jefferson knew the legislators were likely to boggle at such a chancy proposition; indeed, his political opposition in the Federalist Party would object to almost anything he proposed. He therefore chose language that was contrived both to minimize the risks and to render the bait irresistible. He avoided any use of the word "military," pointing out instead the opportunities for "extending the external commerce of the U.S." He spoke enticingly of "great supplies of furs & peltry" to be obtained from the Indians, who up to that time had sold their furs solely to the British Hudson's Bay Company and the North West Company of Canada. As a clincher,

he made the temptation cheap, asking only $2,500 to finance the project (though in the end the actual cost came to $38,722.25).

On February 28, 1803, Congress approved the venture. Jefferson was quietly jubilant. For upwards of two decades as a public servant he had been actively scheming at ways to find out what lay in the great void beyond the Mississippi, and to establish some sort of American presence there. In fact long before he became President, Jefferson, who was both a scientist and a brilliant geopolitician, had made at least two abortive efforts to satisfy his own scholarly curiosity and at the same time to open the door at least a crack for U.S. expansion into the West.

While Minister to France in 1786, he came across an adventurer named John Ledyard. Ledyard struck him as "a man of genius, of some science, of fearless courage and enterprise ... and of a roaming restless character." Jefferson urged him to approach the American West by an outlandish course: across Europe and Asia to eastern Siberia, thence over the Bering Sea to Vancouver Island, down the New World's coast and inland to the Missouri River. Ledyard eagerly undertook the challenge and managed to walk 3,000 miles into Siberia before Catherine the Great got wind of him and, suspecting that he was a spy, had him escorted back to Poland under armed guard.

At that point Jefferson wrote off Ledyard, but not his own curiosity or aspirations. A few years later, by which time he was Secretary of State, he came up with another candidate to traverse the Far West. His new choice was André Michaux, a French émigré who had become a Carolina landowner and sometime botanist and explorer. He claimed that he could find a way across the continent via the Missouri. Encouraged by the man's scientific credentials, Jefferson commissioned him to make the trip. But Michaux, it turned out, *was* a spy — an *agent provocateur* in the service of the notorious, troublemaking French Minister, Citizen Edmond Charles Genêt. Michaux had gotten only as far as Kentucky when he was called back and strongly advised to return to botany.

Jefferson carried his westering ambitions into the White House, and from this lofty vantage point he perceived even more acutely the necessity of establishing a trans-Mississippi foothold for the United States. By that time the British had already accomplished a continental crossing: in 1793 a fur trader named Alexander Mackenzie had blazed a trail across northwestern Canada to the Pacific, and there was some concern that he might try again, this time perhaps along the Columbia River. To further complicate matters, war between France and Britain was imminent, and the President sensed that its destructive waves would probably spill over into North America.

In 1802 Napoleon assigned two powerful armies to service in the New World. The first headed for San Domingo to oust the Negro revolutionary Toussaint L'Ouverture and regain control of the Caribbean island. The second, secretly assembled, was intended to police Louisiana. But yellow fever and the guerrilla tactics of L'Ouverture destroyed the first army in San Domingo, and when it was all but wiped out Napoleon sent the second in relief. That, too, was quickly cut down and it never reached Louisiana.

Overextended and sorely in need of cash to finance his war machine, Napoleon turned to negotiating with Jefferson's emissaries in Paris for the sale of the French possessions in America. In April 1803 the two parties

Jeers for Jefferson's master stroke

In the summer of 1803 Meriwether Lewis was in Pittsburgh supervising the building of a keelboat for the great expedition to the Pacific when a letter arrived from President Thomas Jefferson. It began: "Dear Sir / Last night we received the treaty from Paris ceding Louisiana. . . ." This was electrifying news: in one stroke the size of the United States was doubled. But even more significant to Lewis and his exploring partner William Clark, the Louisiana Purchase transformed what would have been a semiclandestine reconnaissance of foreign territory into a bold survey of American-owned land.

Furthermore, the whole momentous change had happened quite by surprise, growing out of an American bid to France to buy the port of New Orleans. At first negotiations had gone nowhere. Thus when Napoleon's Foreign Minister, Talleyrand, one day announced that the U.S. could have New Orleans if it would take the entire Louisiana territory, the American Minister to France could scarcely believe his slightly deaf ears. Jefferson was even more amazed, and rushed the treaty through Congress despite doubts of its Constitutionality. But economic rather than legal misgivings aroused his political foes, the Federalists. It was the "wildest chimera of a moonstruck brain," they claimed, to pay hard cash, even the bargain sum of $15 million, for lands nobody knew anything about.

On this last point the Federalists were not too far off: though the treaty specified 909,130 square miles, no one knew if that was right (it wasn't; the final survey turned up 800,000). The only certainty was that the territory extended westward to the Continental Divide — but no one knew exactly where that was, either. Now, with the way cleared for Lewis and Clark, Jefferson was going to find out.

Jefferson, whose decision to buy Louisiana was a blatant assertion of executive power, had long been the butt of Federalist attacks like this — on the grounds that he favored limited Presidential authority.

agreed on the terms of the Louisiana Purchase *(map, below)*, by which the United States eventually gained 800,000 square miles between the Mississippi and the Rocky Mountains. Now Jefferson no longer needed secrecy or guile to move westward. As President he had a legitimate duty to examine the new lands.

He was more than ready to do so. By the time the territory was transferred to United States ownership, Jefferson's secretary, young Captain Meriwether Lewis, had assembled all of the equipment for the Corps of Discovery, and his co-commander, Second Lieutenant William Clark, was already at the mouth of the Missouri, drilling the men and selecting additional baggage for the great trip into the hinterland. On March 9, 1804, Captain Lewis, dressed up in the best of his uniform coats for what would be the last time in more than

two years, appeared at the Government House in St. Louis. There, as a witness, he put his signature to the document completing the great land transaction—and removing the last formal barrier to the historic venture. Lewis and Clark and their men would be the first Americans to carve a track across the West all the way to the Pacific; they were the pathfinders for a nation. In their wake would follow the mountain men, prospectors, cattlemen, sodbusters, tracklayers and city builders —the successive generations of an empire.

When Jefferson noted in his message to Congress that the West was "not as well known as is . . . desireable" he was drastically understating the case. In truth, most of the trans-Mississippi territory remained, as French traders called it, *pays inconnu,* unknown land. The best maps Jefferson could obtain for the

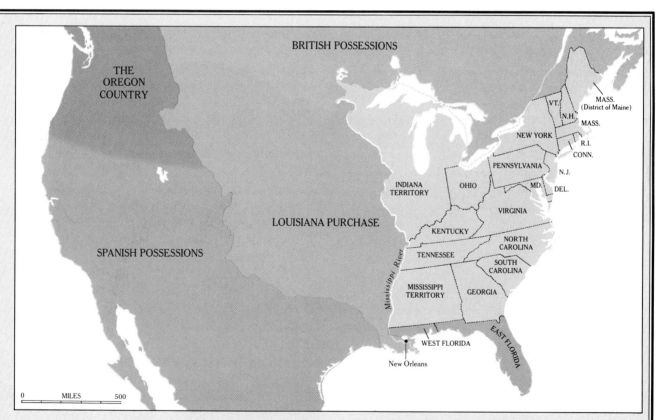

The Louisiana Purchase Treaty of 1803 gave the United States the western Mississippi drainage, extending north to the British possessions and southwest to lands claimed by the Spanish. Although later exploration defined the watershed as shown above, in 1803 the western limits were unknown. However, it was assumed, correctly, that the northwest boundary of Louisiana adjoined the unexplored Columbia River Basin or Oregon country, to which the U.S. held vague claim since the discovery of the river mouth in 1792 by an American fur ship. Together they would provide a broad land corridor to the Pacific.

Corps's guidance represented a mixed bag of geographical information collected here and there over 200 years, and offered little more than outlines and guesswork. The Missouri River had been charted only as far above St. Louis as the Mandan villages in the Dakota region. British, Russian and Spanish explorers had touched tentatively here and there along the Pacific Coast north of California, but no one had charted the Columbia River beyond its mouth. No white man knew the distance from the Dakota region to the Columbia, much less what lay in between.

Because of this vacuum of knowledge fantastic tales had arisen. Some were based on a modicum of fact, others were entirely imaginary. In either case, through repetition and the absence of disproof, they had come to bear the color of revealed truth. Strange and wondrous folk were said to dwell in the vastness. Among these were a tribe of man-hating, arrow-shooting Amazons, each of whom had her right breast removed because it got in the way of the bowstring; and a tribe of Welsh-speaking Indians descended from a Briton who had reached the Americas long before Columbus. One particularly bizarre story had it that in an eerie region called *Les Côtes Brûlées* (the Burnt Cliffs) would be found a community of devils in human form standing only 18 inches high.

Jefferson had no way of knowing the accuracy of most of these reports; indeed, in addressing Congress he had mentioned rumored geographical marvels, including a mountain made entirely of salt. He was determined that the Corps of Discovery must learn what was really out there in the wilderness. And Meriwether Lewis, the man whom he selected to report on the facts, was no dreamer or schemer like Ledyard or Michaux. On the contrary, Lewis' mind was in perfect congruity with that of the President, and for good reason. Jefferson had been grooming him for years.

Meriwether Lewis' family had been neighbors of Jefferson's in Albemarle County, Virginia. After Lewis' father died, his mother remarried and the family moved to the frontier in Georgia. Lewis spent his boyhood on the very fringes of the American wilderness. By the time he returned to Virginia in his teens to manage his father's land, he had acquired an essential qualification of exploration — the ability to live in wild country. The statesman and the young man became fast friends; when-

ever Jefferson felt like talking, he would summon Lewis with a mirror blinking in the sun.

During these early conversations, Jefferson began to share his grand design with Lewis, and the young man responded eagerly, volunteering to go into the wilderness in 1792 when he was only 18 years old. Though Jefferson turned Lewis down at that time in favor of Michaux, nevertheless the President was impressed by his youthful neighbor's boldness; he later recalled that "I told him it was proposed that the person engaged should be attended by a single companion only, to avoid exciting alarm among the Indians. This did not deter him."

In 1794 when the Whiskey Rebellion erupted, Lewis volunteered for the Army. He had risen to captain by the time Jefferson became President in 1801. Upon taking office, Jefferson invited Lewis to be his private secretary, and late into the evenings the two friends developed their scheme for a probe to the Pacific, grounding the adventure in the kind of detailed planning that would become its hallmark.

Jefferson's first priority in setting up the Corps was to pick the right people. In Lewis he had a superb leader with strength of body, woods-wisdom, an inquiring turn of mind, determination and coolness under stress. So well qualified was Lewis that in the whole following century of Western trailblazing only one man came close to matching his abilities. That was Joe Walker, one day to be king of the tough breed called the mountain men, but in 1802 still a small boy growing up on a farm carved out of the Tennessee woods.

But qualities of command were not enough. The ideal man for this journey, Jefferson felt, should possess a knowledge of "botany, natural history, mineralogy & astronomy." Accordingly, Jefferson dispatched Lewis to Philadelphia for instruction at the University of Pennsylvania and at the American Philosophical Society, then the nation's reigning scientific institution.

For a month and a half, beginning in mid-April 1803, Lewis submitted himself to concentrated tutoring. From the mathematician Robert Patterson he learned celestial navigation. Other renowned researchers, such as the naturalist Benjamin Smith Barton, anatomist Caspar Wistar and the physician Dr. Benjamin Rush, drilled him in their various specialties and interests. Dr. Rush urged him to inquire among the Indians into such matters as suicide and murder, burial customs, diet, medicines, menstruation, breast feeding, bathing, fasting, longevity and religious practices. Lewis was asked particularly to determine, if possible, any affinities between Indian religions and Judaism — since it was believed by some people that American Indians might actually be the descendants of lost tribes of wandering Jews.

In addition to priming Lewis with questions about the medical practices of the tribes, Dr. Rush furnished Lewis with a rather impractical list of *Rules of Health,* advising, for example, against marching if the men felt "the least indisposition." He also gave Lewis a generous supply of "Doctor Rush's pills" for "costiveness," or constipation. Lewis and Clark, as physicians pro tem for the Corps of Discovery, were to fall back on this remedy for almost any ailment — including diarrhea.

During his educational marathon, Lewis gave particular thought to the question of who would accompany him as adjutant. At length he chose a Kentucky frontiersman and old Army comrade, William Clark, younger brother of the famous frontier fighter of the Revolution, General George Rogers Clark. Clark accepted with delight — and with deplorable spelling: "I will chearfully join you," he wrote. "My friend I do assure you that no man lives whith whome I would perfur to undertake Such a Trip &c. as your self." In an exchange of compliments, Lewis declared that Clark's authority would be equal to his own. He promised his old friend a captaincy (and later became lastingly bitter at the War Department's refusal of that promotion).

Together, the two men went about the critical work of assembling their crew. When seeking volunteers for the mission, they carefully avoided "Gentlemens sons" who smelled adventure. Lewis declared: "We must set our faces against all such applications and get rid of them on the best terms we can. They will not answer our purposes." Instead the leaders agreed they wanted solid frontiersmen, stable of character, self-reliant but amenable to the harsh discipline that circumstances would impose even if the leaders did not. In addition the men should have a wide array of skills, for the Corps would need hunters to supply meat, boatmen wise in the ways of rivers, carpenters to build winter quarters and blacksmiths to repair equipment. In the end they assembled a party of 30, including 17 regular soldiers, 11 enlistees, a half-breed to serve as an in-

terpreter, Clark's giant Negro servant York and Lewis' dauntless Newfoundland dog Scannon. They picked no drifters, drunks, neurotics or romantics. The proof of their judgment was that during their journey through 7,689 miles of dangerous wilderness only two of the men failed under stress.

Lewis had the job of selecting their gear. Early on, he made a trip to Harpers Ferry, West Virginia, where the arsenal had already received orders to supply his weapons. There, impressed by the accuracy of the Kentucky long rifle but concluding that it was too fragile, he redesigned the piece so effectively that Lewis' "Harpers Ferry Rifle" became the standard weapon and first mass-produced infantry arm for the United States Army. He ordered swivel cannons as heavy armament. And more or less on a whim he also decided to take along a newfangled semi-toy, an air rifle.

In Pittsburgh, Lewis commissioned the building of the Corps's principal transport — a 60-foot keelboat, or barge. Demanding and impatient when it came to seeing the needs of the Corps fulfilled, he was infuriated by the rumpot habits of the boat builder and wrote the President that he had been "moste shamefully detained by . . . unpardonable negligence." Lewis straightened out this situation without Presidential help, but in all matters of preparation and equipment, Jefferson remained a close and fascinated consultant.

The President noted with approval the medicine chest and its contents, which included a supply of opium and laudanum. He concurred with the need for a "Cheap portable Microscope," hydrometers, an iron-framed collapsible canoe invented by Lewis, and a "portable soup" whose recipe was concocted by Lewis with the advice of a Philadelphia chef. (The men later learned to loathe the stuff.)

To help the Corps befriend the Western Indians — and perhaps smooth the way toward future trade — Lewis and Jefferson agreed upon a lavish stock of gifts. In fact the largest cost item on Lewis' supply inventory was $669.50 for presents. These included colored beads, calico shirts, handkerchiefs, mirrors, bells, needles, thimbles, ribbons, sheet metal, kettles and brass curtain rings to be worn on the fingers. Lewis also brought along dozens of peace medals, some of them bearing on one face a likeness of President Jefferson and on the obverse two hands clasped in friendship. ◉

In this 1650 map the island of California floats offshore. The Pacific coastline, from Cape Mendocino north of San Francisco south to the San Diego area, is accurately delineated, but it was many years before chartmakers showed California firmly attached to the mainland.

A menagerie of strange beasts for a land of mystery

A Dutch artist who had never visited America portrayed a slim-waisted, amiable buffalo in 1630.

Until Lewis and Clark returned with their charts and reports of the real West, almost all depictions of the trans-Mississippi land and its creatures came from the imaginations of men who had never been there. European geographers, relying upon the sketchy reports of Spanish soldiers, believed that California was an island, and drew maps accordingly *(left)*. Inland, there were even greater mysteries — and myths. For years, Spanish expeditions blundered about in the Southwest in search of such ephemeral goals as the Seven Cities of Cibola — probably only a group of pueblo villages constructed of adobe. There were other legendary landmarks just as imposing: a mountain of clear salt, another of shimmering crystal, cliffs of unflawed gemstone, and fields — if not cities — where nuggets of pure gold lay scattered like fallen walnuts.

Within this vast and unknown landscape roamed some wonderful mythical animals: unicorns, gargantuan woolly mastodons and beavers that were seven feet tall sitting up. No unicorns ever existed, and the enormous beavers and mastodons that once did in fact roam North America had long been extinct. Thus no sketches of Utah unicorns or Montana mastodons survive, but attempts by Europeans to draw real animals like the actual beaver *(below)* and the buffalo *(above)* resulted in creatures very nearly as astonishing.

This beaver with human eyes appeared in a 1703 volume by a French traveler.

With rocks and medieval-style pikes and bows, Indians of the Southwest defend a jumbled fortress against charging Spanish soldiers (*right*) in this 16th Century Dutch oil. Despite the fictional touches, the painting re-creates an actual incident in which conquistador Francisco Coronado suffered only a dented helmet storming a Zuñi pueblo in 1540.

By the spring of 1804, after the official transfer of the Louisiana Territory to American ownership, the Corps of Discovery was ready to go. Now all the careful planning would be put to the test of the wilderness: Jefferson's decades of political maneuvering and diplomacy, his foresight and boldness and mastery of detail, his wisdom in choosing the man who would lead the mission and, most of all, his instinct about the West as the direction of American destiny. On May 14 the expedition started up the Missouri.

For the next 2 years 4 months and 10 days, the explorers were beyond all advice or support, having rowed, paddled, trudged and ridden horseback quite literally beyond the edge of the known world.

They had scarcely moved beyond the familiar stretches of the lower Missouri when the leaders found much to marvel at. "This senery already rich pleasing and beatiful was still farther hightened by immence herds of Buffaloe, deer Elk and Antelopes which we saw in every direction feeding on the hills and plains," wrote Lewis who, like Clark, tended to improvise spelling. "I do not think I exagerate when I estimate the number of Buffaloe which could be compre[hend]ed at one view to amount to 3,000." Farther on they would see herds of well over 10,000 buffalo, at times "attended by their shepperds the wolves" or feeding in company with other game "in one common and boundless pasture. . . . the buffaloe Elk and Antelope are so gentle that we pass near them while feeding, without appearing to excite any alarm among them; and when we attract their attention, they frequently approach us more nearly to discover what we are."

Lewis and Clark added faithfully to their notes throughout the trip, compiling enormously detailed and flavorful journals. Others of the party fell into a similar habit. Amid the scientific data and personal wonderment in these journals was a measure of straightforward complaining. The men soon learned to detest the serpentine Missouri, with its caved-in banks and treacherous sandbars. Even more annoying were the hordes of gnats that flew into the eyes, and the mosquitoes that sought every patch of open skin. Lewis noted that mosquitoes "continue to infest us in such a manner that we can scarcely exist; for my own part I am confined by them to my bier at least ¾ths of my time. My dog even howls with the torture he experiences from them...

they are so numerous that we frequently get them in our thrats as we breath."

Lewis found an additional early hazard in his own passionate curiosity. He tested mineral deposits by taste, trying suspected alum, cobalt and other ores with his tongue. As a result he fell painfully ill from arsenic or some other metallic poison. A purge with a "Dost of Salts" cured him.

Eleven weeks out the party encountered its first Indians, the Otos. After liberally distributing gifts and peace medals bearing Jefferson's likeness to this amiable tribe, Lewis addressed them in a speech that helped to set the pattern of official United States policy toward the Indians in the West:

"Children. The great chief of the Seventeen great nations of America, impelled by his parental regard for his newly adopted children on the troubled waters, has sent us out to clear the road...[He] has commanded us his war chiefs to undertake this long journey...You are to live in peace with all the white men, for they are his children; neither wage war against the red men, your neighbours, for they are equally his children and he is bound to protect them. Injure not the person of any traders who may come among you....Do these things which your great father advises and be happy. Avoid the councils of bad birds; turn on your heel from them as you would from the precipice of an high rock . . . lest by one false step you should bring upon your nation the displeasure of your great father . . . who could consume you as the fire consumes the grass of the plains."

Though Lewis, by Jefferson's express order, was a good deal more diplomatic than many of those who followed him, nevertheless his basic stance toward the Indians was stern. Be conciliatory, he warned the Indians, or you will be sorry.

In this aggressive approach to diplomacy, Lewis found that his air rifle was an excellent asset. One of the party recorded the occasion. "Captain Lewis shot his air gun, told them that there was medician in hir, and that She would do great Execution. They were all amazed at the curiosity and as soon as he had shot a fiew times, they all ran hastily to see the Ball holes in the tree and they Shouted aloud at the Site of the execution she would do."

Seventy-five miles beyond the meeting place with the Otos, death struck the party for the first and only

The first white man to span the trackless wilderness

A dozen years before Lewis and Clark made their historic expedition across the North American continent, a Scottish fur trader had quietly beaten them to it. In 1793, Alexander Mackenzie pierced the western Canadian wilderness and became the first white man to surmount the Rockies and reach the West Coast overland. An employee of the Canadian-owned North West Company, Mackenzie set out to discover the Northwest Passage, a mythical water route to the western ocean. Through it, he planned to open the lush fur country of the coast for his company—and at the same time claim all promising territories for Britain.

He had first conceived the idea during a tour of duty at a remote fur-trading outpost on Lake Athabasca, in what is now northern Alberta. Excited by Indian tales that the Pacific was not far to the west, Mackenzie determined to make a probe in that direction. In the summer of 1789, the 25-year-old trader set off with eight men (plus four Indian wives) in three birchbark canoes. They paddled up the Slave River to Great Slave Lake, then onto another broad river (later named for Mackenzie himself) that swung north at the Rockies. As they floated onward, the landscape became bleak and forbidding. For 40 days they continued until the river spilled into the tidal edges of a vast icebound body of salt water. Mackenzie had reached an ocean, but it was the Arctic Ocean. Bitterly disappointed, he turned around and, in a race with the waning sun, managed to get back to the post before winter.

The directors of the North West Company were not at all pleased. But in May 1793, the company gave him one more chance. This time, taking nine men in a 25-foot birchbark canoe, he headed upstream from Fort

Alexander Mackenzie reached the Pacific—and the Arctic Ocean as well.

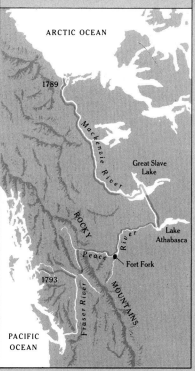

Fork, situated on the more southerly trending Peace River. As the party headed into the Rockies, the stream grew narrow and roilsome; the canoe had to be hauled through the tumbling white water and portaged around

falls. For a week the men struggled up the slopes, then wandered for more than another week from stream to stream in a series of alpine canyons. At one point (and without suspecting it) Mackenzie crossed the Continental Divide. Up to this time he had been plagued by difficulties; but now his luck ran out entirely. In the furious rapids of the Bad River (later called the Fraser), the party's canoe capsized, and only a lucky current swept the men into shallow water and saved them from drowning.

Defeated by the river, Mackenzie and his men trekked westward over the Coast Mountains. On July 20, 73 days after embarking on the Peace River, the exhausted party, having begged a last ride in the canoes of some Bella Coola Indians, floated into an arm of the Pacific just north of Vancouver Island. Mackenzie had finally found his Northwest Passage —but an unnavigable, useless one.

After a quick return trip (he was back at Fort Fork in a month), he tried to convince the directors of the North West Company that just one more try would find the easy route they wanted. They turned him down. Eventually, Mackenzie left the company and went to England to drum up government support for his plans. To that end he published a book in 1801 called *Voyages from Montreal,* which included the diaries of his two journeys and an epilogue urging Great Britain "to secure the trade of [Western Canada] to its subjects."

The Crown was as uninterested as the North West Company had been. However, Thomas Jefferson was fascinated by Mackenzie's tale, of which he pored over every word. Three years later, when he sent Lewis and Clark to seek out a transcontinental route for the United States, a copy of Mackenzie's book went with them.

time. Many of the Corpsmen had begun suffering from boils and stomach disorders, which Lewis attributed to the Missouri's scummy water. The symptoms of Sergeant Charles Floyd seemed especially ominous. On August 19 when the party was camped near the site of the present-day Sioux City, Iowa, Floyd started vomiting and became violently diarrheal. The leaders were at a loss for a remedy. The next day, the ailing sergeant called Clark to him and said, "I am going away. I want you to write me a letter." Before Clark could lay hands on his writing materials, the sergeant was dead. The cause was recorded as the "Biliose Chorlick."

Even while Floyd lay on his deathbed, Lewis had to deal with the first and worst disciplinary crisis of the expedition. A few days earlier, Moses Reed, a volunteer, had asked for and received permission to backtrack to the party's last camp to search for a lost knife. When he did not return Lewis realized Reed might be deserting. Quickly, Lewis dispatched a group after Reed "with order if he did not give up Peaceibly to put him to Death." They found Reed back among the Otos. He tried to wheedle a guard into letting him flee but the Corpsman was adamant.

Upon being returned to the expedition's camp, Reed was punished for his attempted desertion in a manner that created a permanent impression on his fellow Corpsmen. Clark described the matter tersely: "[We] proceeded to the trial of Reed, he confessed that he 'Deserted & stold a public Rifle Shot-pouch Powder & Ball' and requested we would be as favourable with him as we Could consistantly with our Oathes — which we were and only Sentenced him to run the Gantlet four times through the Party & that each man with nine Swichies Should punish him and for him not to be considered in future as one of the Party."

On only one other occasion, more than 400 miles farther up the Missouri, were the commanders put to the necessity of severely punishing a malingerer. The culprit this time was John Newman, an army private; he was sentenced to 75 lashes and discharge from the expedition (he was later sent back to St. Louis). The meting out of the lashes was witnessed by Indians. Clark recorded the reaction of the chief. "The punishment of this day allarmd. the Indian Chief verry much, he cried aloud (or effected to cry)." Clark explained to the chief the necessity of making an example

and maintaining discipline; the Indian agreed that discipline was necessary but "his nation never whiped even their Children, from their burth." How then, Clark inquired, would the chief have made an example in a similar case? The chief's advice was simple: kill him.

Near the spot where this unhappy episode occurred, the Corps leaders' firmness was put to a different kind of test. All the way upriver, Lewis and Clark had anticipated with some apprehension a possible confrontation with the Teton Sioux, who dominated a long stretch of the upper Missouri and were reputed to be both warlike and arrogant. For years they had terrorized neighboring tribes and exacted tribute from any traders who came their way.

At the mouth of the Teton River in South Dakota, the Corps did indeed encounter a party of Teton Sioux. In an effort at frontier diplomacy Lewis and Clark invited the chiefs on board their keelboat. However, the Indians showed little inclination to be friendly, and at last Clark and a few of the men rowed them back to shore. At this point, one pugnacious young chief became deliberately provocative. As Clark's journal recounted the episode, the Indian "was verry insolent both in words & justures (pretended Drunkenness & staggered up against me) declareing I should not go on, Stateing he had not receved presents sufficent from us, his justures were of Such a personal nature I felt My self Compeled to Draw my Sword (and Made a Signal to the boat to prepare for action)."

Seeing this dangerous turn of events from the keelboat, Captain Lewis ordered his men to arms. Some of the Sioux warriors, meanwhile, strung their bows and drew arrows. But before letting fly they hesitated, perhaps because the swivel cannons and all the rifles on the keelboat were aimed right at them. At that point Clark coolly dismissed his own men, ordering them to row back to the keelboat. He stood alone on the shore until Lewis sent reinforcements.

As soon as the additional men arrived, the Indians withdrew a short distance. Clark turned on his heel and walked straight toward the boat without a backward glance. Utterly outfaced, some of the Indians begged to be taken on board for a fresh start at negotiations. Clark granted their request, but he was still seething. "We proceeded on about 1 Mile & anchored out off a Willow Island placed a guard on Shore to protect the Cooks

Ruddy and vigorous, William Clark posed for the Philadelphia painter Charles Willson Peale, who executed this matched pair of portraits of the explorers to hang in his museum of natural history.

In painting Meriwether Lewis, Peale caught some of the dreaminess of the moody and idealistic leader. Together with Clark, Lewis greatly enriched Peale's Museum with Western curiosities.

& a guard in the boat . . . I call this Island bad humered Island as we were in a bad humer."

Thereafter the Teton Sioux, though they remained basically hostile, never again mounted a serious threat to the Corps. Puzzled but clearly impressed by these firm-handed white men, the tribe took to begging and offering women for the explorers' beds. "A curious custom," wrote Clark, "is to give handsom squars to those whome they wish to Show some acknowledgments to." The offers were not always refused, either here or later. Among the Arikaras, Lewis observed that the women were "handsome and lively and disposed to be amorous." Clark confided to his diary that he had never seen more friendly and persistent "squars"; they were "verry fond of caressing our men." On one occasion upriver, however, a warrior had second thoughts about the policy; after giving his wife to a Corpsman for one night, he became so enraged when she attempted to stay with the expedition that he threatened to kill her. The woman was promptly returned and her irate husband soothed with presents.

For most of the journey, Lewis felt that it was wisest to allow the men these diversions with Indian women. However, when the Corps reached the Pacific, where the Indians had already encountered other white adventurers and their diseases, Lewis warned against any contact. But several men were infected—one of them by a woman who bore upon an arm the tattooed brand of a former white admirer, "J. Bowman."

In the mid-autumn of 1804 the party reached the mouth of the Knife River in the future state of North Dakota. There they decided to make winter camp among the Mandan Indians. The men of the Corps set to work erecting a fort, a sturdy log structure sheltered from the wind both by woods and the rimrock along the river's edge. Again the emphasis on caution and thoroughness paid off, for the winter of 1804-1805 was a bitter one; Lewis recorded temperatures down to 45° below and, on one really cold day, noted that some of the expedition's hard liquor that had been left outside froze solid in 15 minutes.

Nevertheless the resourceful commanders were able to put the long, enforced halt to good use. During the five months at Fort Mandan, as they called their quarters, Clark found a chief named Big White who claimed to know the terrain far ahead. Clark spent hours trans-

The fanciful drawings on these pages appeared in the first published account of the Lewis and Clark expedition, a set of journals kept by Sergeant Patrick Gass. The unknown illustrator had a quaint concept of the journey. Above, to depict the capsizing of a canoe, he drew men, dressed for dinner, sinking after their bewildered horses—which had apparently fit snugly into the craft.

lating the chief's crude maps, drawn in the sand, into a chart of the upper Missouri and its tributaries. One piece of information from Big White and the other Mandans was particularly exciting. They "inform us, that the Missouri is navigable nearly to it's source," wrote Lewis, "and that . . . at a distance not exceeding half a days march, there is a large river running from South to North . . . We believe this stream to be the principal South fork of the Columbia river." That river, he knew, would lead to the Pacific Ocean.

While Clark occupied himself with geography, Lewis cultivated Indian friendship. Playing the role of diplomat and the first American landlord of this newest extension of United States territory, Lewis ordered the expedition's blacksmith to help mend Indian hoes and battle-axes, and he donated fragments of a burned-out iron stove to make new tools and weapons. He gave away an iron gristmill, hoping to ease the women's work in grinding cornmeal. But the warriors had other ideas; they broke the machine into fragments and shaped the metal into arrowheads.

While wintering over with the Mandans, Lewis recruited two new crew members from a neighboring village of the Minnetaree tribe. One turned out to be a

craven nuisance, the other a prize beyond any price. The nuisance was Toussaint Charbonneau, a French-Canadian whom Lewis hired to interpret; the prize was his wife Sacajawea—a name that later generations of schoolchildren came to know by heart as the beautiful and courageous Indian princess who helped to lead America westward.

Sacajawea (Lewis and Clark commonly wrote of her as "the Indian Woman" because they could not spell her name) was a Shoshoni. She had been captured by the Minnetarees when about 11 years old, and later sold to Charbonneau as a slave. Now, at 16, she was married to him and hugely pregnant. Perhaps hoping to see her own people once more, she seemed anxious to go upriver with the Corps. Lewis consented to take her along because he thought—with superb intuition as it turned out—that she might be useful if the expedition did indeed meet the Shoshonis to the west.

When her time came that February, she underwent a long and agonizing labor. Although Lewis' clinical skills were by now improving (he had successfully amputated frostbitten toes) he was out of his depth in obstetrics. Luckily a fur trader who was visiting the Mandans suggested a dosage of rattlesnake rattles as

In this illustration, the man perched in the tree is hunter Hugh Mc-Neal, and the furry, doglike creature gazing up at him represents a grizzly bear. In the actual event, McNeal's horse reared at the sight of the grizzly and threw his rider at the bear's feet. McNeal smashed his gun on the bear's head and scrambled up a tree, where he stayed for three hours until the bored animal wandered away.

proper therapy. "Having the rattle of a snake by me I gave it to him and he administered two rings of it to the woman broken in small pieces," Lewis reported. "I was informed that she had not taken it more than ten minutes before she brought forth."

On April 7, 1805, the Corps of Discovery gathered its gear and again headed West. Lewis noted with astonishment that in this virgin land beavers swam fearlessly in their streams in broad daylight. One day a buffalo calf followed him about like a pet dog. On the riverbank, he saw for the first time huge pawprints of the "white bear"—the dreaded grizzly.

Out hunting a few weeks thereafter, Lewis shot a buffalo. He stood watching the animal die, not thinking to reload his gun, and a grizzly came within 20 steps before Lewis saw it. Later he recounted the next few terrifying moments: "It was an open level plain, not a bush within miles nor a tree within less than three hundred yards . . . the river bank was sloping . . . in short there was no place by means of which I could conceal myself from this monster . . . he pitched at me, open mouthed, and full speed, I ran about 80 yards and found he gained on me fast, I then run into the water the idea struck me to get into the water to such debth that I

could stand and he would be obliged to swim, and that I could . . . defend myself with my espontoon [an old-fashioned, spear-pointed weapon that Lewis used to steady his rifle when shooting] . . . the moment I put myself in this attitude of defence, he sudonly wheeled about . . . declined to combat on such unequal grounds, and retreated with quite as great precipitation as he had just before pursued me."

On May 26 Lewis came within first sight of one of the greatest landmarks on the journey. He had climbed a hill near what is now Cow Creek in Montana when he saw, far off, a range of peaks. He later confided his feelings to his journal. "These points of the Rocky Mountains were covered with snow and the sun shone on it in such a manner as to give me the most plain and satisfactory view. while I viewed these mountains I felt a secret pleasure in finding myself so near the head of the heretofore conceived boundless Missouri; but when I reflected on the difficulties which this snowey barrier would most probably throw in my way to the Pacific, and the sufferings and hardships of myself and party in them, it in some measure counterballanced the joy I had felt in the first moments in which I gazed on them. But as I have always held it a crime to anticipate evils I will

Negotiating with the Indians at the beginning of the expedition, an overdressed Lewis speaks to a group of underdressed Oto and Missouri tribesmen. As he did with all the Missouri tribes, Lewis told these people they were now bound to obey the President of the United States, the "Great Chief" and "only Great Father." The Indians replied they were well pleased with the arrangement.

believe it a good comfortable road untill I am compelled to believe differently."

He was soon prompted to so believe. Proceeding up the Missouri, the party came to a fork that did not seem to fit with the map Clark had drawn with the Mandans. Here two streams of apparently equal volume joined. Which was the real Missouri? Most of the Corpsmen picked the northerly branch as the correct one, for a sound reason: that stream was as silt-laden and generally repulsive as the rest of the Missouri. The south branch ran clear.

But Lewis and Clark were not so sure, and now they displayed yet another dimension of their leadership qualities: a refusal to accept the obvious. They suspected that the clarity of the south fork indicated an origin in the high barren Rockies. To double-check, each man picked a branch to explore with a small party. Lewis took the muddy fork. Seeing that its course continued northward he concluded that he was not on the main stream, and that if the expedition took this fork it would soon be wandering futilely into the endless plains of Canada. On a quirkish impulse, he named the tributary Maria's River (later spelled Marias) for a girlfriend back home, although he felt obliged to remark that "the hue of the waters of this turbulent and troubled stream but illy comport with the pure celestial virtues and amiable qualifications of that lovely fair one."

Then he returned to camp, where he found that Clark had confirmed his own conclusions. They took the south fork and upon this carefully weighed decision turned the fate of the Corps of Discovery. A wrong choice, wrote Lewis, "would not only loose us the whole of this season but would probably so dishearten the party that it might defeat the expedition altogether." Lewis was particularly gratified that the men, despite their doubts about the south fork, were so willing to trust the judgment of the commanders.

The next hurdle, formidable indeed, confronted the Corps of Discovery in the form of the Great Falls of the Missouri. The sight of the roaring falls dumfounded Captain Lewis. Noting that the torrent was 300 yards wide and at least 80 feet high, he wrote, "The water after decending strikes against the butment . . . on which I stand and seems to reverberate and being met by the more impetuous courant they roll and swell into half formed billows of great hight."

The portage around the falls covered more than 18 miles, over rough terrain grown with spiky cactus that

Fighting with Indians on the return trip, Lewis fires into a small band of Piegan Blackfeet who had stolen some rifles and tried to escape with the party's horses. During the fatal skirmish — the only violent one connected with the expedition — Lewis killed an Indian. The artist again showed Lewis attired in parade-ground style. Actually he had shortly before bartered his last coat for a canoe.

tormented the men through their double-soled moccasins. To move the heavy equipment, Lewis set a crew to hewing primitive cart wheels from the 22-inch trunk of a cottonwood tree. These wheels, he noted in his journal, "with couplings, toungs and bodies . . . might either be used without the bodies for transporting our canoes, or with them in transporting our baggage." They were used for both, although getting the entire load around the Great Falls took 24 days and left the Corps close to exhaustion.

But soon they were again "under way much to my joy," as Lewis wrote. And now they were in the high country where the Shoshoni tribe lived — and where Sacajawea had spent the first 11 years of her life until the Minnetarees had captured her in a raid. The Indian woman had already demonstrated great courage and presence of mind when her husband, who could not swim and whom Lewis described as "perhaps the most timid waterman in the world," allowed one of the smaller boats to be nearly capsized in a squall, then froze at the tiller in a panic. With the boat "topsaturva," light objects among their gear spilled overboard. While Charbonneau was "crying to his god for mercy," Sacajawea alertly retrieved the equipment from the water.

Lewis gratefully recorded her "fortitude and resolution."

As the party neared the source of the Missouri, Sacajawea proved her ultimate value. She recognized landmarks and helped to guide the Corps up into the mountains. Moving quickly, the Corps reached the roof pole of the continent of North America — the Continental Divide. Just short of it one member of the expedition, Hugh McNeal, ostentatiously spread his legs and straddled a stream that he took to be the headwaters of the river they had followed for 2,400 miles (the actual source lay up another stream). In his journal Lewis recorded how McNeal had effusively "thanked his god that he had lived to bestride the mighty & heretofore deemed endless Missouri."

From that point Lewis swiftly led his men two miles over a ridge and through the later-named Lemhi Pass. After descending a short way, he paused to slake his thirst at a sparkling rivulet. "Here," he wrote proudly, "I first tasted the water of the great Columbia river." The brook was not the true Columbia but it was indeed a tributary. At long and arduous last, the Corps was on the Pacific slope.

Lewis was particularly anxious to meet with Sacajawea's people. Having been forced to abandon the boats,

Preparing for the winter of 1804-1805 on the upper Missouri, top-hatted members of the Corps of Discovery work on a slightly lopsided version of a building later named Fort Mandan. Since di-arist Gass was originally hired for his abilities as a carpenter, he is probably one of the men shown building what was then the westernmost military outpost of the recently expanded United States.

the expedition needed horses to continue the journey; their only hope of getting them quickly was to make friends with the Shoshonis. But the tribe at first proved "affrighted" and evasive. When at last the Corps did make contact with them, the Indians remained uneasy and ready to vanish into the forest until, suddenly, a woman rushed to embrace Sacajawea. They had been girlhood friends. The Shoshonis relaxed somewhat and a formal powwow began. Suddenly Sacajawea ran forward and threw her arms around the chief, Cameahwait: she had just recognized him as her brother. Beginning on this happy note, negotiations with the Indians proceeded smoothly, and the Shoshoni chief eventually agreed to supply the white men with horses. In late August the Corps of Discovery set off again. Sacajawea chose to go with them. She, her husband and infant son would stay with the party until they once again returned to the Minnetaree village 13 months later.

Although the horses obtained from the Shoshonis greatly eased the burden of baggage and the Corps was now headed downhill, the trek itself continued hard. The precipitous western face of the Rockies was cut by torrents, steep slopes and ribbed ledges that seemed all but impassable. Worse still, virtually all wild game

seemed to have vanished. And though the Columbia, whose course they now followed, was full of salmon, the fish had already spawned. They were generally dead or dying and unfit for horse fodder. Even dogs, whose flesh Lewis had found more to his taste than most any other meat, were hard to find among the little-known Indians the party now came upon.

Despite the hardships of the way and their own personal discomfort, Lewis and Clark kept the men moving, and continued to record their impressions of each new tribe. Lewis openly admired the Nez Percés for their pride of bearing but even more for the splendid Appaloosa horses they pastured. The coast-dwelling Chinooks and Clatsops, on the other hand, he learned to regard with a sort of exasperated contempt; he judged them to be shiftless beggars and thieves. In meeting Indians, Lewis—now thoroughly weatherworn and suntanned—had to roll up his buckskin sleeves to establish his identity as a white man.

Then, quite suddenly, on November 7, 1805, came the climactic moment for the Corps of Discovery. Far off the men heard for the first time the rumble of Pacific breakers. Clark wrote, "Great joy in camp we are in *view* of the *Ocian,* this great Pacific Octean which we been so long anxious to See. and the roreing or noise made by the waves brakeing on the rockey Shores (as I suppose) may be heard distictly."

By December 7, 1805, they had camped on the south bank of the Columbia near its mouth. From this spot, they could keep watch over the heaving Pacific and hail any ship that might come by. For it had occurred to President Jefferson, who seemed able to think of everything, that if the journey out proved very dangerous, the Corps might have to come home by ship, intercepting some trader's vessel on the West Coast. Accordingly he had furnished Lewis with a letter of credit authorizing him to draw upon United States envoys anywhere — including Java, the island of Mauritius and the Cape of Good Hope. This unrestricted line of credit from the nation's treasury was perhaps the ultimate expression of the President's confidence in the youthful leader of the expedition.

By January 1 the Corps had hewed a stockade and winter quarters which they named Fort Clatsop. Clark had already fallen out of love with the Pacific, whose noise he could not bear. "The sea," he wrote, "which is imedeately in front roars like a repeeted roling thunder and have rored in that way ever since our arrival in its borders which is now 24 days . . . I cant say Pasific as since I have seen it, it has been the reverse."

No ship hove over the horizon and, in any case, Lewis longed to conduct further investigations of the land on the way home. Impatient for spring, the men broke camp on March 23, 1806, and headed east.

In psychological terms, the six-month journey back was easier. This time the party knew the way and, more fundamentally, they knew there *was* a feasible route. But the trip itself included all the physical stress that had accompanied the Corps's westering. Moreover the homeward journey produced two incidents representing the only grievous violence of the entire expedition. Both involved Lewis, who, with six men, had separated from Clark in order to reconnoiter fresh country. Camped with some seemingly amicable Blackfeet, Lewis awoke at a cry of alarm to discover that the Indians were stealing rifles from the sleeping explorers. In the ensuing melee one Blackfoot was stabbed to death and another wounded by a shot. Though Lewis was in no logical sense to blame, any hope for peaceful relations with the Blackfeet was shattered. For decades af-

terward, the tribe made war upon the pioneers who came westward on the Lewis and Clark trail.

The other mischance was also a shooting — and Lewis himself was the victim. While hunting meat, a member of the party, who had only one eye, mistook Lewis for an elk or bear and shot him in the buttocks. For weeks Lewis was in considerable pain, and had to be carried in a litter.

Lewis was reunited with Clark near the mouth of the Yellowstone in mid-August, and he was still suffering from his wound when, on September 20, 1806, far downstream on the Missouri once more, the Corps passed a French settlers' village called La Charette — the first visible sign of white man's civilization they had seen in nearly two and a half years. Clark entered in his record, "we saw some cows on the bank which was a joyfull Sight to the party and caused a Shout to be raised for joy."

It was a shout of jubilation, of relief and of triumph. They were home from the wilderness. They were alive and safe. They had vindicated a President's faith and judgment. With strength, endurance, discipline and the exercise of uncommon common sense, they had opened the way to half a continent. Moreover, they had gone into the unknown and brought back knowledge and solidified the American title to lands that had doubled the size of the nation.

Word of their return spread rapidly (most people had given them up for lost) and newspapers across the land rushed into print with summaries of their achievement. The *Columbia Centinel* of Boston carried this capsule account: "A Letter from *St. Louis (Upper Louisiana),* dated *Sept. 23,* 1806, announces the arrival of Captains LEWIS and CLARK, from their expedition into the interior. — They went to the *Pacific Ocean;* have brought some of the natives and curiosities of the countries through which they passed, and only lost one man. They left the *Pacific Ocean* 23rd March, 1806, where they arrived in November, 1805; — and where some American vessels had been just before. — They state the Indians to be as numerous on the *Columbia* river, which empties into the *Pacific,* as the whites in any part of the U.S. The winter was very mild on the *Pacific.* — They have kept an ample journal of their tour; which will be published, and must afford much intelligence." Much intelligence indeed.

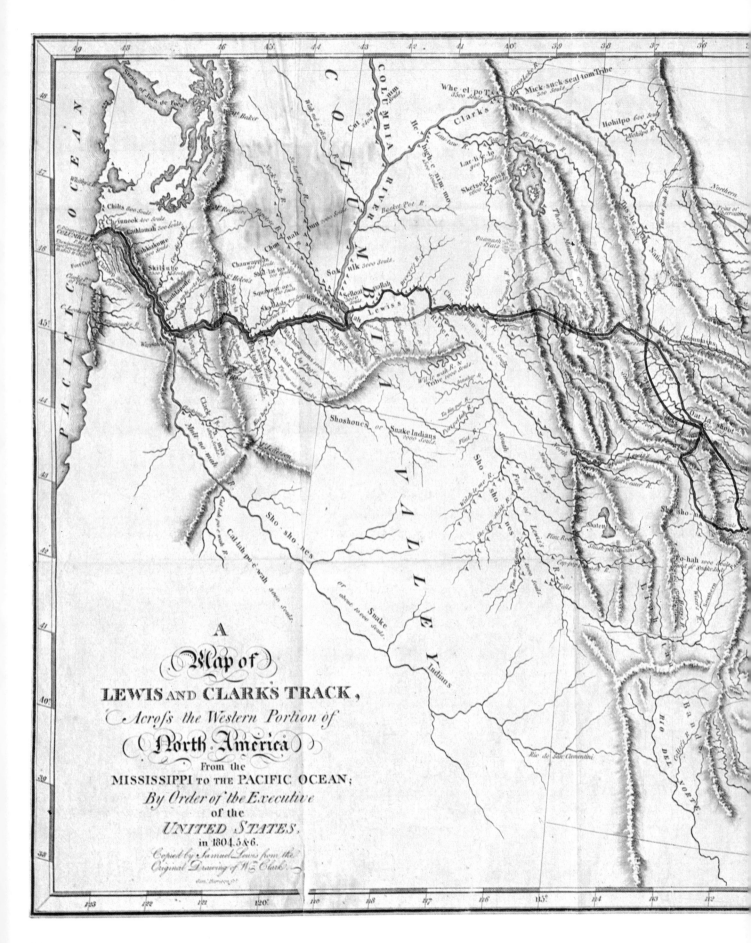

A
Map of
LEWIS AND CLARK'S TRACK,
Across the Western Portion of
North America
From the
MISSISSIPPI TO THE PACIFIC OCEAN;
By Order of the Executive
of the
UNITED STATES,
in 1804, 5 & 6.
Copied by Samuel Lewis from the
Original Drawing of W.m Clark.

A rich haul of Western knowledge

The object of your mission is to explore the Missouri River, & such principal stream of it, as, by it's course & communication with the waters of the Pacific Ocean…may offer the most direct & practicable water communication across this continent for the purposes of commerce.

This sentence of President Thomas Jefferson's, written in his vigorous 18th Century style, comprised the first of an extended list of instructions that he laid down for Meriwether Lewis and William Clark as they set off into the Western wilderness. They were gone so long on their voyage of discovery —nearly two and a half years—that many people supposed them dead. Yet when on September 23, 1806, they reappeared in St. Louis after traveling 7,689 punishing miles through trackless country, they had carried out every one of the President's charges.

Most important, Lewis and Clark had found the way West, and had brought back annotated topographical sketches as the basis for the first detailed map *(pages 34-36)* showing Americans just how to get to the Pacific. As Jefferson had instructed, they filled over a dozen notebooks like the one below. The entries varied from meticulously thorough scientific notes to casual—and wonderfully misspelled —daily observations like Clark's mention of "a fine morning calm and worm musquetors & knats verry troublesom."

The expedition also collected hundreds of plant and animal specimens, many of them new to the scientific world, and for each specimen they diligently appended a list of characteristics. So highly did later naturalists regard Lewis and Clark's pioneering work that they named several birds after the explorers and created two brand-new Latin categories of plants, which they called *Lewisia* and *Clarkia*.

Finally, the expedition leaders made a special effort to meet peaceably with the Indians, to understand their customs and attitudes, and to establish cordial relations between the tribes and the U.S. government. In this latter enterprise they were so successful that several delegations of Indian notables *(page 44)* went out of the wilderness to meet with Jefferson even before Lewis and Clark themselves had returned.

This notebook, bound in elkskin, is one of the original journals kept by Lewis and Clark. The entry for the 26th of October, 1805, contains several columns of figures recording the positions of the sun and moon—the explorers' way of determining their exact location.

Area covered by expedition's map

The first official map of the country opened by Lewis and Clark was compiled from Clark's encyclopedic navigational reckonings. Finally published in 1814, it satisfied Jefferson's principal directive, indicating the previously uncharted courses of the upper Missouri and Columbia River systems.

The published map was enlivened by Clark's own capsule notations. Clark, for example, labels Fort Mandan as the "Wintering post of Mess.rs Lewis and Clark in 1804 and 1805." On the Oregon coast, Clark observed that Fort Clatsop, their next wintering place, was in an area settled by "200 souls."

Because the expedition's route on the original map was too dimly delineated to follow, it has been emphasized here with colored lines. Lewis and Clark made the entire westward trip together (red line). On the return journey, however, they split up so that Lewis (green line) could reconnoiter the Marias River while Clark and the main group (purple line) went down the Yellowstone to its juncture with the Missouri. At that point the parties met (blue line) for a triumphal return to St. Louis.

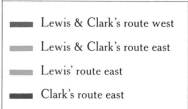

Lewis & Clark's route west

Lewis & Clark's route east

Lewis' route east

Clark's route east

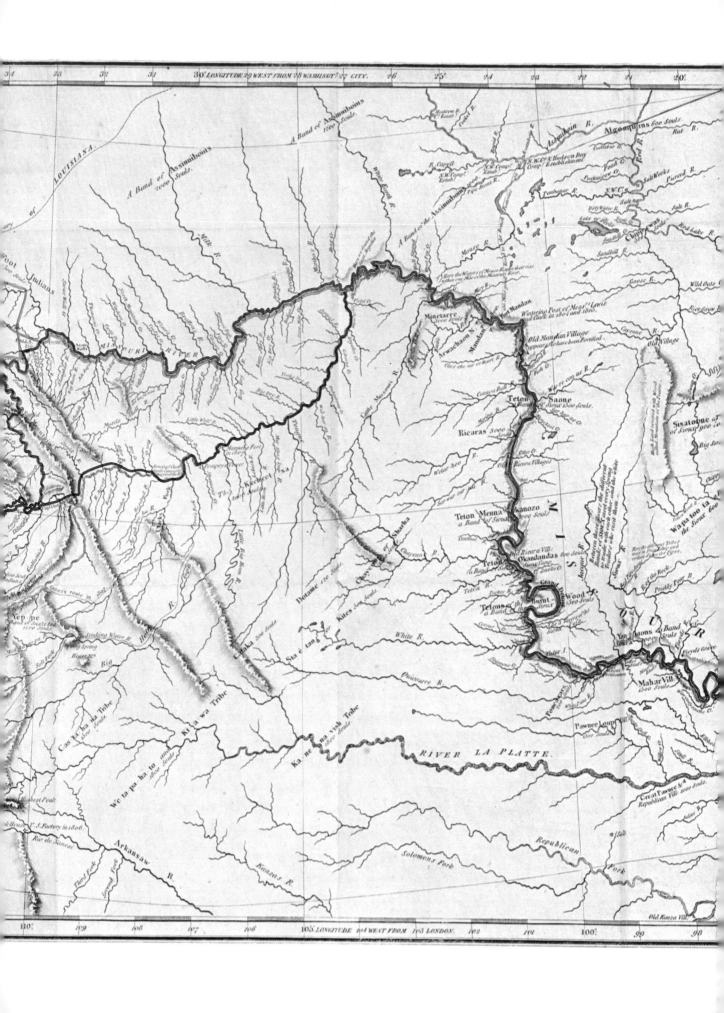

Other objects worthy of notice will be the soil

& face of the country, it's growth & vegetable productions...

On their way through the wilderness of the Louisiana and Oregon territories, Lewis and Clark identified so many botanical specimens that they were able to add nearly 200 species to the world's roster of known plants. Their botanical investigations also had an immediate practical value, since many of the plants collected were edible or contained powerful medicines. The carrot-shaped roots of the bitterroot plant, for example, could be boiled, and when the bitter-tasting peel had been removed, they were palatable and nutritious. Indians of the mountain tribes liked the taste of these starchy roots so much they would often trade a horse for a sackful of them. The roots also had curative powers; the Indians would dry and chew them to relieve sore throats.

The Chinook Indians of Oregon crafted rain-repellent headwear out of this bear grass.

In the Rocky Mountains Lewis picked this blossom of the bitterroot plant and carried it thousands of miles back to St. Louis.

Clark's description of an Oregon grape leaf growing along the Pacific Coast included measurements down to a fraction of an inch.

Indians boiled the flowers of the penstemon plant to use for treating sores and burns.

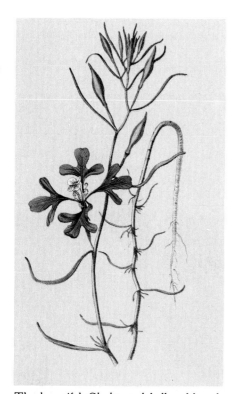

The beautiful *Clarkia pulchella,* although named for Clark, was discovered by Lewis.

Lewis and Clark learned to eat the chestnut-flavored roots of this Western Spring Beauty.

The party also sampled the roots of this wild turnip, a staple food of the Plains Indians.

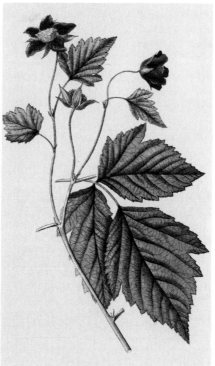

Despite its name the Oregon grape, discovered by Lewis, is actually an evergreen shrub.

Lewis found the fruit of the salmonberry was "reather ascid tho' pleasantly flavored."

The salal plant produced berries that were a favorite fruit of Indians in the Northwest.

Though they were not trained naturalists, Lewis and Clark came across enough unfamiliar birds, animals and reptiles to fill a zoo. In keeping with Jefferson's orders they took careful note of 122 species and subspecies that were unknown to science and in many cases native only to the West. Clark made sketches of any particularly intriguing creature. He and Lewis also collected animal hides and horns, and bird skins with such care that a few of them were still intact nearly two centuries later. While Lewis and Clark failed to meet the mythological monsters reputed to dwell in the West, they did unearth the bones of a 45-foot dinosaur. Furthermore, some of the living beasts they did come upon, such as the woolly mountain goat and the grizzly, were every bit as odd or fearsome as any myth. (Lewis was soon noting ruefully that he "had reather fight two Indians than one bear.") In their collectors' enthusiasm they even floated a prairie dog out of its burrow by pouring in five barrelfuls of water, then shipped the frisky animal to Jefferson alive and yelping.

This bird, first sighted on the approach to the Rockies, was later named Lewis' woodpecker. Another bird native to the same area came to be called Clark's crow.

In his journal Clark described a "large buzzard" with a wingspread of nine feet two inches. It was the California condor, largest bird on the North American continent.

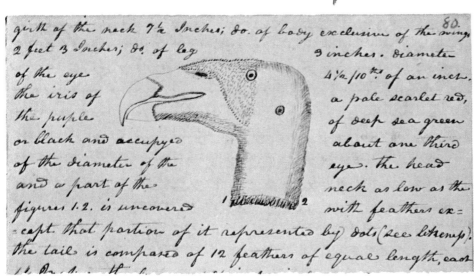

40

The first animal that Lewis stuffed for shipment to the President from Fort Mandan was this Western subspecies of the badger.

The grizzly, weighing up to a thousand pounds, existed only in the West. Lewis had to dive into a river to escape one of the bears.

Typical of animals found occasionally east of the Mississippi but flourishing in the West were the red fox *(top)* and the coyote.

Another exclusively Western animal, the Rocky Mountain goat, provided the Indians with woolly hides that they used for clothing.

The expedition's accounts of abundant beaver *(top)* and muskrat helped trigger a fur-trapping boom that led to further exploration.

The meat of the bighorn sheep was rated tender and delicious by the Corpsmen. Indians used the male's circular horns in making bows.

*You will endeavor to make yourself acquainted...with
the names of the nations & their numbers; the extent &
limits of their possessions; their relations with other tribes....*

For many months Lewis and Clark and their party were the only white men in a wilderness dominated by Indians. They encountered over 50 tribes, from the warlike Sioux of the mid-Missouri to the intriguing Chinooks along the Oregon coast, whose bizarre customs *(below)* fascinated the two leaders.

In becoming acquainted with these people, one real master stroke by Lewis and Clark was their decision to adopt into the Corps a Shoshoni girl, Sacajawea, who not only interpreted for them but helped the two young Americans to understand Indian customs. As a result, Lewis and Clark were able to fulfill Jefferson's mandate even more successfully than he had hoped, returning to Washington, D.C., with many magnificent examples of Indian culture.

Like many Northwest tribes, the Chinooks put their babies in a viselike contraption during their first year of life, producing the slope-headed adults shown in this drawing by Clark. He mistitled them Flatheads; actually, the Flathead tribe of the western Rockies did not practice such disfiguration.

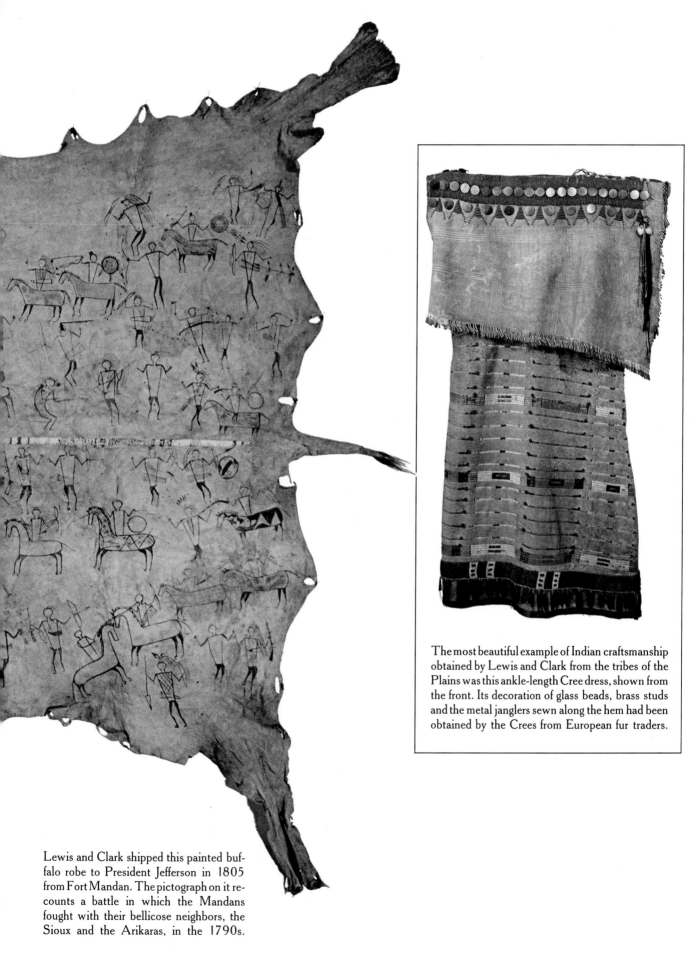

Lewis and Clark shipped this painted buffalo robe to President Jefferson in 1805 from Fort Mandan. The pictograph on it recounts a battle in which the Mandans fought with their bellicose neighbors, the Sioux and the Arikaras, in the 1790s.

The most beautiful example of Indian craftsmanship obtained by Lewis and Clark from the tribes of the Plains was this ankle-length Cree dress, shown from the front. Its decoration of glass beads, brass studs and the metal janglers sewn along the hem had been obtained by the Crees from European fur traders.

If a few of their influential chiefs, within practicable

distance, wish to visit us, arrange such a visit with them,

and furnish them with authority to call on our officers....

Throughout their journey Lewis and Clark were careful to call upon the more important tribal chiefs, pointing out to them with the most formal oratory *(page 24)* the advantages of being allied with the Great Father in Washington. After the speechmaking Lewis would fire his air gun; then he and Clark would pass out gifts and silver medals *(right)* bearing Jefferson's likeness. The explorers also invited some of the Indian dignitaries to visit the United States, as Jefferson had instructed them to do.

Between 1804 and 1806, three different delegations traveled to Washing-ton, D.C., using their peace medals as passports when they first met up with U.S. Army officers in St. Louis. At the Capitol, they were entertained by Jefferson, fitted out with gold-trimmed uniforms, and had their portraits painted by French émigré artist Charles Fevret de Saint-Memin, whose lifelike representations of three Osages are shown on these pages. Jefferson, impressed by the dignified bearing of these Indians whom he termed "the finest men we have ever seen," expressed the hope that America's westward expansion would prove to be beneficial for the Indians as well as for the whites.

Jefferson had medals struck for Lewis and Clark to give as peace tokens.

Saint-Memin drew an Osage with his medal hung around his neck.

An Osage chief poses in an officer's uniform with gold epaulets.

Painted and caparisoned in ceremonial dress, Osage men like this warrior pranced through war dances before delighted Washington crowds.

2|The mountain man's domain

The second wave of exploration in the American West was led by a tough, ragtag assortment of fur trappers who did not think of themselves as explorers. Called mountain men, they spilled through the Rocky Mountains searching for beaver—and finding new land and bold adventure. They ranged into remote valleys to discover lakes of salt and geysers of steam. They tangled with grizzly bears and when they returned to tell what they had seen and done, the trappers' reports were often too much for civilized ears. "They said I was the damndest liar ever lived," complained Jim Bridger, one of the boldest of the mountain men. "That's what a man gets for telling the truth."

Two mountain men set beaver traps in the shallows of an icy pond.

Driven off their trap lines by an attacking party of Blackfoot Indians, two fur hunters head into the timber to take a stand. The Blackfeet remained implacably hostile to white explorers after Meriwether Lewis shot a brave in 1806.

In this lithograph based on an actual event, mountain man S. E. Hollister battles with a she-bear whose cubs he had tried to capture. Though horribly bitten, Hollister nevertheless managed to kill the huge bear with his hunting knife.

LA CACCIA DEI CASTORI.

The fur seekers who opened a wilderness

On August 15, 1806, en route back to civilization, Lewis and Clark encountered two men, Joseph Dickson and Forrest Hancock, who were headed up the Missouri River to trap beaver in the Yellowstone country. During the meeting on the upper Missouri, Dickson and Hancock made a remarkable proposal: they invited John Colter, one of the expedition members, to go back into the wilderness with them as a sort of technical adviser. Colter asked his two captains if he could accept the offer.

In their customary sober manner, Lewis and Clark considered the matter for a time. They realized that Colter now belonged to the only group of white men who had firsthand knowledge of the country behind — knowledge that could have a high cash value. The captains granted Colter's request, with the understanding that no other member of the party would ask for a premature discharge. Lewis and Clark did not regard Colter as a fool for returning to the hellish country he had only just escaped; they obviously thought that he had received an attractive offer.

So it was that after two years of brutal hardship and high risk, John Colter turned back into the Western wilderness. He was to remain in the bush continuously for the next four years. And during those years he established a claim to being the precursor of the mountain men — the tough, wide-ranging fur trappers and traders who first made Americans aware of the kind of land they had in the Rockies.

These adventurers pioneered a new phase of one of the oldest and most intriguing businesses in North America. For more than two hundred years, the fur trade had been *the* trade of the North American wilderness, simply because the beaver and the mink, the marten and the otter were the only things of value thought to exist there. As early as 1600 French *coureurs de bois,* the pioneer fur men of North America, paddled log canoes into the continent's interior, where they built trading posts, collected pelts and, in many cases, lived permanently with Indian wives. In 1763 the British conquered Canada and inherited the profitable commerce, exploiting it through two great fur companies: the North West Company, which opened up the Canadian West by explorations like those of Alexander Mackenzie *(page 25);* and the Hudson's Bay Company, based in the East and glorying in the special patronage of the British crown.

Yet by one of the ironies of history, the people of the United States (and before that the colonies) had profited very little from the early fur boom. To begin with they had been blocked by both the French, with their Indian allies, and later by the Canadian monopolies. But more important, the Americans were mainly concerned with nation-building, clearing land, industry and agriculture; what trapping they did was casual and part time. One of the first serious attempts to bring the United States into the Western fur trade — the establishment of John Jacob Astor's trading post, Astoria, on the Pacific Coast — proved abortive *(page 58).*

Seen in this light, the decision made by Dickson, Hancock and Colter to become beaver trappers takes on a special historical significance. Colter, who proved to be the most durable and venturesome of the three (Dickson and Hancock disappear from the historical record after one short winter in the mountains), was not consciously trying to place the United States in competition with Canada for half a continent of unexplored land. He was simply a man who had a certain

Hudson's Bay Company officials hand out guns to Indians at a Red River fort. The British-owned company tried to maintain cordial relations with Indians, who not only brought in furs but made valuable allies.

taste and talent for the wilderness, and wanted to make some money trapping beaver. Nevertheless his activities during the next few years were of a kind that Thomas Jefferson, a great geopolitician, would have applauded. By his example, John Colter stimulated other men to compete for the fur trade of the West and create a counterbalance to British claims in the region. In addition, he cut some astonishing trails through country no white man had yet trod — or at least lived to describe.

Colter himself was a man to match his achievement. A lean, six-foot-tall Virginian, he had fought Indians west of the Alleghenies before signing on with Lewis and Clark. When he set out with Dickson and Hancock in 1806, he had already learned how to travel light, carrying little more than his leggings and loose, quill-fringed buckskin shirt, the buffalo robe he used as a bed, a tiny store of salt, some trinkets for trading with Indians, and the rifle with which he got his food.

During his first winter in the wilderness, Colter set up a base in the valley of the Yellowstone and, with his partners, trapped successfully for a season. Next spring he started home for the second time. Once again he did not reach St. Louis. Instead, he received an offer to turn back into the wilderness, as counselor and guide to another party of fur seekers.

After John Colter's long winter of hard work, it must have taken an extraordinary man to turn him round once more — and the leader of this second expedition, Manuel Lisa, was indeed extraordinary. In his own freewheeling, entrepreneurial way, he made unique contributions both to the U.S. fur business and to the exploration of the Western mountains. However, Lisa

The trade account of a Hudson's Bay fort for 1715 lists all the skins acquired and then gives their value in beaver pelts. The beaver was so basic to the fur trade that all prices were reckoned in beaver skins.

is remembered chiefly through memoirs written by his enemies, who apparently included most of his acquaintances. "Rascality set on every feature of his dark-complexioned Mexican face," was a comment in the diary of one Lisa employee.

Lisa was indeed a violent man of rare ruthlessness and few principles other than those of self-interest. A Spaniard of unknown antecedents and rather mysterious resources, he had arrived in St. Louis some dozen years before. There he seems to have dabbled in government contracts and bribes, spied a little for anyone who wanted to pay for his services, and organized an abortive smuggling venture to run contraband goods to Santa Fe, deep in Spanish territory. With a partner, François Benoît, he undertook to provision Lewis and Clark for their westward journey, and by accident or design so fouled up the arrangements as to earn the captains' intense dislike. "Damn Manuel and triply damn Mr. B.," wrote Lewis to Clark. "They give me more vexation and trouble than their lives are worth."

Lisa was undisturbed; and while the Corps of Discovery was in the field he clearly was giving serious thought to what its success might mean in terms of commercial possibilities. By 1806, when Lewis and Clark returned to St. Louis, Lisa had already begun preparations to send a party of fur trappers into the mountains. That winter he hired several ex-Corpsmen and, early in the spring of 1807, loaded 60 men into keelboats to start up the Missouri. It was on the upper river that Lisa met John Colter and persuaded him to return to the wilderness as his employee.

On Colter's advice, Lisa pushed on to the point at which the Bighorn River flows into the Yellowstone, and there he built a combined trading post and fort. Working out of this post, Colter, Lisa and the others had a successful trapping season. But Colter did more than trap beaver. During the winter of 1807-1808 he made what may be the most extraordinary solo exploration of any American in the history of the West.

Colter's objectives were simply to deal with the Indians of the West, and to search for beaver water. Traveling alone, he set off on a mighty trek through land that was neither accurately charted nor named. He skirted the eastern flank of what would later be called the Absaroka Range, ascended the Wind River Valley, crossed the Continental Divide at Union Pass, descend-

ed the Pacific slope and crossed and recrossed the Snake River and the Tetons. In a circuit through what is now Wyoming, Montana and Idaho, he was almost continuously in virgin wilderness. He was the first to come upon such wonders as the hot springs, boiling mudholes and geysers near what is now Yellowstone Park. Having seen these marvels, Colter returned to Lisa's fort and settled down to trapping for a while.

But his phenomenal endurance and courage were to be tested again. In the fall of 1808 Colter was trapping near the Jefferson Fork of the upper Missouri with a companion when the two men were surprised by some 500 Blackfeet. The partner tried to resist and was killed on the spot, his body bristling with arrows. Colter was captured, stripped and tormented casually while the Blackfeet discussed various ingenious methods of dispatching him. After several alternatives had been rejected as lacking in artistry, a chief asked Colter how fast he could run. Having lived long enough near the mountain Indians to know something about their taste in entertainment, Colter (who in fact had a reputation as being exceptionally fast on his feet) allowed that he was a terrible runner, slow as a turtle. Thereupon the Blackfoot sports told him to run for his life; the war party would follow in about 30 seconds with the intention of making mincemeat of him.

Fully motivated, Colter sprinted off barefoot through the prickly-pear thorns and rocky scree of the canyon rim, making for the Jefferson Fork, six miles away. After three miles, he had outrun all of his pursuers but one; however, that one was steadily improving his position. When the warrior pulled close, Colter turned and tripped him, dispatched him with his own lance, then ran on until he reached the bank of the Jefferson. Immediately, he leaped into the river and hid under a raft of driftwood while the Blackfeet scoured the shore. That night, he swam downstream five miles or so, hit the beach and resumed running. Seven days and some 200 miles later, naked, blistered and dehydrated from the sun, all but starved, his feet flayed from the rocks he had run across, his body full of festering thorns, he arrived safely at Lisa's fort on the Bighorn River. Characteristically, after only a few weeks of rest Colter re-outfitted and again went back into the mountains, there to stay for another two years of trapping, roaming and—whenever opportunity offered—cheerfully bushwhacking Blackfeet.

By that time his employer Manuel Lisa was getting ready to expand. In the summer of 1808, leaving most of his men behind, Lisa went back to St. Louis with his furs. In the frontier town he was treated with considerably more respect, if no more cordiality, than before. He might still be a scoundrel: on his return he found himself charged with a murder for having ordered the death of one of his own men; he somehow wriggled out of the fix by claiming that the man was a deserter, and therefore "a rascal who got what he deserved." But he was now indisputably a very rich scoundrel, and some of the shrewder gentry of St. Louis were apparently willing, even eager, to become partners in his ventures. No less an old adversary than William Clark agreed to become the president of Lisa's fur company,

EVERYTHING ANYONE WANTED TO KNOW ABOUT BEAVER

In 1743 James Isham, a Hudson's Bay trader, made this attempt to satisfy European curiosity about beaver. Besides sketching all possible details of beaver and beaver hunting in his composition, Isham wrote the following interpretation, keyed to the images.

(1) A Beaver house; (2) the thickness made of stone, mudd, & wood & c.; (3) where the Beaver Lyes within the house; (4) when the Beaver are Disturb'd, or hear a noise they make into the water, from 3 and 6; (5) where their food Lyes; (6) the half Beaver or small Beaver Lyes; (7) a Indian breaking the house

op'n with a Chissel, tied to a Long stick; (8) the Beaver making out of the house hearing a noise and makes to the Vaults; (9) netts sett in the Creek with a string and a stick at the End to catch the Beaver as they come out of the house; (10) a Indian sitting by a fire watching a Nett, with a stick by him to Kill them as he hauls them out; (11) Dam's made by the Beaver, that the water show'd not Run too fast upon them; (12) Vaults the Beaver makes into when Disturb'd. out of the house, they Run abt. 12 or 14 foot in Land (i.e.) and abt. 2 foot under the Ground; (13) a Beaver hawling a tree by the teeth into the water; (14) a

stop'age made by Inds. with stakes to Keep the Beaver from going into the River; (15) a Beaver cutting a tree Downe with his teeth; (16) the stump where cutt Down; (17) the tail of a beaver; (18) the Castor under wch. Lyes the oyly stones or 2 bladder's; (19) the penis and stones; (20) the Gutts or Interials; (21) the heart & Liver; (22) the Lights; (23) the fore feet; (24) Inds. tent in the woods; (25) a Indian going a hunting; (26) willows on the Edge of the creek; (27) a flock of partridges; (28) thick woods; (29) a stick Lying by the Indn. to Kill Beaver & c.; (30) the Creek which Runs into the Large Rivers & c.

The bloody failure of a grand scheme

On September 8, 1810, the brig *Tonquin,* carrying 33 members of John Jacob Astor's newly incorporated Pacific Fur Company, sailed out of New York bound for the Oregon coast. Astor subsequently dispatched 64 guides and trappers from St. Louis to make their way overland and meet up with the *Tonquin* at the mouth of the Columbia River.

Astor was already the dominant force in the fur trade east of the Mississippi; now he was attempting to expand his operations into the Northwest. His aim was to establish a fur-

trading outpost near the site where Lewis and Clark had spent the winter of 1805-1806. To be called Fort Astoria, Astor's post was intended as a permanent settlement.

At the helm of the *Tonquin* was a headstrong former Naval officer, Jonathan Thorn. As soon as the brig reached the Columbia on March 22, 1811, Thorn recklessly attempted an immediate landing, despite high seas. Seven men drowned *(below)* before the remainder were able to reach shore. Thorn then left less than half of the party behind to build the fort

and sailed northward to trade with Indians. During a bargaining session, he lost his patience and struck a Salish chief. A few days later the Indians returned to the *Tonquin,* butchering Thorn and almost everyone aboard. But one gravely wounded sailor who had concealed himself in the hold touched off the *Tonquin's* store of gunpowder, and with a thunderous roar the 290-ton brig was blown to splinters. (The ship's fate was later revealed by the Indians.)

Seven months after the disappearance of the *Tonquin,* Astor's overland

Pounded by leaping storm waves, the *Tonquin's* longboat capsizes while the brig itself struggles at the mouth of the Columbia.

party began straggling into the fort with their own tale of misadventure. They had been led by a New Jersey merchant who knew nothing of the wilderness. After crossing the Rockies, they made the mistake of embarking on the Snake River in canoes. The river grew faster and rougher by the mile, and soon the party was marooned beneath the sheer, mile-high walls of Hell's Canyon. Four men drowned in the rapids and one went mad before the remainder managed to scale the icy rock walls, leaving nearly all their gear behind. Only 45 of them made it to Fort Astoria alive.

On May 8, 1813, the supply ship *Beaver* arrived at the fort with reinforcements and supplies. At last it seemed that Astor's project might work out after all. The trappers, recovered from their ordeals on sea and land, were buying furs by the thousands. The future seemed secure.

But now international events undid them. Far to the east, the United States and Britain were at war. Fearing attack by a British warship, the Astorians sold their furs to Canadian competitors at a debased price. On December 13, 1813, Captain William Black of the H.M.S. *Raccoon* landed, ran up the Union Jack and changed the name of the outpost to Fort George. It was a pyrrhic victory for the British, for 12 months later the Treaty of Ghent that settled the War of 1812 gave the fort back to the U.S. But by then Astor wanted nothing more to do with the little settlement. Though it helped to establish America's claim to the Pacific Coast, Fort Astoria passed into history as a catastrophic endeavor that consumed 65 lives while yielding no profits.

Fort Astoria appears deceptively bucolic in this engraving, depicting the troubled outpost just before it was captured by the British.

and put some of his own money into the business.

To his new partners and investors, Lisa outlined a novel and effective system for collecting furs. He was convinced that the old French and British techniques of encouraging Indians to bring pelts from their tribal lands would never work in the American West. The Plains and mountain Indians were mainly horsemen who felt that slogging about in a beaver swamp was a far less attractive way of life than buffalo hunting and brigandage. Therefore, Lisa would hire his own white trappers, paying them to go wherever beaver were to be found, regardless of tribal—or any other—boundaries. Having made their catch the trappers would bring it to a single, central point—Lisa's fort, at the mouth of the Bighorn—for shipment to St. Louis. This system not only freed Lisa from dependence on the Indians, always an unstable element in the fur trade, but also made it unnecessary to maintain a number of small posts, most of whose custodians could be expected to double-cross their boss whenever it was profitable.

Though Lisa was deliberately cutting out the Indians from any direct participation in the fur trade, nevertheless he had to keep on friendly terms with the tribes whose lands his trappers were traveling and exploiting. And as it turned out, he was very successful at keeping peace in the wilderness. On his outward journeys he carried gaudy, inexpensive gifts for important chiefs. He accepted the Indian life style—including, perhaps as much for reasons of business as passion, at least one Indian wife (which hardly helped his reputation with the more prudish citizens of St. Louis, where he also had a wife). The result was a temporary but workable Indian-white truce on the middle Missouri.

Lisa did not extend his operations much beyond the eastern Rockies—the area that John Colter had first entered as a trapper in 1807. One reason was that not even he could make any permanent arrangement with the Blackfeet, whom Lewis and Clark had antagonized back in 1806. But Lisa and his men, including Colter, did consolidate the information collected by Lewis and Clark, converting much abstract geographical knowledge into the practical means of travel and survival. By 1812 or a little later, the river routes from St. Louis to the Continental Divide were fairly well known. It was still a long, hard and dangerous trip from the mouth of the Missouri to, say, the Wind River, but it was no longer blind bushwhacking; all the difficulties, risks and alternatives had been established, and could be considered before embarking on the journey.

John Colter by this time had acquired his fill of the wilderness. Early in 1810 he managed one more hairbreadth escape from the Blackfeet, while five men were shot down around him. For the last time, Colter made his weary way back to Lisa's fort. There he threw his hat to the ground and solemnly announced to the assembled company: "If God will only forgive me this time and let me off I will leave the country day after tomorrow—and be damned if I ever come into it again!" Whereupon he got in a canoe and in a month paddled 2,000 miles downriver to St. Louis.

Despite the many trails he had blazed, Colter received little credit for his discoveries, mainly because he had created no charts nor kept a journal. Again and again he tried to describe the wonders he had seen, first to other trappers, later to the polite society of St. Louis. But his reports—and particularly his tales of geysers, hot springs and boiling mud—seemed preposterous. Public opinion was willing to entertain the possibility that there might be mountains of crystal, exotic dwarfs and mammoths in the West. However, people would not swallow the story that the Inferno, too, was located out there somewhere, and the "discovery" was given the derisive name of "Colter's Hell."

The only willing ear was that of his old commander, William Clark. Colter told Clark about his travels and from memory helped fill in the appropriate section on a private map that Clark maintained and improved as his former frontier companions checked in with him. This was the nearest thing to a permanent record Colter ever left behind him, and at best it was a sketchy, incomplete record, which would scarcely enable a stranger to retrace his heroic route.

As for Manuel Lisa, he left the actual recording of geography to others while he reaped his own rewards from the fur trade. Until his death (miraculously, in bed, at a health spa) in 1820, Lisa had at least a piece of virtually all the fur action originating in St. Louis.

Very quickly, however, Lisa was to be surpassed on all counts by a Virginia gentleman named William Ashley, who took the crucial step of pushing the American fur trade—and expanding geographical knowledge—into the heart of the Rockies, and beyond. A member of the St. Louis establishment, Ashley had been a judge, a munitions maker in the War of 1812 and subsequently a real-estate speculator. In 1821, when Missouri entered the Union, Ashley was elected lieutenant governor. From that influential position he found it easy to snap up the pieces of the Lisa fur empire. With Andrew Henry, a former Lisa partner, Ashley proceeded to organize his own outfit, which came to be known as the Rocky Mountain Fur Company.

On February 13, 1822, Ashley inserted a memorable ad in the help-wanted section of the *Missouri Gazette and Public Advertiser,* soliciting the services of "enterprising young men" willing to go into the wilderness. From this advertisement and a similar one that appeared the next season *(page 64),* Ashley recruited an astounding group of men whose names in later years would read like a roll call of great Western adventurers and explorers: Jed Smith, Jim Bridger, Tom Fitzpatrick, Hugh Glass, the Sublette brothers, James Clyman, Edward Rose. But at the time the most striking fact about Ashley's crew must have been their great variety and their utter inexperience in the ways of mountain life.

Some of them were respectable enough. Young Jim Clyman was working as a surveyor, one of the most honorable of professions on the frontier; William Sublette was serving as the underpaid constable of St. Charles, Missouri (he sold his most valuable possession, a bedstead, for one dollar upon joining Ashley). But William's brother Milton, only 21 years old, had not done much of anything; Jim Bridger had never risen above the station of apprentice blacksmith. And Edward Rose was a Cherokee-Negro who came to Ashley after a career as a Mississippi pirate and bandit.

In the spring of 1823 Ashley led these tough but green men and some 62 others out of St. Louis, planning to follow the Missouri north to the Yellowstone country, where the party would disperse and set about trapping beaver. (The previous spring Andrew Henry had taken some of the men up to the mouth of the Yellowstone, where they built a fort.) On May 30 they arrived at the river villages of the Arikara Indians, near the present border of North and South Dakota—and promptly blundered into the most significant of all the battles between Indians and mountain men.

The immediate causes of the fight have never been really clarified. One known fact is that the Arikaras had for years been generally hostile to white men; more specifically they bore a grudge against some fur traders who had protected two or three Sioux warriors a few weeks earlier, at a time when the Sioux and the Arikaras, old and bitter enemies, had been on the warpath. When Ashley's party arrived, the Arikaras were still in a warlike mood, and had some 600 warriors holed up in their villages. Ashley had a force of only 70 men.

On the morning of June 2 the Arikaras sallied out in force, apparently without provocation. About three fourths of the Indians, Ashley reported in a letter from the front, were "armed with London Fuzils that carry a ball with great accuracy, and force, and which they use with as much expertness as any men I ever saw handle arms; those that have no guns use bows and arrows, war axes, & etcetera." With this weaponry the Arikaras completely routed the Americans, killing 12 and forcing the others to flee, leaving most of their dead lying on the sands of the Missouri.

Ashley immediately retired downstream and sent off an urgent plea for help. In response, Colonel Henry Leavenworth assembled six companies (about 200 men) of the U.S. Sixth Infantry, armed them with two cannons and several small swivel guns in addition to their own rifles and pistols, and started upriver. As the relief force—which came to be called, rather grandly, the Missouri Legion—proceeded upstream, it picked up some 700 Sioux allies. Various trappers and other white men also joined the Legion en route, and when the force finally reached the Arikara villages in early August it totaled no less than 1,100 men. Yet for all his overwhelming superiority in numbers and weapons, Leavenworth proved to be at best a timid commander. After some skirmishing, the Arikaras slipped out of their villages at night, leaving the Missouri Legion maneuvering around the approaches to their empty huts.

By outfighting and outmaneuvering the trappers and their allies, the Arikaras damaged white prestige among all the river tribes. The traditional river routes to the mountains were now closed to fur seekers. To the north lay the trapping grounds of the Hudson's Bay Company and Astor's American Fur Company—whose proprietor had by now recovered from his unhappy Pacific venture. Both were too powerful for Ashley to challenge. If he still wanted to get into the fur business his only option was to head directly west, overland. ◉

The fashion that stimulated Western exploration

Beaver hat and fur-collared cape

The opening of the mountains and forests of the West owed much of its impetus to a small and frivolous item: the beaver hat. From the early 17th Century to the middle of the 19th, no proper European gentleman appeared in public without one; hatters like the Zurich manufacturer whose label is shown above could scarcely keep up with the demand. In 1760 alone, the Hudson's Bay Company exported to England enough North American beaver pelts to make 576,000 hats. Americans shared this sartorial taste, and a man of fashion in New York would happily pay $10 for a beaver hat.

In addition to the almost insatiable demand for beaver, the North American fur business enjoyed a growing market for its other product lines. By the 1830s, splashes of ornamental furs —not only beaver, but marten, fox and otter — were appearing on the collars, sleeves, hems, gloves and boots of ladies and gentlemen alike. At the height of the craze even a sober ladies' bonnet *(right)* was not thought *comme il faut* unless adorned with a dash of fur.

(696)

(864)

Silk pelisse robe with marten trimming

Taffeta dress with fox shawl

Fur-trimmed fichu

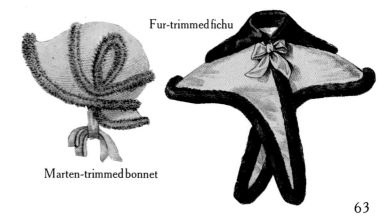

Marten-trimmed bonnet

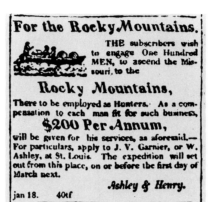

For the Rocky Mountains.
THE subscribers wish to engage One Hundred MEN, to ascend the Missouri, to the
Rocky Mountains,
There to be employed as Hunters. As a compensation to each man fit for such business,
$200 Per Annum,
will be given for his services, as aforesaid. For particulars, apply to J. V. Garnier, or W. Ashley, at St. Louis. The expedition will set out from this place, on or before the first day of March next.
Ashley & Henry.
jan 18.   40tf

In the fall of 1823, Ashley put the survivors of the Arikara defeat on horse- and muleback and sent them deep into the Rockies. This act of simple necessity turned out to be yet another permanent feature of the new-style Western fur business: moving men, supplies and furs between the mountains and the lower Missouri by pack trains and wagons. As with so many other developments in the fur trade, it also produced a fresh burst of land exploration. Within a year a trapping party led by tough, swashbuckling Tom Fitzpatrick had forced its way to the head of the remote Wind River country where a convenient notch enabled the group to get through to the other side of the Rocky Mountain wall. The notch was later to be named South Pass, and became a major portal to the Far West for tens of thousands of emigrants traveling along the Oregon Trail. For now, however, South Pass opened up virgin trapping grounds in the heretofore unexplored Green River country where, except for the relentless Blackfoot warriors, there was little interference from marauding Indians.

In order to keep contact with his far-flung fur brigades, and possibly to be sure they would not be tempted into trading with any itinerant rivals, Ashley told his men that in July 1825 he would meet them at Henry's Fork on the Green River with a caravan-load of equipment from St. Louis. There he would pay them off for their previous months' work, pick up their furs and re-outfit them for the 1825-1826 season. At the same time, since no trapping was done in midsummer, they could lounge around the river for a few weeks, gamble a little, drink a lot of whiskey and pursue any Indian girls who happened to be in the vicinity. Finally, Ashley let it be known that if Indians, white freelancers and employees of other fur companies cared to sell their furs at Henry's Fork, pick up supplies and join in the fun and games, they would be more than welcome. Thus it was that the rendezvous — soon to be the best-known social and business institution of the American mountain men — came into existence.

In almost every subsequent year, the rendezvous site was changed, and the Rocky Mountain Fur Compa-ny's trappers remained free to search out new beaver country. Encouraged to wander, the Rocky Mountain men became great pathfinders in their own right.

Historians are still trying to figure out exactly where all of them wandered. It is certain that by the mid-1830s American trappers had explored the mountains of the West from the eastern slopes of the Rockies to the Sierra passes into California, and from the Columbia River to the Mojave Desert. They were the first white men to look upon such wonders as the badlands of the Great Basin, the chasm at Yosemite, the redwoods of California.

What tales they had to relate! Hugh Glass used to tell of the time a wounded grizzly charged him three times and mauled him so badly that two rescuing comrades, having killed the bear, wrote Glass off as too mangled to carry out and sat down to await the moment of the burial chore. But Glass took so long about it that they finally just left him lying on the ground. Whereupon, still refusing to die, he somehow managed to crawl to a Sioux village, where he was taken in and nursed back to health.

Jim Bridger liked to boast that he was the true discoverer of the Great Salt Lake. One winter night in 1825 a party of trappers including Bridger, Ashley and Henry camped at Cache Valley just west of the present Wyoming border. Two men in the party made a friendly wager about the ultimate course of the nearby Bear River and, to settle the matter, Bridger ran the river until it emptied into what looked like a great shallow bay. Tasting the water he found it salty, and he returned to the trappers' camp to report that he had come upon an arm of the Pacific Ocean. None of the men ever revealed the resolution of the bet; but the following year four other trappers went down the Bear, paddled around the entire body of water, and estab-

The brute realities of a trapper's life were dramatized in this illustration from *Harper's Weekly*. Besides attending to the business of trapping beaver, a mountain man spent his days hunting big game such as moose or cougar, being hunted by bear and on leaner days shooting crows for food.

SCENES IN THE LIFE OF A TRAPPER.—[Sketched by W. M. Cary.]

A proud young man, his weather-beaten partner and a pet bear cub approach the end of a fur-gathering journey in this romanticized tableau, *The Trappers' Return,* by George Caleb Bingham. Although their life was never as idyllic as shown here, the end of a trip was often carefree as the trappers floated down the Missouri with a large bundle of pelts in their dugout canoe and the lights of St. Louis ahead.

lished once and for all that it was a salt-water lake.

Jim Beckwourth became a war chief of the Crow tribe, took several Indian wives and boasted forever afterward of the battle honors that he won among his adopted people. Once, according to his own account, when he was engaged in lone combat with a number of enemy warriors he was swiftly reinforced by a large party of Crows. "I despoiled my victim of his gun, lance, war-club, bow and quiver of arrows. Now I was the greatest man in the party, for I had killed the first warrior. We painted our faces black, and rode back to the village bearing eleven scalps."

Anticipating that some whites might find fault with both his behavior and his associations, Beckwourth doughtily rose to his own defense: "I fought in their behalf against the most relentless enemies of the white man. If I chose to become an Indian while living among them, it concerned no person but myself; and by doing so, I saved more life and property for the white man than a whole regiment of United States regulars could have done at the same time."

Bold words—but mountain men usually talked big —and very often lived the same way.

There was, of course, no single mold from which these varied rogues and heroes emerged, but as a group they developed a distinctive style based partly on the necessities of their work and partly on a certain community of taste. Most contemporary descriptions of them were romanticized, bowdlerized or otherwise inaccurate, but a convincing account of the typical mountain man was contributed by Rufus Sage, himself a mountain trapper and small trader during the 1830s.

"His skin, from constant exposure, assumes a hue almost as dark as that of the Aborigine, and his features and physical structure attain a rough and hardy cast. His hair, through inattention, becomes long, coarse, and bushy, and loosely dangles upon his shoulders. His head is surmounted by a low crowned wool-hat, or a rude substitute of his own manufacture. His clothes are of buckskin, gaily fringed at the seams with strings of the same material, cut and made in a fashion peculiar to himself and associates. The deer and buffalo furnish him the required covering for his feet which he fabricates at the impulse of want. His waist is encircled with a belt of leather, holding encased his butcher-knife and pistols—while from his neck is suspended a bullet-pouch securely fastened to the belt in front, and beneath the right arm hangs a powder-horn traversely from his shoulder, behind which, upon the strap attached to it, are affixed his bullet-mould, ball-screw, wiper, awl, &c. With a gun-stick [a homemade ramrod] made of some hard wood and a good rifle placed in his hands, carrying from thirty-five balls to the pound, the reader will have before him a correct likeness of a genuine mountaineer when fully equipped."

Few things came easily in this man's life. A mountain man was meagerly equipped even by the low woodland standards of his time. For an entire winter's work he dressed pretty much as Colter had done, in buckskins, with one extra set of leggings. He usually carried several knives, a pipe, tobacco and perhaps some reading matter for idle moments (the Bible, Shakespeare and books of poetry occasionally turned up in trappers' camps). Spare locks and flints, some 25 pounds of powder, a hundred pounds of lead and his gun made up the rest of his baggage. The gun was usually a heavy .40- to .60-caliber rifle, preferably one of the pieces made by hand for the mountain trade by the Hawken brothers of St. Louis. A Hawken rifle was said to be accurate at distances up to 200 yards and was powerful enough to knock down a buffalo, a grizzly bear or a Blackfoot. Pistols and fusils (short-barreled shotguns) were sometimes added to the armament.

Except for a little flour, coffee, tea and salt, the mountain man carried no food. Instead, he lived almost exclusively off the land. Occasionally a trapper might gather wild plums and nuts, and in hard times he would eat whatever else came to hand—roots, bark, even boots. But as a matter of preference and convenience he was carnivorous. Almost any creature might go into the pot; buffalo, deer, elk and antelope were the most common prey, but a bobcat, rabbit, wolf or hawk would do. (*Le mal de vache,* a form of dysentery caused by a steady diet of fat meat, was a frequent and occasionally fatal mountain complaint.)

Next to his guns, the most important possessions of a mountain man were four to six beaver traps, which cost him about $12 to $16 apiece. They were put to work during two trapping seasons. The first was in the fall, after the summer fur had become prime; it lasted until the ice and snow made travel and trapping impossible. The second began in the spring, when the ice began to break up, and continued until the quality of the fur deteriorated because of warm weather. At both seasons the water in which the trapper worked was freezing. Rheumatism brought on by constant immersion in ice water was another occupational ailment.

The standard trapping procedure was to wade into the muck of a pond or swamp and set a trap under the surface in such a way that the animal would be held under the water and drowned. (Many a beaver managed to escape by gnawing off his imprisoned foot.) The trap was baited with a bit of greenery or a daub of scent. All that remained was to check the trap every few days, haul a 40-pound beaver carcass out of the mud and cold water now and then, and repeat the process.

When foul weather finally closed down the ponds and streams, the trapper retired for the winter to a crude camp; again, the best description is by Rufus Sage:

"It is usually located in some spot sheltered by hills or rocks, for the double purpose of securing the full warmth of the sun's rays, and screening it from the notice of strolling Indians that may happen in its vicinity. Within a convenient proximity to it stands some grove, from which an abundance of dry fuel is procurable when needed; and equally close the ripplings of a watercourse salute the ear with their music.

"His shantee faces a huge fire, and is formed of skins carefully extended over an arched frame-work of slender poles, which are bent in the form of a semicircle and kept to their places by inserting their extremities in the ground. Near this is his 'graining block,' planted aslope, for the ease of the operative in preparing his skins for the finishing process in the art of dressing; and not far removed is a stout frame, contrived from four pieces of timber, so tied together as to leave a square of sufficient dimensions for the required purpose, in which, perchance, a skin is stretched to its fullest extension, and the hardy mountaineer is busily engaged in rubbing it with a rough stone or 'scraper,' to fit it for the manufacture of clothing."

Often the trappers bought or otherwise obtained an Indian girl to take to the mountains for pleasure and to perform some of the dirtier winter camp chores. Indian girls were regularly and willingly sold by the tribesmen at rendezvous. The price might be as little as a jug of whiskey or a horse; but one mountain man claimed to have paid $2,000 in beaver skins for a chief's daughter. In an especially detailed account of the Mandan tribe, the artist and traveler George Catlin listed some fairly standard rates of exchange: "Their women are beautiful and modest . . . and if either Indian or white man wishes to marry the most beautiful girl in the tribe, she is valued only equal perhaps to two horses, a gun with powder and ball for a year, five or six pounds of beads, or a couple of gallons of whiskey." But even with this sort of companionship, four or five winter months in a smoky, leaky hut must have been a tedious time—a long season of short rations, bitter cold, wet gear and grubby tasks. All in all, there was precious little glamor, less profit and a surfeit of danger in the life of an ordinary mountain man.

Nevertheless some men not only achieved hero status for their mountain-roaming exploits, but later in their lives emerged to prominence in other roles. Bill Sublette worked his way up from ordinary trapper to trader, became a partner in the Rocky Mountain Fur Company, and ended his days as a wealthy man selling supplies to his onetime companions. Jim Clyman, wandering ever westward, eventually left the fur trade to become a founding father of the new state of California. A young mountain man named Christopher (Kit) Carson later made a glittering name as the West's greatest freelance Indian fighter and the only brigadier general in the United States Army who could write nothing beyond his own name and could read nothing at all (he was appointed head of the First New Mexico Volunteer Infantry during the Civil War).

Not surprisingly, the mountain man's world had ample room for misfits and eccentrics. There were remittance men like Benjamin Harrison, son of one United States President and uncle of another, whose family sent him West to spare themselves the embarrassment of his "drunkenness and recklessness." There was the Cherokee-Negro Edward Rose, one of Ashley's original crew, who in 1832 turned up in a Crow village at the mouth of the Stinking River enjoying the rank of a chief and a harem of four wives. And there was "Old Bill" Williams, a religious fanatic who lived by choice completely alone in the wilderness, emerging from time to time with fabulous loads of prime furs from secret trapping grounds. Williams gained a bad reputation among the mountain men: he was believed to have practiced cannibalism on at least one occasion. ◉

This West Coast trapper dressed himself up in a gaudy but warm Cossack costume.

THE
TRAPPER'S GUIDE;
A MANUAL OF INSTRUCTIONS

FOR CAPTURING ALL KINDS OF FUR-BEARING ANIMALS, AND CURING THEIR SKINS; WITH OBSERVATIONS ON THE FUR-TRADE, HINTS ON LIFE IN THE WOODS, AND NARRATIVES OF TRAPPING AND HUNTING EXCURSIONS.

To aspiring 19th Century trappers, the title page above introduced the imaginative works of Sewell Newhouse, an Oneida, New York, businessman who tried to cash in on the fur boom by his own unique methods.

Newhouse's manual, *The Trapper's Guide,* was dedicated to "poor men who are looking out for pleasant work and ways of making money." Not only was trapping profitable, he told readers, but it would transform anyone into "a stouter and healthier man." The author admitted that he had a vested interest in boosting fur trapping since he manufactured a widely sold steel trap *(below)*. But he also itemized equipment such as snowshoes, tents and even canoes that could be bought from other sources.

While Newhouse's idealized trapper at right bore little resemblance to rugged mountain men — even to those who had developed into backwoods dudes *(left)* — nevertheless *The Trapper's Guide* was genuinely useful. Newhouse advised would-be trappers to work in pairs, each packing 50 pounds of equipment including traps, fishing tackle and plenty of food. Such a team, he said, could "make five hundred dollars in a trapping season."

The Newhouse beaver trap was a major improvement over previous snares. When an animal stepped on the disk, the steel jaws snapped shut and the leaf springs on either side flew up to lock them as shown.

"Snowshoes are indispensable to the trapper wherever deep snows prevail," Newhouse advised. To put on a snowshoe, the trapper wound the strap around his boot, then knotted the ends behind his ankle.

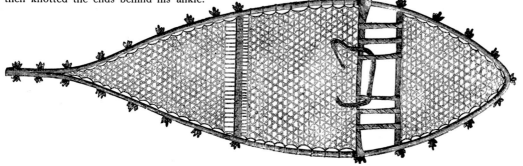

This illustration from *The Trapper's Guide* showed a highly romanticized view of a grubby, uncomfortable profession. Not only was this dandified trapper absurdly clad for the wilderness, but real trappers did not shoot their prey, because bullets tore up the fur.

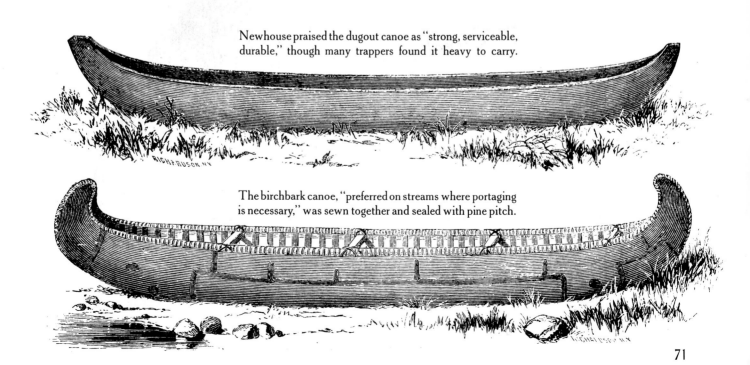

Newhouse praised the dugout canoe as "strong, serviceable, durable," though many trappers found it heavy to carry.

The birchbark canoe, "preferred on streams where portaging is necessary," was sewn together and sealed with pine pitch.

Most trappers were ordinary men—ordinary, at least, before they went into the mountains. The basic requirements for a mountain man were much the same as for a farm laborer: a strong back, a good constitution and some experience with tools and weapons. It is not surprising that many of them were ex-farm hands who had grown bored with the agricultural life. One such was a youngster named Zenas Leonard. He was a minor figure in the fur brigades, but happened to be in places where action occurred and could write pretty well. In 1839 he published in his hometown newspaper, the *Clearfield Republican,* a journal of his experiences that is perhaps the most intriguing original document of the mountain-man period.

According to his own account, Leonard grew up on a farm in Clearfield County, Pennsylvania. It was poor mountain land, and in the spring of 1830, on the morning of his 21st birthday, Leonard told his father, "I can make my living without picking up stones," and left. Eventually he got to St. Louis, where he was hired by a small trapping outfit led by one John Gantt, who had been dishonorably discharged from the Army for embezzlement. In the spring of 1831 Leonard went west with Gantt's men. He was to remain there for the next four years, engaged in hardships and adventures beyond the imaginings of a Pennsylvania farmboy.

In the fall of 1831, as they searched out a site for their winter camp, the Gantt party was trapped in the deep snows of a canyon far up the Laramie River. Leonard and 17 other men tried to walk 800 miles through the mountains to Santa Fe, though none of them was certain of the city's location. "Here we were in the desolate wilderness," Leonard wrote, "uninhabited by even the hardy savage or wild beast—surrounded on either side by huge mountains of snow, without one mouthful to eat save a few beaver skins—our eyes almost destroyed by the piercing wind, and our bodies at times almost buried by the flakes of snow which were driven before it. Oh! How heartily I wished myself home."

Leonard and a few other men in Gantt's party survived the winter, not by stratagem or woodcraft but because they ate beaver skin, were lucky enough to stumble on two starving buffalo and had an incredible capacity for brute endurance.

Their experience was terrible, but not unusual. Beyond the routine problems of survival in rugged countryside and brutal weather, mountain men were confronted with a great variety of special ones endemic to their work. Jim Bridger, for example, once went about for three years with a long, barbed Blackfoot arrowhead buried in the muscles of his back. Finally Bridger ran into the missionary-physician Marcus Whitman, who dug out the arrowhead, presumably without any anesthetic except, perhaps, a bottle of whiskey.

Josiah Gregg, a Santa Fe trader, was with a trapping party when one of its members was accidentally wounded in the arm by a rifle ball. The wound turned gangrenous, and to save their companion the trappers performed an amputation. "Their only case of instruments," Gregg later reported, "consisted of a handsaw, a butcher's knife, and a large iron bolt. The teeth of the saw being considered too coarse, they went to work and soon had a set of fine teeth filed on the back. The knife having been whetted keen and the iron bolt laid upon the fire, they commenced the operation, and in less time than it takes to tell it the arm was opened round to the bone, which was almost in an instant sawed off; and with the whizzing hot iron the whole stump was so effectually seared as to close the arteries completely. Bandages were now applied and the company proceeded on their journey as though nothing had occurred. The arm commenced healing rapidly and in a few weeks the patient was sound and well, and is perhaps still living to bear witness to the superiority of the hot iron over ligatures, in taking up arteries."

Such wounds by gun, arrow or other weapons were common in the lives of the mountain men, largely because of the implacable hatred of many Indians—most notably the Blackfeet and the Arikaras. Some of the violence might have been avoided if the invading whites had been more experienced and skillful in either woodsmanship, diplomacy or battle tactics. Time and again, the mountain men fought when they should have parleyed, fled when they should have fought, were treacherous when honesty would have served their interests better. Their problems were tragically illustrated by the so-called Battle of Pierre's Hole, in which their opponents were the Gros Ventres, prickly and pugnacious allies of the Blackfeet.

In the summer of 1832 a band of about 150 Gros Ventres, who had been off on a visit to the Arapahos of the southern Plains, were returning to their northern

The rambunctious capital of the fur trade

All of the energies of the fur trade came to a coruscating focus in St. Louis. Located on the western bank of the Mississippi just below the mouth of the Missouri, St. Louis was in a perfect position to command Western trade. From its port, steamboats transported men and supplies out to beaver country and carried back peltry by the ton. From 1815 to 1830 the brown gold passing through musty waterfront warehouses brought $3,750,000 into St. Louis.

Citizens found little difficulty in spending the money. The waterfront was lined with taverns and grogshops where trappers, rivermen, wagoners, ex-soldiers and drifters met to drink, gamble, boast and very often fight. A visitor in the 1830s noted that "the reckless mountain boys who had returned from their summer campaigns were the life and terror of the place."

Above the raucous levee was a different sort of world that still retained the sophisticated ways of the original French settlers. Wealthy fur merchants rivaled one another in erecting limestone residences sumptuously furnished with mahogany, crystal, velvet and lace. One leading trader, Auguste Chouteau, who as a young man had chopped trees for the first settlement in 1764, lived in a mansion with black walnut floors; his servants were instructed to apply a fresh coat of wax every day. And when one of the "Bostons," as the Americans were called, made a fortune, he usually copied the grand style. In 1818 William Clark erected a house that included an imposing room measuring 100 by 35 feet. This was his council cham-

Thick steamboat traffic churns in and out of St. Louis, as seen from the Illinois shore.

ber where, under massive chandeliers, he displayed all the Indian artifacts he had gathered over the years.

By 1820 the city supported three newspapers and a bookstore. For those whose taste ran to more lively entertainment, 50 plays were put on that year, and there were enough dances and parties to keep four hairdressers and several professional musicians profitably employed.

But even the refined lives of the elite suffered an occasional outburst of anger. Unlike waterfront ruffians who were quick to use their fists, however, the gentlemen of St. Louis got redress through duels. After a challenge was issued, the two principals and their seconds would row out to the local field of honor, Bloody Island, in the Mississippi. There they would pace off their positions, raise their pistols and coolly fire — a decorous procedure

that left at least seven prominent citizens dead between 1810 and 1831.

St. Louis had plentiful growing pains. In 1823, the streets were in such a primitive state that a local newspaper writer sardonically offered "Hints for the Mayor and Aldermen," in which he urged: *"By all means prevent the paving of Main Street.* That street is the only navigable watercourse *through* the city for craft of the larger size." Crime was rampant. Thieves, thugs, even kidnappers prowled the city at night; and as late as 1838 there was still no regular, paid police force.

All this led to the common saying in St. Louis that "God would never cross the Mississippi." Whatever His reservations about the city, the census count indicates that by the year 1840 some 16,000 Americans had found its array of temptations irresistible.

lands. Their route took them close to Pierre's Hole, a valley in the Tetons where the trappers were holding their annual rendezvous. Bad blood already existed between the two groups; on the way north the Gros Ventres had been making whatever trouble they could, and at one point they had tried unsuccessfully to bushwhack Billy Sublette and Tom Fitzpatrick.

On July 17, when the rendezvous ended, Milton Sublette led a party of trappers in the direction of the Snake River. Seven miles from the rendezvous site he encountered the wandering band of Gros Ventres. Temporarily outnumbered, Sublette asked for a parley. A Gros Ventre chief rode out to meet the trappers, represented by Antoine Godin, a notable Blackfoot-hater whose father had been killed by the tribe, and by a friendly Flathead Indian who had been at the rendezvous. As Antoine extended his hand in peace to the Gros Ventre negotiator, he ordered the Flathead to shoot. The Gros Ventre fell dead, Godin seized the victim's scarlet robe and the two murderers fled back to their own party.

The Gros Ventres immediately drew back to a grove of willows and began to dig rifle pits and throw up a breastwork. This was taken as a most hostile gesture by the mountain men, who were soon reinforced by 200 more trappers and 500 Flatheads and Nez Percés from the rendezvous camp. Billy Sublette took charge of the operation, deciding that, since the trappers and their Indian allies outnumbered the Gros Ventres by about 7 to 1, the mountain men had a golden opportunity to wipe out the whole war party.

Zenas Leonard was in the first wave sent by Sublette to storm the Gros Ventre position. "In a case of this kind," Leonard later wrote, "any man not evincing the greatest degree of courage and every symptom of bravery, is treated as a coward; and the person who advances first, furthest and fastest, and makes the greatest display of animal courage, soon rises in the estimation of his companions. Accordingly with the hope of gaining a little *glory* while an opportunity offered, I started into the brush in company with two acquaintances (Smith and Kean) and two Indians. We made a circuitous route and came towards the fort from a direction which we thought we would be least expected. We advanced closer and closer, crawling upon our hands and knees, with the intention of giving them a select shot; and when within about forty yards of their breastwork, one of our Indians was shot dead. At this we all lay still for some time, but Smith's foot happening to shake the weeds, as he was laying on his belly, was shot through. I advanced a little further, but finding the balls to pass too quick and close, concluded to retreat. In passing by, Smith asked me to carry him out, which met my approbation precisely, for I was glad to get out of this unpleasant situation under any pretext —provided my reputation for courage would not be questioned."

Actually, Leonard was overly modest. In comparison with most of the other men, he proved himself something of a tiger, for he probably got closer to the Gros Ventres than the great majority of the would-be attackers. Throughout the day the outnumbered, surrounded Indians held off the mountain men, giving better than they got. (The final casualty figures were 26 Gros Ventres including the murdered chief, 32 in the army of the trappers.)

That night, the Gros Ventres began to sing their death songs, but they were not quite ready to give up the ghost entirely, for they had one final trick to try. They interrupted their sad songs long enough to shout across the breastwork to a Flathead Indian that they would soon be revenged, since a party of 600 to 800 warriors was about to descend upon the scene of battle and chew up the trappers. The simple stratagem worked with remarkable success. A few of the mountain men remained in the woods, but the great majority of them panicked. "Every man," wrote Leonard, who was one of the men who stayed, "thought only of his own security and ran for life without ever looking around

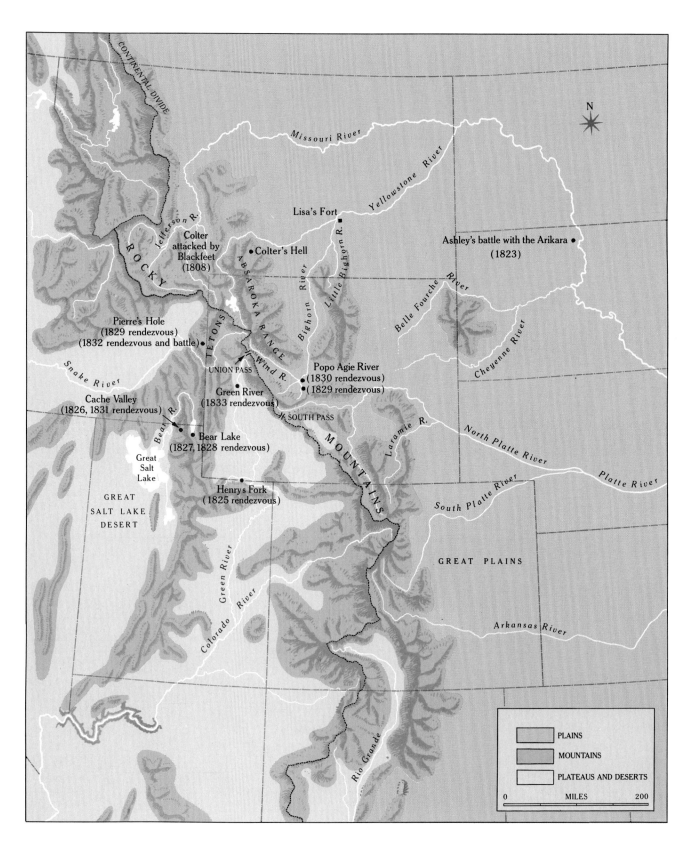

Colter attacked by Blackfeet (1808)

Colter's Hell

Lisa's Fort

Ashley's battle with the Arikara (1823)

CONTINENTAL DIVIDE

Missouri River

Yellowstone River

Jefferson R.

ROCKY

ABSAROKA RANGE

Bighorn River

Little Bighorn R.

Belle Fourche River

Cheyenne River

Pierre's Hole
(1829 rendezvous)
(1832 rendezvous and battle)

TETONS

UNION PASS

Wind R.

Popo Agie River
(1830 rendezvous)
(1829 rendezvous)

Green River
(1833 rendezvous)

Snake River

Cache Valley
(1826, 1831 rendezvous)

Bear R.

SOUTH PASS

Laramie R.

North Platte River

Platte River

Bear Lake
(1827, 1828 rendezvous)

MOUNTAINS

Great
Salt
Lake

Henrys Fork
(1825 rendezvous)

GREAT
SALT LAKE
DESERT

South Platte River

GREAT PLAINS

Green River

Colorado River

Arkansas River

Rio Grande

	PLAINS
	MOUNTAINS
	PLATEAUS AND DESERTS

0   MILES   200

N

which would at once have convinced him of his folly."

Most of the mountain men ran all the way to the rendezvous camp. In the morning they began to creep back to the scene of battle, only to find that the Gros Ventres, presumably laughing all the way, had slipped out of the fort and disappeared. The rage of some of the mountain men, reported Leonard, "was unbounded, and approached to madness. For my own part, although I felt much regret at the result after so much toil and danger, yet I could not but give the savages credit for the skill they displayed in preserving their lives, at the very moment when desperation, as we thought, had seized the mind of each of them."

On that day, at least, most of the mountain men left the field alive. At other times, even when no Indians were near, trapping could be a lethal occupation. Men died of drowning, infected injuries, dysentery, smallpox, hydrophobia, tetanus and accidental or intentional gunshots by their companions. They also fell off mountains, were bitten by rattlesnakes and, like Hugh Glass, were mauled by grizzly bears. James Ohio Pattie, a trapper in the southern mountains in 1826, claimed that of the 116 men who left Santa Fe that season, only 16 survived until the next. In later years trapper Antoine Robidoux, then 62, was able to count only three living men from 300 he knew to have roamed the Rockies.

Why, then, did the mountain men go out again and again? Adventure, in many cases. Escape, in others — a yearning to be alone in the wilderness when it was still truly wild. Some men simply liked the life, while a few, such as Beckwourth, cherished the company of Indians, both male and female, or relished the notion of playing Indian themselves for a while. Most commonly, however, the motivation was much the same as it has always been with so many men everywhere: money. A good

THE MOUNTAIN MEN'S VIOLENT WORLD

By the early 1830s, fur trappers were intimately — and often violently — acquainted with a vast area of the West stretching from the Missouri River through the Central Rockies and on to the Great Basin beyond. The map at left describes their far-flung world. Brawling with Indians, resupplying at a rendezvous each summer and always pushing into the unknown, the mountain men in less than three decades ferreted out every glade and stream in the kingdom of the beaver. As one trapper said fondly of the newly opened terrain, it came to be a "home in the wilderness."

trapper would come back to rendezvous with three or four hundred pelts; a very good and very lucky one might double this figure, as Jed Smith did in his big year of 1825 when he brought in 668 pelts. After a mountain man unloaded his furs at the beginning of a rendezvous he might have between a thousand and two thousand dollars in his pocket, at a time when a skilled worker, such as a carpenter or a mason, could hope to earn little more than $1.50 a day.

Of course, the money did not stay in his pocket long. In fact, it seldom lasted through the month of the rendezvous. The business structure of the rendezvous all but guaranteed that the men who supplied trappers would grow rich while the trappers themselves remained poor. The trapper had no choice but to offer his pelts to Ashley, Bill Sublette (after he succeeded Ashley) or whoever else came to monopolize the rendezvous concession. Throughout the boom days of the Rocky Mountain Fur Company, trappers sold beaver pelts at rendezvous for two to four dollars a pound that would later be resold in St. Louis for six to eight dollars.

The trapper could do nothing to raise the price because the rendezvous was the only market. Furthermore, he had to buy all his goods for the next season from the agents of St. Louis suppliers, who operated a floating version of the company store, complete with sky-high prices. Whiskey, an essential commodity at a rendezvous, was bought in St. Louis for 30 cents a gallon, cut with water and sold to the mountain men, frequently in short measure, at three dollars a pint. The average St. Louis price for tobacco, coffee or sugar was 10 cents a pound, lead 6 cents and gunpowder 7 cents. In the mountains each of these items cost two dollars. And for trade goods to mollify the Indians (calico, beads and the like) the markup was usually 2,000 per cent or more. If a trapper had anything left after buying his supplies, he usually blew it on the local Indian girls.

In effect the trappers worked 11 months for the sake of a debauch at rendezvous. Many of them thought it was worth it. At the rendezvous they found what they had yearned for all year: company, conversation, new clothes, dry shoes, a variety of women, tobacco and booze. For one glorious month they talked, bragged, fought, gambled, fornicated and drank in a mighty exhibit of manliness before, broke and drained, they turned back into the mountains for another perilous year.

Mountain men and Indians join a supply caravan on its way to the annual fur rendezvous, where the trappers would sell their pelts, reprovision and carouse. The dashing rider on a white horse is Sir William Drummond Stewart, a Scottish gentleman who often attended the rendezvous as a lark.

A picture gallery of hardscrabble heroes

Son of a Southern planter and a Virginia slave, Jim Beckwourth discovered a High Sierra pass that became part of a major emigrant route to California.

The mountain men who marked the first trails through the Rockies flourished only briefly. Sizable numbers of them did not start probing the wilderness for beaver until the 1820s; by 1840, with the fur-bearing animals largely trapped out, their day was over. Yet these trappers and back-country entrepreneurs made an indelible impression on the American imagination.

As early as 1846 books appeared in the East featuring mountain men embroiled in all sorts of derring-do. Kit Carson was a particular favorite of the publishers; he was the star in dozens of dime novels bearing such titles as *Kit Carson, the Guide; or, Perils of the Frontier.* In one, Kit surrounded an entire Indian camp singlehanded by creeping around it at night and firing potshots from different vantage points.

The fact was that the true lives of the mountain men, while perhaps not quite so flamboyant as depicted in the novels, were sometimes every bit as perilous. By the most conservative estimates, one in every five trappers died on the trail. Nevertheless a number of them survived into distinguished old age —long enough to have their features recorded by the newfangled art of photography. Such rugged characters as Jim Beckwourth *(left)* and Jim Bridger *(overleaf)* fell in with the contemporary fashion for photographic *cartes de visite* and had their pictures printed on calling cards so that people could see what a real mountain man looked like.

Jim Baker turned from fur trapping to become an Army scout and a guide to emigrant trains; he died a Wyoming farmer in 1898.

Jim Bridger had this *carte de visite* made in the 1860s. He was still guiding in the Rockies at the time.

Long a trapper and guide, Kit Carson joined the Army at 52 to become a top Indian fighter.

A mountain man at 18, Joe Meek later became U.S. Marshal for Oregon Territory.

Albert Boone, grandson of Daniel, was described by Kit Carson as "a man who isn't afraid of anything."

Fur trader Augustin Grignon posed with a tomahawk-like pipe, circa 1850.

A shrewd field boss for Hudson's Bay Company, John McLoughlin later became a leading citizen of Oregon.

3 | King of the trailblazers

Having completed this painting at a rendezvous in the 1830s, Alfred Jacob Miller gave it a cryptic title: *Bourgeois W----r & His Squaw*. But to anyone familiar with the mountain men, the title was perfectly clear. In the fur trade, the term "bourgeois" designated a person who commanded a group of trappers. And the artist simply assumed that viewers would know "W----r" to be Joseph Reddeford Walker, perhaps the most talented of all mountain men.

Most mountain men spent their lives in hard trapping, grim winter confinement and brief rendezvous blowouts, but a few broke out of the grueling cycle. Among these few were men like Walker, who journeyed beyond the Rockies to the coast of California.

Sometimes the path-breaking seemed to occur almost by accident. Thus, in a hunt for beaver water deep in the Southwest, a band of trappers led by Jedediah Smith blundered into the Mojave Desert, and from there suffered onward through desiccating heat to the coast. Joe Walker, whose story is told in the chapter that follows, was cut from a different cloth. His expedition to California was carefully planned and superbly led. In later years, the trails he blazed through the wilderness became great highways to the Far West.

Followed respectfully by his Indian wife, Joe Walker rides in to a rendezvous.

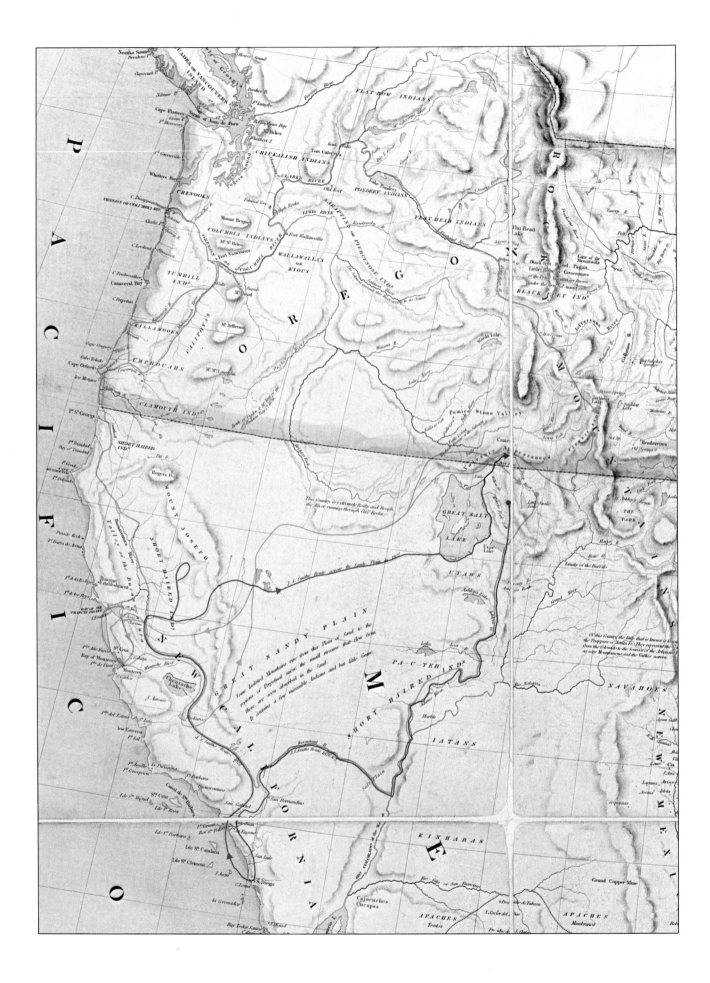

The man who "didn't follow trails but made them"

Of all the rough-and-ready mountain men gathered on the Green River for the fur trappers' rendezvous of 1833, the toughest and most picturesque was Joseph Reddeford Walker. Then 34 years old, Walker was in his physical prime and cut a truly impressive figure. He measured six feet tall, weighed more than 200 pounds and was blue-eyed and handsome in a craggy, hawk-beaked way. He wore his hair long in the Indian style, had a full beard, and in the fashion of his time and place he was something of a clotheshorse. His leggings, hunting shirt and plumed slouch hat were elegantly worked by Indian girls, of whom Walker was always fond and who were fond of him. Even among so many colorful figures, and in the midst of a wild rendezvous, Joe Walker stood out as a kind of beau ideal of the mountain man.

He was already a veteran of both the Southwest and the Rockies—a man who had helped survey part of the Santa Fe Trail and had led a 100-man party of mountain men through two tough seasons of trapping in the Salmon and Snake River countries. This year, Joe Walker had something very interesting to say to the fur men assembled at Green River: he called for men to join him on an expedition into the dimly known, trackless lands to the west, perhaps all the way from the ren-

Joseph Walker

dezvous site to the coast of California.

Walker's announcement created a sensation. Such a trip had been tried only thrice before—by another mountain man, Jedediah Smith, in 1826 and 1827, and in 1829 by Peter Ogden, an energetic leader in the Hudson's Bay Company. Smith and Ogden had followed more or less the same southern route into California—a route that was neither direct nor safe, taking them across bleak desert lands.

Nevertheless, Joe Walker had no difficulty in finding the men he wanted. However terrible the trip might be, the trappers had heard rumors of California's warm winter sun, mission wineries and passionate Mexican girls. Another inducement, at least as strong as any of these rumors, was Joe Walker's reputation as an even-tempered and successful field commander, perhaps the best wilderness trailblazer of them all. In short order, Walker chose some 40 men—including young Zenas Leonard, one of the chroniclers of the fur trade, who had come to the rendezvous after spending a hard, profitless winter in the Rocky Mountains. Leonard was glad to sign on as a clerk, and in his account of the expedition he summed up the general opinion of its leader: "Mr. Walker was a man well calculated to undertake a business of this kind. He was well hardened to the hardships of the wilderness—understood the character of the Indians very well—was kind and affable to his men, but at the same time at liberty to command without giving offense—and to explore unknown regions was his chief delight."

Joe Walker's prestige as a frontiersman would grow steadily throughout his life. For 50 all-but-incredible years, spanning the whole period from the rise of the

A detail from an annotated 1839 map traces the routes to California of mountain man Jed Smith in 1826 *(red)* and 1827 *(green)*. The new trail laid down in 1833 by Joe Walker *(superimposed in blue)* was more direct and far less hazardous.

The site of the Green River rendezvous provided a serene setting for this landscape by Alfred Jacob Miller, showing the scene a few days before mountain men arrived. Miller noted that "Indians encamped for the rendezvous were all about us, for this gathering brings them from far and near."

93

mountain men to the coming of the cowboys, he roamed the trans-Mississippi country from the Rockies to Mexico, from desert to ocean, leading his own expeditions and turning up in moments of crisis to extricate lesser men from their difficulties. He was a geographical genius with a remarkable intuitive sense for the shape, texture and topographical details of the Western wilderness. A trapper named George Nidever stated flatly: "He could find water quicker than any man I ever knew." One incident indicates the respect other frontiersmen felt for him: a man named Daniel Connor, trying to catch up with Walker somewhere in the southern Rockies, asked a friend the direction of the trail Walker was following, and was told that Walker "didn't follow trails, but rather made them."

The expedition to California would test to the utmost Walker's gift for making trails. In 1833, a vast area of the West — present-day western Utah, northern Arizona, virtually all of Nevada and eastern California — was largely unexplored. The Great Basin had been seen and noted as a terrible-looking place, but its extent and the nature of its western boundary were matters of surmise. There was particular confusion about the relationship between the Rockies and the Sierra Nevada. The Sierra had often been seen from the California side, but its size and difficulty were greatly underestimated. Joe Walker and his party would soon learn the truth about this formidable chain of mountains.

Walker's life up to 1833 seemed almost designed to prepare him for this great adventure. He had been born into a remarkable frontier clan in the Tennessee mountains. His father had pushed across the Piedmont to join the first settlers in the Appalachians. One brother was to die at the Alamo with Davy Crockett; another led wagon trains across the continent.

Joe Walker himself came west to Missouri in 1818. Two years later he hitched up with an American party attempting to carry trade goods from Missouri to Santa Fe. The venture was manifestly illegal and dangerous, since it would take the traders into Spanish territory, which was guarded against American incursion. But Walker — typically — turned adversity to advantage. He and the other Americans with him were imprisoned by the Spanish authorities, then released at Walker's suggestion in order for them to help wage a campaign against marauding Pawnees. In return for his assistance the Spaniards granted special trade concessions to the American party, and Walker set off for American territory in high spirits. On the way, by sheer coincidence, he ran into his brother Joel, headed for New Mexico with another Missouri trading party. Joel's description of the meeting suggests that Joe had already been transformed by his travels in the outback: "I saw as I supposed, an Indian with his hair flying up and down. He came up and to my immense astonishment I saw he was my brother, Captain Walker, who had started the year before trapping."

Four years later Joe Walker could be found with a surveying team mapping and marking part of the route to New Mexico, a task that was undertaken on commission from the federal government. Having thus helped to establish what would become the Santa Fe Trail *(page 103)*, Walker went home to Missouri. There, in 1827, he was elected the first sheriff of Jackson County, Missouri. The most important part of his bailiwick was Independence, the county seat and one of the earliest of a notorious series of wide-open Western boomtowns. He was a good lawman, a famous shot who seldom drew his gun, a convivial man who could turn steely cold on occasion. His imposing presence and air of command were enough to keep the lid on Independence, more or less. After serving two terms he was asked to run a third time, but declined on the grounds that the pay was low and the work confining.

Upon laying down his badge, Walker — unlike so many Western gunslingers — did not choose to earn an easy living or bolster his ego by turning bully or hoodlum. Instead, in 1831 he set off on a horse- and cattle-buying trip that took him to Fort Gibson in the Cherokee Nation. There he met Captain Benjamin Bonneville, an enigmatic figure in the history of the early West. Bonneville was then beginning an extended leave of absence from the Army, organizing what he claimed would be a private trapping and trading venture. Perhaps trapping and trading were all he had in mind, perhaps his real intentions lay in the covert realm of espionage *(page 95)*; for whatever reason, Benjamin Bonneville did lead a well-equipped party of 110 men into the West in 1832, and he took Joe Walker with him as his field commander.

They spent two full seasons in the mountains, trapping on the Salmon River in the fall and on the Snake

Benjamin Bonneville: fur trader or secret agent?

Benjamin Bonneville, the man who hired Joe Walker and sent him on his trailblazing expedition to California, was an Army captain on leave who spent more than three years trapping in the West. Just what drew him to the region and why he did what he did there are questions that have puzzled historians ever since.

It was odd to begin with that Bonneville, at 38, suddenly decided to interrupt his promising military career and enter the fur trade. Competition in the field was cutthroat, and he had neither money nor experience in the mountains. Nevertheless, in 1831 he applied to the Army for a leave of absence; his request went through bureaucratic channels with unusual rapidity—whereupon a group of Manhattan businessmen swiftly and inexplicably agreed to provide him with ample funds for his venture.

Out in the mountains, Bonneville proved to be a failure as a fur trader. Arriving in 1832, he built a trading post at a point far north on the Green River. Perhaps because it was near a stronghold of hostile Blackfoot Indians, he fortified it with a sturdy log breastwork. But trappers, resentful of this well-heeled neophyte, shunned his fancy fort, and he had to abandon it, to the jeers of veteran mountaineers who dubbed it "Bonneville's Folly."

He continued to display a singular lack of concern about profits. For his next move, he dispatched the well-outfitted Walker expedition to California; although the venture yielded no furs, Bonneville seems to have been entirely satisfied. Later, Bonneville himself twice led parties to the

In later life, Bonneville became a general.

Columbia River in Oregon, though he was aware that the region was the trapping turf of the powerful British-owned Hudson's Bay Company. On both occasions the Britishers promptly sent him packing.

In September 1835, Bonneville returned to Washington, all set to re-enter the Army. But he found himself discharged, for he had overstayed his leave by almost two years, and the Army had never received the request for an extension that he claimed to have sent in earlier. He asked for reinstatement, but his case threatened to become mired in the military bureaucracy. Then, once again, obstacles were almost miraculously swept from his path. President Andrew Jackson himself interceded and ordered the captain reinstated.

How did this obscure officer, who had left the service of his country to pursue his own private interests, rate

such extraordinary Presidential concern? The answer, perhaps, is that Bonneville never actually did leave the service of his country.

In his original application for a leave of absence, Bonneville had declared that he planned to gather data on the topography of the region west of the Rockies and north of Mexico, and on the size and disposition of its Indian tribes. Such information would, of course, have been valuable to the government, especially in planning westward expansion. The government would have been even more eager to learn the strength of the British in the Northwest and of the Mexicans in California. It might even have known some businessmen who, in exchange for sharing the information, would bankroll an effort to get it.

Certainly Walker's trip to California and Bonneville's two forays into Oregon paid off handsomely in this kind of intelligence. Even the fort on the Green River, although a commercial failure, could be construed as a strategic master stroke. It was ideally situated to control the passes of the central Rockies.

No records exist to show whether Bonneville, who spent the rest of his life in the Army, was indeed engaged in espionage. Yet he must have felt a kind of satisfaction when, in the 1850s, he received command of a post in Oregon, by then U.S. territory. After all, he had written a report to the Army 20 years earlier, while he was still out in the mountains, urging that "if our Government ever intends taking possession of Oregon, the sooner it shall be done the better."

River in the spring, and having a hard time of it all around. There was the almost inevitable trouble with the Blackfeet; one night the Indians staged a raid on Walker's horses and mules while the men who were supposed to guard them played "Old Sledge," a card game among the mountain men. The Indians were driven off and no horses were lost, but bad luck continued to plague the party. Trapping was so poor that during two seasons the men took only 23 packs of beaver, hardly enough to pay their wages.

Yet, possibly because his attention was already focused on a more challenging matter, Joe Walker seemed undisturbed by that lackluster record when he came to the rendezvous of 1833 and, as Bonneville's guide and executive officer, began to organize the trip to California. As with all the affairs of his employer, the motive for this venture remains uncertain. But in purely economic terms, there were compelling reasons for the mission. By 1833 the mountains were full of competing trappers and beaver were declining; a probe toward California might yield new opportunities, for in that direction lay the last large tracts of unexplored wilderness and a possible trade route to the coast.

Walker's basic plan for the probe was clear enough. He would head west into the Great Basin from the Great Salt Lake, and make a trail to central California. But one thing was certain: he would *not* go to California by the route or in the manner of Jedediah Smith.

Smith had reached the West Coast a few years earlier by a roundabout route. He traveled southwest from the Great Salt Lake into what is now western Arizona and crossed the desert country into California, entering the region well south of the Sierra. As exploration, Smith's journey represented the typical mountain man's way of doing things—a kind of muddling-through approach (or, in several cases, not quite muddling through). Part hero and part tragic bungler, his style presents many contrasts to that of Joe Walker.

Smith's early deeds were promising. A native of New York State, he turned up in St. Louis at the age of 23, and there he answered William Ashley's advertisement for enterprising young men to serve as fur trappers. Smith caught Ashley's eye as one of the most enterprising of his crew. During the fur traders' battle with the Arikaras in 1823, Ashley apparently noted Smith's coolness and bravery, for shortly afterward he appointed the young man a squad leader in his fur brigade.

Another contemporary, a trapper named William Waldo, described Smith as "a bold, outspoken, professing, and consistent Christian [Methodist], the first and only one known among the early Rocky Mountain trappers and hunters." It was said of Smith that his Bible and his rifle were his inseparable companions, and Waldo added: "No one who knew him well doubted the sincerity of his piety." Jed Smith seems to stand out in the history of the early West as a kind of classic Yankee figure: a grim, inflexible, high-minded man, perhaps a bit of a prig. Certainly his short, violent career reflected the traditional Yankee vices and virtues.

After the Arikara debacle Smith worked in the mountains for Ashley during the next four seasons and became an excellent trapper; the 668 pelts he took in the 1824-1825 seasons may rank as the record for a single mountain man. In 1826, having just turned 27, Smith joined Billy Sublette and David Jackson to buy Ashley out. It was agreed that while the two other partners worked the central Rockies, Smith would explore the country to the southwest, looking for new trapping country. In August 1826, he left the Cache Valley rendezvous at the head of a party of 15 men.

The party passed the Salt Lake and, in the Utah Valley, Smith encountered a band of Ute Indians. To them he handed out a typical bag of mountain-man gifts — some red ribbon, a razor, a couple of knives, half a pound of tobacco and the like. From them he got next to nothing; if they had any information to give him about the country south of Utah Lake he either did not ferret it out or did not understand it. With no clear destination or line of march in mind, Smith and his little band pushed ahead. For the next month they wandered southward through the Wasatch Mountains on the eastern rim of the Great Basin, getting deeper and deeper into what Smith himself called "a Country of Starvation." The forests of the north had turned to scattered clumps of sagebrush, the soil to reddish sand. Clearly, this was not beaver country.

Eventually the party crossed the Colorado River and followed the left bank into the Black Mountains of northwestern Arizona. Short of water and food, traveling in a "remarkably barren" country, the wandering men were now in real danger. In his own account of the expedition, Smith mournfully noted that he "had lost so many Horses that we were all on foot — my men & the remainder of my Horses were worn out with fatigue & hardships & emaciated with hunger." In fact, more than half of the horses died during this stage of the journey.

Emerging from the Black Mountains, Smith and his starving men stumbled into a broad valley, glinting with the green of willow and mesquite. There they were hospitably received and resupplied by Mojave Indians. By this time Smith had, quite sensibly, given up all hope of finding beaver water, but the long trip back to the rendezvous site seemed too formidable to risk again. Figuring that the way ahead had to be easier than the way back, he continued to travel westward. From one of the Mojave Indians, according to a letter in which he described his journey, he learned that "it was not far to some of the Missions of California & I detirmined (as this was the only resort) to go to that place as soon as my men & horses should be able to travel."

This last leg of Smith's trip took him through the lethal heart of the Mojave Desert. For 15 grueling days of constant thirst and hunger his men trudged across a flat, salt-crusted plain blazing in the autumn sun. They tried to follow the westward course of the Mojave River, but the stream had a disconcerting habit of ducking beneath the surface of the ground for miles at a time (in his account of the expedition he named it the Inconstant River). And whenever the river went underground, the willows that lined its banks gave way to the prevailing scrub of yucca and spiny cactus. It was an exhausted and soul-weary group of men that, in mid-November, arrived in the vicinity of Los Angeles.

In this Mexican territory Smith was, of course, an illegal entrant into a foreign country, without a passport. Despite his shaky position he asked that his party be given horses and permitted to travel freely through California. The Governor-General of the province, José Echeandía, soon brought him to San Diego for questioning. Perhaps because the beaver-trapping trade was all but unknown in California, the nearest category that the governor could find for Jed Smith was *pescador,* "fisherman." Smith found himself completely unable to convince the governor "of the truth that I was only a hunter & that Dire necessity had driven me here." He was kept in San Diego under house arrest until January. Fortunately for him the captains of three American ships in San Diego harbor interceded for him. As a condition of his release, Smith agreed to leave California by the same route that had brought him there. But he did nothing of the sort. Instead, he took his men northward and spent the winter in the San Joaquin Valley.

In May 1827, Smith tried to lead his men eastward across the Sierra; the deep snows soon turned him back, and he left five horses dead behind him. He then tried a second time, taking only two companions with him while the remaining 11 (two of the original party had deserted) stayed behind in a camp on the Stanislaus River on the western slope of the Sierra. On the second occasion he succeeded in crossing the mountains, probably through what is now known as Ebbetts Pass. In the torrid desert east of the Sierra the three men came very close to death, and the heroic side of Smith's character emerged. On the 25th of June the strength of one of the men, Robert Evans, gave out completely. Smith and the other man temporarily abandoned Evans because, as Smith later wrote, "We could do no good by remaining to die with him," but they found water

The parched, salt-covered flats of the Mojave Desert, shown here in an 1853 painting by Lieutenant George Brewerton, created a fearsome barrier to Jed Smith's westward journey. To cross the desert, Smith probably followed a trade route used by the Mojave Indians to bring valuable, brightly colored sea shells from the California coast.

three miles further on, and Smith brought back a drink that saved Evans' life and enabled him to continue. The three men reached Bear Lake, the site of the 1827 rendezvous, on July 3.

Smith realized the importance and the value of what he had done. He stayed at Bear Lake long enough to write a letter *(page 107)* to William Clark, his great predecessor in exploration, telling the full story of his harrowing trip and carefully describing "a country which has been, measurably, veiled in obscurity, and unknown to the citizens of the U. States." But now Smith had a new responsibility and a new mission. After less than 10 days, he left the rendezvous with a party of 18 men and two women to relieve the 11 men he had left in California. He chose to go by much the same route he had followed the previous year, despite its difficulties, for he would not face the grim crossing of the Great Basin again. The southward trip was no easier the second time—and the Mojave Indians, who had helped them earlier, were now in an ugly mood. After his force came out of the mountains, they embarked upon what should have been a peaceful crossing of the Colorado River. But the Mojaves fell upon them and killed 10 of the men and took the two women prisoners. At the moment of attack, Smith and the eight remaining men were on rafts in the middle of the river, and thus escaped. However, they were left with only five rifles and little ammunition or other supplies.

The subsequent journey through the Mojave Desert was as bad as always, and made even worse by the fact that for a time Smith lost the trail he had followed the previous fall. As they so often did, the mountain men endured what had to be endured, and they reached the Mexican settlements of California in late August.

During the next few months Jed Smith provided a textbook example of how men who do not understand history—even their own—are forced to relive it. Not only had he illegally entered California a second time but, because he had violated his parole the year before, he was now a felon and a fugitive. Yet once again he was arrogant in his dealings with the local authorities. Once again they arrested him, and on this occasion they actually threw him into jail. Once again he was released because of the good offices of a diplomatic American sea captain, but only on the understanding that he would leave California immediately and forever.

And once again, Smith broke his word. Picking up all of his men, including those from the stranded 1826 party, he went as far as the Sacramento Valley, where he spent most of the winter.

The following summer, Smith slipped out of the province, traveling northward along the coast toward the Columbia River. As they moved up the coast, the party bickered with Indians and on one occasion threatened to garrote a member of the Kelawatset tribe who had stolen an ax. On July 14, 1828, while Smith and two other members of his party were off on a scouting trip on the Umpqua River, the Indians retaliated. They attacked the unsuspecting trappers and killed 15 of them, leaving only one survivor, Arthur Black. Stripped of supplies, Black eventually limped into Fort Vancouver, followed two days later by Smith and his two companions. The four men spent the winter there; in the spring, their despised rivals, the men of the Hudson's Bay Company, reoutfitted the Americans, and Smith and Black made their way back to the United States. (The other two men, heartily sick of the whole adventure, remained behind.)

Over a period of three years Jed Smith had taken a total of 33 men with him on his California expeditions. Twenty-six of them had been killed, two others had deserted him. Yet he had little to show for all the expense of blood and energy. In 1830 he returned to St. Louis to make maps of the country through which he had traveled, but before he got around to this chore he set off on a trading expedition to Santa Fe. It was to be his last adventure. With a party of 83 men he traveled into a section of Cimarron River country that was known to be almost waterless. Smith and the others had not taken sufficient supplies of water, apparently feeling that their mountain-man instincts would lead them to a spring or stream. However, their instincts failed, and the party soon had to break up and scatter across the desert in search of a water source. A hunting party of Comanches, seeing Smith alone and weakened, shot him. Yet even his death, at the age of 32, had a feckless but heroic quality to it. Before he died he had a chance to get off just one shot—and with it he killed the chief of the band that had attacked him.

Joe Walker would have had the foresight and good sense not to be out there alone in the first place. And Walker's trek to California, one of the most fruitful explorations ever conducted by a mountain man, was typical of his endeavors — a model of good planning and efficiency. Walker and his men left the trappers' rendezvous on the Green River on August 20, 1833. Each man was mounted, and each led three additional horses packed with "every article necessary for the comfort of men engaged in an expedition of this kind." The words are those of Zenas Leonard who, having put in his time with some of the scruffiest outfits in the mountains, was understandably pleased by the thoroughness of Walker's preparations.

Actually, the abundance of horses was a kind of trademark for any party led by Joe Walker. Of all the mountain men, Walker seems to have been the best and most knowledgeable stockman. Throughout his life, in slack periods, he would buy, sell, trade and drive horses and cattle. Unlike most mountain men he had horse sense in the literal meaning of the words: he used animals often, used them carefully, took pains to find enough forage for them and did not ride them into the ground — though like all Western explorers he regarded spare animals as emergency rations, and knew that on the hard trails and high mountains he would inevitably lose some of his stock.

On the Bear River, four days after they had left the rendezvous, Walker halted the group while they were still in well-watered, wooded country and set them to hunting. He kept them at this work until each man had added 60 pounds of dried and jerked meat to his pack. Ordinary mountain men probably would have neglected this elementary precaution; they tended to gorge themselves on a day when hunting was easy, then starve a week later when they could not find game.

Walker's prudence was again displayed when he reached the Salt Lake vicinity, three weeks after leaving the Green River. Here he adopted a tactic used by all his successful predecessors, from Coronado to Lewis and Clark. He stopped, sought out a band of local Indians, and interrogated them on the character of the country and the best routes west.

Combining the advice he received from these Bannock Indians with the earlier rumors he had heard about the Great Basin, he sifted all of the information through his intuitive sense of what simply smelled right and finally picked a route that proved to be the best possible one through the desolate country. North of the Salt Lake the party had headed almost due west toward what is now called the Humboldt River. Walker continued on in this direction, across the parched plains of northern Nevada. The going was hard (Leonard wrote that "Our men, who were in such fine spirits when we left the rendezvous, began to show symptoms of fatigue and were no longer so full of sport"). But it would have been far worse if Walker had turned south into the salt desert west and southwest of Salt Lake.

The party's beeline path across the dry lands intersected the Humboldt near its source. Walker then followed the river downstream to the swampy Humboldt Sink, in what is now western Nevada (years later the first transcontinental railroad, the Central Pacific, followed the same route across the Great Basin).

Approaching the bogs and lakes early in September the mountain men began to encounter Digger Indians. Although numerous they were a poor, scrawny lot, still dependent upon a Stone Age technology; they lived by grubbing up roots, beetles and lizards, and hunting small game. They were amazed by the possessions of the Walker party, particularly the metal tools. Coveting these marvels, the Diggers buzzed around the white men like mosquitoes, stealing when they had the chance, threatening when circumstances were suitable.

Soon after meeting the Diggers, a group of Walker's men, out hunting for game, killed two or three of the Diggers who had stolen some of their traps. When Walker heard about the killings he raged at the men for needlessly provoking the Indians. But the damage was done. With their desire to steal reinforced by a desire for revenge, the Diggers hung close to the expedition, their numbers increasing ominously. They continued to gather until some eight or nine hundred of them surrounded the 40 mountain men.

Walker quickly built a breastwork and drew his men up behind it. He acted none too soon. According to the apprehensive Zenas Leonard, the horde of Indians marched straight at the fortification, "dancing and singing in the greatest glee" in an unconvincing pretense of friendliness. As Leonard told the story: "When within about 150 yards of us, they all sat down on the ground, and despatched five of their chiefs to our camp to inquire whether their people might come in and smoke with us. This request Captain Walker very prudently refused, as they evidently had no good intentions." ◉

Zebulon Pike and the road to Santa Fe

Lieutenant Zebulon M. Pike

Long before the mountain men charted ways to California, American explorers and traders were forging a solid southerly link with Spanish domains. In 1806 a young Army lieutenant named Zebulon Montgomery Pike left St. Louis to explore the vaguely defined southern border of the Louisiana Territory. Traveling along the Arkansas River with a party of 15 men, Pike decided to climb the towering peak that bears his name *(below)*, thinking it was only a few miles away. Several days later and 40 miles farther on, Pike was still far from his goal. He gave up and in an outburst of defeatism declared "no human being could have ascended to its pinical." Pike may have had short-comings as trailblazer and speller, but he proved to be an excellent propagandist. His published account of the rich Spanish towns in the Southwest sent traders scurrying there. The Spanish responded to their initiative by throwing them in jail.

The traders had better luck after Mexico took over the area in 1821. In 1824 expansionist-minded frontiersmen demanded that a federal surveying team provide a well-marked road from Missouri to New Mexico. Although the wind erased the mounds of earth the surveying crew (including a young Joe Walker) threw up as waymarks, thousands of wagon tracks soon incised into the prairie the famous Santa Fe Trail.

Pikes Peak looms straight up from the level plains. It was scaled by three other explorers 14 years after Pike said it could not be done.

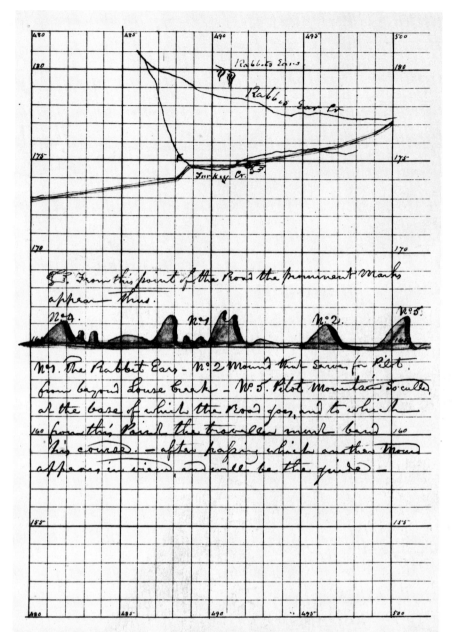

A page from the field notes of Joseph C. Brown, the surveyor of the Santa Fe Trail from 1825 to 1827, maps a section of the road through desert lands. From one spot he sketched the profile of a group of mountains, including a double-peaked one called Rabbit Ears. Besides giving directions, his notes included such vital information as where to find water, firewood, game animals and grazing areas for wagon teams.

Pike's Army expedition *(black line)* followed a meandering route because he made detours to visit Indian villages, wandered about in the vicinity of his namesake peak and returned from Santa Fe by way of Mexico. Despite the distance he traveled, he failed to locate the headwaters of the Arkansas and Red Rivers, which constituted the boundary with Spanish territory. The traders' trail to Santa Fe *(gray line)* led in an almost straight line for some 800 miles across the southern Plains. On the approach to Santa Fe, traders usually took the Cimarron Cutoff since the mountain route was almost impassable to wagons.

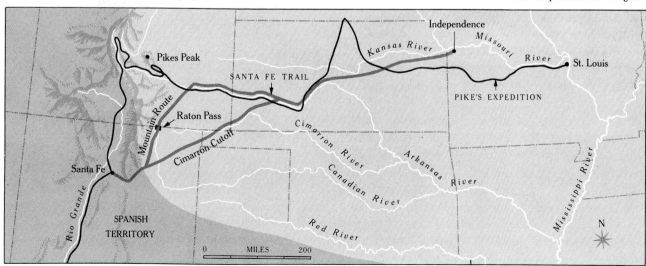

Nestled at the foot of the Sangre de Cristo range of the Rockies, the little whitewashed city of Santa Fe was the center of a region rich in silver, furs and livestock. Spain had jealously guarded this northern part of its Mexican province first from French traders and then, after 1803, from the few American traders who braved the Plains.

When the Mexicans declared their independence from Spain in 1821, an entrepreneur named William Becknell happened to be near the border planning to trade with Indians. Hearing the news, he rushed to Santa Fe, sold his wares and hurried back home to Missouri with bags bulging with silver dollars. Four months later he was on the trail again, but this time he had three wagons loaded with luxuries—colorful cottons, an assortment of cutlery, silk shawls and mirrors.

Since the rugged Raton Pass in the mountains was really suitable only to pack mules, Becknell turned southwest toward the headwaters of the Cimarron River and struck off into a forbidding region of rock and sand. While relatively level, the terrain proved so arid that the members of Becknell's party were forced to slash their mules' ears to quench their thirst with blood. But Becknell reached Santa Fe and made a 2,000 per cent profit. Other wagon trains, better prepared for a desert ordeal, quickly followed in Becknell's path. For his discovery of the Cimarron Cutoff, shorter than the old route by 100 miles, Becknell became known as the "Father of the Santa Fe Trail."

Waving hats and firing guns, exultant traders head into Santa Fe in this anonymous drawing from the 1840s. The long journey from Missouri often took more than a month and subjected the travelers to hunger, thirst and sporadic Comanche attacks.

The Indians massing outside Joe Walker's encampment refused to be put off when Walker saw through the pretended peace efforts of their chiefs. Instead they continued to move toward the mountain men's breastwork. At this point Walker's men signaled to the Indians "that if they advanced a step further it was at the peril of their lives. They wanted to know in what way we would do it. Our guns were exhibited as the weapons of death. This they seemed to discredit and only laughed at us." One problem in dealing with these Indians was that they had only a vague knowledge of rifles, hence little fear of them. So, by way of instruction, Walker organized a shooting exhibition in which his men riddled a beaverskin target and killed a few ducks floating in the lake that protected their rear. The Diggers, though astonished, failed to draw the logical conclusion.

The trouble came to a boil next morning, after Walker's men resumed their march through the Humboldt Sink. About a hundred of the boldest Diggers began to make threatening feints against them. Leonard reported: "This greatly excited Captain Walker, who was naturally of a very cool temperament, and he gave orders for the charge, saying that there was nothing equal to a good start in such a case." The mountain men accordingly attacked the Diggers and killed 39 of them. At last the Diggers understood what guns could do, and they instantly stopped threatening the Walker party.

Having settled with the Diggers, Walker continued west, passing what came to be called Carson Sink. But now his men found themselves confronting the most forbidding barrier to westward travel in the whole continent. Before them lay the unbroken mass of the Sierra Nevada, stretching almost 400 miles from north to south, with peaks more than 14,000 feet high.

Slowly, the men began to work their way up the range, probably following one of the southern tributaries of a river later named the Walker. Leonard described the climb from its beginning: "As we advanced, in the hollows sometimes we would encounter prodigious quantities of snow. When we would come to such places, a certain portion of the men would be appointed alternately to go forward and break the road, to enable our horses to get through; and if any of the horses would get swamped, these same men were to get them out. In this tedious and tiresome manner we spent the whole day without going more than eight or ten miles."

The climb was so punishing and prospects of finding food so dim that some of the men began to question the wisdom of continuing on. The majority opted to stay on course, but a few members of the party insisted that they be allowed to retrace their steps to more hospitable country. Walker considered denying them horses or ammunition for their retreat, but this tactic might have provoked outright mutiny, and he found a happier solution. The men were permitted to butcher two horses that were on their last legs. That night, every member of the party ate his fill. Morale lifted immediately and the disciplinary crisis was over.

The crossing of the Sierra took almost three weeks, and the men suffered constantly from cold and hunger. At one point Leonard recorded that "several parties were despatched on search of a pass over the mountain, and to make search for game; but they all returned in the evening without finding either. . . . We were at a complete stand. No one was acquainted with the country, nor no person knew how wide the summit of this mountain was. We had traveled for five days since we arrived at what we supposed to be the summit—were now still surrounded with snow and rugged peaks—the vigor of every man almost exhausted—nothing to give our poor horses, which were no longer any assistance in traveling, but a burthen, for we had to help the most of them along as we would an old and feeble man."

At last the men reached the crest, then inched their way westward along the divide between the Tuolumne and Merced Rivers. Immediately before them lay one of the great moments of all Western exploration. It was described almost casually by Zenas Leonard: "Here we began to encounter in our path, many small streams which would shoot out from under these high snowbanks, and after running a short distance in deep chasms

---

Though Jed Smith's journal of his California expedition was impounded by Mexican authorities, he set down at least one permanent record of his wanderings in this letter to William Clark, reprinted in a St. Louis newspaper. During the years after the Lewis and Clark expedition, Clark had been accumulating geographical knowledge of the West, and Smith's letter abounds in details of the kind he needed. Along with descriptions of the Mojave Desert, the San Joaquin Valley and the Great Basin, the letter contains identifications of a number of rivers, mountains and Indian tribes.

MISSOURI REPUBLICAN.

ST. LOUIS, (THURSDAY,) OCT. 11, 1827.

We have been politely favored by Gen. CLARK, Superintendent of Indian Affairs, with the perusal of a letter, written by JEDEDIAH S. SMITH, who has been for several years engaged in hunting and trapping in the Upper Missouri, and who has visited that extensive barren country on the West, not heretofore explored. From this letter, written in a plain style, we extract the following, which, we trust, will be found interesting to our readers:

"My situation has enabled me to collect information respecting a country which has been, measurably, veiled in obscurity, and unknown to the citizens of the U. States. I allude to the country South West of the Great Salt Lake, and West of the Rocky Mountains.

About the 22d of August, 1826, I left the Great Salt Lake, accompanied with a party of fifteen men, for the purpose of exploring the country to the south west, which was then entirely unknown to me, and of which I could obtain no satisfactory information, from the Indians who inhabit the country on its north east borders. My general course on leaving the Lake, was S. W. and W., passing the Little Uta Lake, and ascending Ashley's River, which empties into it, where we found a nation of Indians, calling themselves Sampatch, who were friendly disposed towards us. After leaving the Little Uta Lake, I found no further sign of Buffalo—there were, however, a few of the Antelope and Mountain Sheep, and an abundance of Black Tailed Hares. Leaving Ashley's River, I passed over a range of mountains, S. E. and N. W., and struck a river, running S. W., which I named Adams River, in compliment to our President. The water of this river is of a muddy cast, and somewhat brackish. The country is mountainous to the east, and on the west are detached rocky hills and sandy plains. Passing down this river some distance, I fell in with a nation of Indians, calling themselves Pa Utches. These Indians, as well as the Sampatch, wear robes made of rabit skins: they raise corn and pumpkins, on which they principally subsist—except a few hares, very little game of any description is to be found. About ten days march further down, the river turns to the S. E., where, on the S. W. of it, there is a remarkable cave, the entrance to which is about ten or fifteen feet high, and five or six feet in width: after descending about fifteen feet, it opens into a large and spacious room, with the roof, walls and floor of solid rock salt, (a piece of which I send you, with some other articles which will be hereafter described.) I followed Adams river two days travel further, where it empties into the Seeds Keeder, which I crossed and went a south course down it, through a barren, rocky and mountainous country. In this river are many shoals and rapids. Further down, a valley opens, from five to fifteen miles in width. The land on the river bank is furtile and timbered. I here found another tribe of Indians, who call themselves Ammuchiebes. They cultivate the soil, and raise corn, beans, pumpkins and mellons in abundance, and also a little wheat and cotton. I was now nearly destitute of horses, and had learned what it was to do without food; I therefore concluded to remain here fifteen days, to recruit my men; and in the mean time, succeeded in changing my few remaining horses, and was enabled to purchase others, from a party of runaway Indians, who had stolen them from the Spaniards. I here obtained some information respecting the Spanish country—obtained two guides—recrossed the Seeds Keeder, and travelled a west course fifteen days, over a country of complete barrens, and frequently travelling from morning until night without water. Crossed a salt plain eight miles wide and twenty long. On the surface of the ground is a crust of white salt, underneath is a layer of yellow sand, and beneath the sand a few inches, the salt again appears. The river Seeds-Keeder, I have since learned, empties itself into the Gulf of California, about 80 miles from the Amuchiebes and is there called the Collerado.

On my arrival in the province of Upper California, I was eyed with suspicion, and was compelled to appear in the presence of the Governor, residing at St. Diego. from whence, by the assistance of some American gentlemen, (and particularly Capt. W. H. Cunningham, of the ship Courier, from Boston,) I was enabled to obtain permission to return with my men, by the route I had come. I also obtained permission to purchase such supplies as I stood in need of. As the Gov. would not permit me to travel up the sea coast towards Bodago, I proceeded eastward of the Spanish settlement. I then turned my course N. W., keeping from 150 to 200 miles from the sea coast. I travelled three hundred miles in this direction, through a country somewhat fertile, and inhabited by a great many Indians, mostly naked, and destitute of fire arms, and who subsist upon fish, roots, acorns and grapes. These Indians, unlike, in this respect to any others that I have seen, cut their hair to the length of three inches.

I afterwards arrived at a river, which I named (after a tribe of Indians residing on its banks) Wim-mel-che. I found here a few beaver and elk, deer and antelopes in abundance. I made a small hunt, and then attempted, with my party, to cross Mount Joseph, and join my partners at the Great Salt Lake. In this, however, I was disappointed. I found the snow so deep on the mountain, that my horses could not travel. Five of my horses having already perished for want of food, I was compelled to return to the valley. Here leaving my party, I set out on the 20th May, accompanied by two men, and taking with us seven horses and two mules, which were ladened with hay, and provisions for ourselves, and in eight days we succeeded in crossing Mount Joseph, with the loss of only two horses and one mule. The snow on the top of this mountain, was from four to eight feet deep, but so solid that our horses only sunk into it from six to twelve inches.

After travelling twenty days from the east side of Mount Joseph, I struck the S. W. corner of the Great Salt Lake. The country between the mountain and this Lake, is completely barren, and entirely destitute of game. We frequently travelled two days, without water, over sandy deserts, where no sign of vegitation was to be seen. In some of the rocky hills we found water, and occasionally small bands of Indians, who appeared the most miserable of the human race. They were entirely naked, and subsisted upon grass seeds, grass-hoppers, &c. On arriving at the Great Salt Lake, we had but one horse and one mule remaining, and they so poor, they could scarcely carry the little camp equipage we had with us. The balance of the horses we were compelled to eat as they gave out."

Yosemite Valley was first seen by white men in 1833, when Joe Walker's party passed high above it along the divide between the Merced and Tuolumne Rivers. This painting by Albert Bierstadt, done 39 years later, depicts the valley from its floor, with a neck of the Merced in the foreground and the great Cathedral Rocks in the distance.

108

109

which they have through ages cut in the rocks, precipitate themselves from one lofty precipice to another, until they are exhausted in rain below. Some of these precipices appeared to us to be more than a mile high. Some of the men thought that if we could succeed in descending one of these precipices to the bottom, we might thus work our way into the valley below — but on making several attempts we found it utterly impossible for a man to descend to say nothing of our horses."

Walker and his men were gazing upon the Yosemite Valley, never before seen by white men. No route to the bottom seemed open at first, but finally the men searched out a spot where descent was feasible. "We brought our horses, and by fastening ropes round them let them down one at a time without doing them any injury. After we got our horses and baggage all over the rocks we continued our course down the mountain, which still continued very steep and difficult."

The floor they reached was more than seven miles long, studded with great granite monoliths and lined with feathery cataracts as high as 1,500 feet. So spectacular was the scenery that forever afterward many of the 40 men remembered the moment as the supreme experience of their long journey — or, perhaps, of their lives. When Joe Walker died in 1876 and was buried in California, the epitaph on his headstone included the words: "Camped at Yosemite, November 13, 1833."

Soon after reaching the valley the Walker expedition came down the western slope of the Sierra, following the Merced to the San Joaquin River. They were now in the heart of California, savoring its flowering warmth. Here they found acres of acorn mast, and Leonard noted that the nuts, "when roasted in the ashes or broiled, are superior to any chestnuts I ever eat." (In an afterthought he admitted, somewhat ruefully, that "a person subsisting upon very lean horse meat for several days is hardly capable of judging with precision in a case of this kind.") In the parklike, oak-studded meadows there was easy forage for the tired horses, and there were deer, elk and bears for the pot. Everywhere, every day, the soft autumn sun of California caressed them. They were the first Americans to see the giant redwood trees, "some of which would measure from sixteen to eighteen fathom round the trunk at the height of a man's head." One night they saw a spectacular meteor shower. "This was altogether a mystery to some of the

men," wrote Leonard, "but after an explanation from Captain Walker, they were satisfied that no danger need be apprehended from the falling of the stars."

At about the same time they encountered another mystery: "Soon after the men went to rest and the camp had became quieted, we were startled by a loud distant noise similar to that of thunder. Whilst lying close to the ground this noise could be distinctly heard for a considerable length of time without intermission. When it was at first observed some of our men supposed it was occasioned by an earthquake, and began to fear that we would all be swallowed up in the bowels of the earth; and others judged it to be the noise of a neighboring cataract. Captain Walker, however, suggested a more plausible cause, which allayed the fears of the most timid. He supposed that the noise originated by the Pacific rolling and dashing her boisterous waves against the rocky shore. The idea of being within hearing of the *end* of the *Far West* inspired the heart of every member of our company with a patriotic feeling for his country's honor, and all were eager to lose no time until they should behold what they had heard." The explanation was plausible enough, but patently impossible. At that moment, Walker and his men were encamped some 70 miles from the Pacific. Very likely they had indeed experienced a minor earthquake.

Late in November they skirted the eastern shore of San Francisco and San Pablo Bays, and crossed the low coastal range — and then "the broad Pacific burst forth to view. The first night we encamped quite close to the beach near a spring of delightful water." From there Walker led the men southward toward Monterey, the capital of Upper California. But before bursting unannounced and unprepared on the provincial officials, he stopped his party near the mission in San Juan Bautista. "Here Captain Walker deemed it prudent to halt for a few days," wrote Leonard, "in order to ascertain the disposition of the people, and make further inquiries with respect to the country, &c., lest we might be considered as intruders and treated in a way that we would not much like. It was our desire to keep on peaceable terms with the Spaniards, at least no one desired to give the least offense of any kind." After getting a passport in San Juan Bautista, Walker continued on to Monterey, where his reception contrasted sharply with the one given Jed Smith seven years earlier. From the start, Walker was hospitably received and became something of a social lion. This, too, was characteristic of Joe Walker: on the trail he was perhaps the most business-like and disciplined of all the mountain men; off duty he let his long hair down and indulged in whatever pleasures were available.

For the next three months the Walker party unwound, drinking and eating often and well. They went to bull-roping contests and bear fights, the chief weekend sports on the ranchos; they were treated to demonstrations of the Mexicans' skilled horsemanship. They soaked their feet in salt water, their bodies in California sun; and they became friendly with a variety of California girls. Zenas Leonard does not elaborate on this aspect of their stay; perhaps his social life cut into his time for journal-keeping. From the notes he did make, it would seem that California must have amounted to a kind of mountain man's dream of Lotus Land. Certainly it must have been difficult to leave that golden land. In fact, six of Walker's men were permanently seduced; they asked for their discharges and stayed behind.

But Joe Walker, as Leonard had said, was a man whose "chief delight" was "to explore unknown regions." The Mexicans offered Walker a 50-square-mile tract of land if he would stay on and bring in "fifty families, composed of different kinds of mechanics" to settle there—an offer that, had it been accepted, would have made Walker a wealthy man and a major figure in California's colonial society. He declined. Late in January he collected his men, put them under field discipline and turned back to face the mountains again.

In the San Joaquin Valley he set his men to hunting. Finally on February 14, 1834, driving 340 horses, 47 head of cattle and 30 dogs (brought along, like the cattle, as a food supply), Walker headed east. At the base of the Sierra he turned south, parallel to the mountains, looking for a less taxing crossing than the one he had used on the westward trip. He soon found it—and it was one of the most significant of his discoveries. Above the headwaters of the Kern River the expedition entered a notch later named Walker Pass, which took them through the mountains at the easy elevation of 5,200 feet. In a few years Walker Pass would become a point of entry for emigrants bound for California.

Though the homeward crossing of the Sierra was less difficult than the outward one, the Nevada badlands were as bad as ever. Some of the stock died of thirst and, lacking any other liquid, the men drank the blood of these animals. Again they sweated, suffered and cursed; again every one of them survived.

The party moved north along the western edge of the desert, until they picked up their outward route near the Humboldt Sink. Once more they encountered the Diggers, who proved to be forgetful. In an eerie replay of the affair of the previous autumn, the Diggers again began to pester the mountain men. Again Walker did his best to avoid violence, but the slow-learning Diggers continued to harass him. In mid-June he and his men wheeled upon the Diggers and rode them down, killing 14 more of the unfortunate Indians. From then on, the last leg of the trip to the Bear River rendezvous of 1834 was something of a cakewalk for the trail-hardened travelers. They arrived at the rendezvous on July 12. They had been gone a full year.

Walker and his men had thrown an invisible but invaluable line across a large portion of the Western void, and they had done it skillfully and safely. Though Walker's expedition passed through some of the worst country in North America and had several brisk engagements with Indians, his party suffered no fatalities. In the end, Walker returned with a group of men who knew something about the Great Basin crossing and the Sierra passes. These men could serve as guides and advisers for others who might want to go that way. Finally, Walker and his men had all had a grand time in California. Among mountain men and others they later acted as boosters of the virtues and the pleasures of the Golden State.

The on-to-California urge would grow steadily stronger in the succeeding decades; it was, indeed, to become a cornerstone of America's expansion. But the seeds of this expansion had already germinated when, mulling over the matter in 1833, Zenas Leonard wrote: "Yes, here, even in this remote part of the great West before many years, will these hills and valleys be greeted with the enlivening sound of the workman's hammer, and the merry whistle of the ploughboy. Our government should be vigilant. She should assert her claim by taking possession of the whole territory as soon as possible—for we have good reason to suppose that the territory *west* of the mountain will some day be equally as important to a nation as that on the *east.*"

A watercolor of Mission San Carlos Borromeo in Carmel was painted by an English naval officer on an 1827 visit.

At trail's end, a garden of pleasures

The roughhewn mountain men who blazed the first overland trails to California found at the end of their journeys a land that seemed like a veritable pleasure garden compared with the wilderness they had left behind. Life in the balmy Mexican territory was centered around two fascinating institutions: the ranchos, with their fiestas and daredevil cattle-handling techniques *(following pages);* and the pastoral missions, where Indians were converted to Christianity and trained in the arts of farming and cattle raising.

A string of 21 Franciscan missions stretched from San Diego 570 miles north to Sonoma. They were so large — around 100,000 acres each — that they constituted small kingdoms. On Christmas Day, 1833, Joe Walker and his mountaineers were welcomed for a two-day stay at the one shown here. Inside, they found some converted Indians at exuberant "devotional exercises," which, wrote Zenas Leonard, consisted of "unbounded transports of joy" followed by "weeping and lamentation."

Prosperity on a grand scale had touched California by the time the mountain men got there. Much of its territory was divided among 50 cattle ranches, each sprawling over at least 50,000 acres. Visiting these huge private estates, the Americans were awed by the California cowboys, called vaqueros, who skillfully rounded up or cut out cattle from herds so huge that they reached half a mile from center to circumference. Their way with a rope was downright dazzling. The mountain men, whose sense of artful exaggeration was finely tuned, would have appreciated the local boast that "A Californian can throw a lasso as well with his foot as a Mexican can with his hand."

Making a sport of the chore of ridding the rancho of a predator, vaqueros in spiffy work dress rope a bear. It was a consummate bit of horsemanship, since the scent of bear made horses well-nigh unmanageable.

On a horseman's holiday, two vaqueros race their horses down a dusty rancho by-lane. Rancho horses were so numerous that they were allowed to wander around freely, trailing ropes that made catching them easy.

115

No se apure — "take your time" — was a phrase visitors to any rancho quickly picked up. But if the mountain men thought the slow-paced daily routine on a rancho lacked vigor, they had only to wait for the next fiesta. The wait would be short, for all year long there were events that called for three or four days of uninterrupted revelry: weddings or wakes, strawberry harvesting or communal drives to destroy the ubiquitous mustard plant.

The biggest social affair was the rodeo, an annual roundup to separate the ranchero's cattle from his neighbors'. Rodeos were held in the spring, by each rancho in turn, starting in San Diego and going north to Santa Barbara. Presumably the work of rounding up the cattle got done, but at the same time the days were filled with flashy riding competitions, cockfights, gambling and bull-and-bear baiting. During the nights, when the Californians gratified their passion for dancing, the girls got a chance to show off. One popular dance was the *bamba,* in which a señorita balancing a glass of water on her head had to step into a hoop, raise it to her knees and whirl it around while stamping her feet in time to a fast guitar strum.

Fandango, which Charles Nahl painted in the 1850s, shows a rancho couple coyly pointing toes in the traditional Spanish courtship dance. At right, a vaquero and his girl set off for a joyride on a palomino, the Mexican-bred horse introduced into California by the original Spanish settlers.

4 | Sightseers and scholars

Hardly anyone who journeyed West during the early decades of the 19th Century traveled about in quite the high-fashioned style of the German naturalist Prince Maximilian and the dashing Swiss artist Karl Bodmer (*right*) who accompanied him. But a number of dedicated men did go there for much the same reasons as this incongruous pair. They went, as Maximilian said in his *Travels in the Interior of North America,* to investigate the "character of the natural face of that remarkable country"—the wildlife, the Indians and the look of the land itself.

Unlike the trappers and traders who broke paths across the wilderness in order to exploit it, this new breed of explorers won a lasting gain. In notebooks and sketch pads and on their canvases, men like Bodmer, Maximilian, the botanist Thomas Nuttall and the artist George Catlin caught and preserved the wonders of the wilderness.

After his return Karl Bodmer painted this scene of himself *(right)* and Prince Maximilian meeting a band of Minnetarees.

No 76. √ 1, 2. Western blue Bird. √ 3, 4, Arctic blue bird. 5, 6 Black throated Gray W.ᵃ
Plate 380. Sialia occidentalis, Townsend. Sylvia arctica. S. nigrescens, Townsend. Plant

7, 8. Hermit W.ᵃ Calycanthus florida
Sylvia occidentalis, Towns ing. — Carolina allspice

9. Townsend's W.ᵃ. — 10, 11. Audubon's W.ᵃ
Sylvia Townsendi, Aud. Sylvia Audubonii, Nuttall.

120

"Animals, vegetables, minerals, Indian curiosities, etc."

On the upper Missouri one day in 1811, a party of westward-bound trappers and traders looked up from their keelboats to see the east bank swarming with distinctly unfriendly Sioux. Earlier reports had indicated that there might be as many as 600 warriors painting themselves for battle in the vicinity. The white men took no chances. The boats sculled to the west bank; their swivel gun and two howitzers were charged and loaded. All hands were ordered to ready their own weapons.

Dutifully, one member of the party, a 25-year-old Yorkshireman named Thomas Nuttall, primed and loaded his rifle. Happily for the future of American science, the Sioux chose to parley rather than fight that day, and Nuttall was not required to fire. A neophyte botanist, he had been using the weapon to dig plants along the Missouri shore. The barrel was clogged with sod and seeds; one shot, and the man who was to become the father of Western botany would have been blown to bits.

This almost comic performance was typical of the career of Thomas Nuttall, in whom genius, luck and unworldliness were mixed in approximately equal measure. No one could have looked more out of place in a land that hardened men through every imaginable kind of trial and tribulation. Nuttall seemed the very opposite of a wilderness traveler; in fact, he fitted the stereotype of the armchair intellectual. He was short and slender, with a high-domed, bulging forehead and intense, deep-set eyes. His behavior was gentle, absent-minded and withdrawn. But Thomas Nuttall was the exemplar of a new breed of explorers of the West, men who possessed a special toughness of their own—an almost fanatical devotion to the task of learning about all things in the wilderness, animate and inanimate.

The fact is that filling in the great trans-Mississippi void required two kinds of men. The blank spaces on the maps were the concern of the geographical explorers—the military and mountain men, the traders and, later, the settlers. But the West was also a blank in terms of its natural history, and that job of identification fell to botanists, ornithologists, mammalogists, ethnologists, paleontologists, geologists, meteorologists. In those less specialized days, they were collectively known as naturalists.

The ranks of the naturalist-explorers of the Western void included a disparate array of wealthy eccentrics, impoverished researchers, young enthusiasts and aging professionals. Some were primarily patrons and supporters of investigators who did the real work. There were a German prince and a Scottish laird among them. There were artists like Karl Bodmer and George Catlin, who painstakingly recorded the reality of frontier scenes; and others like Alfred Jacob Miller, who evoked the grandeur of the landscape.

The naturalists' interests lay in the length of fishes, the diameter of trees, the color of birds' wings, the customs and attire of Indians, and the aspect of the terrain itself. Not surprisingly, those interests and their accomplishments won them few headlines. They were memorialized instead in textbooks and museums, and particularly in the nomenclature of American flora and fauna—there is a Nuttall's Woodpecker, for example, and a Townsend's Warbler, named for Dr. John Kirk Townsend, ornithologist and protégé of Nuttall. The naturalists carried plant presses, books and drawing materials rather than beaver traps and bullet molds. Yet

Two ornithologists' work resulted in the medley of Western birds at left: John Kirk Townsend found the birds and sent them East, where John James Audubon, aided by his son, painted them. Fittingly, one is named for Townsend, one for Audubon.

they investigated the Old West as extensively as the geographical explorers, and far more systematically; and they exposed themselves to the same dangers and hardships. Considering where they went and what they endured, there is no question that they were brave men. But they were not dashing men of action. Theirs was to reason why, not to do or die. Consequently they labored largely in obscurity.

Of all the naturalists who, in their unglamorous way, won the West, Thomas Nuttall became preeminent. He seemed a most unlikely candidate for such a role. Born in England, he was groomed for a career in the family printing business. To the exasperation of his parents, the boy obviously preferred to spend his time looking for plants, bugs, rocks and fossils in the countryside. When he was 21, he announced that he had had enough of printing and intended to head west to become a naturalist in America.

In the spring of 1808, Nuttall arrived in Philadelphia, at that time an excellent place for a would-be naturalist to make his start. Philadelphia was the leading intellectual center of the New World. Its American Philosophical Society could claim some of the most prominent scientists and scholars of the country. The overriding interest of this intellectual community lay in natural history, particularly in classifying the flora and fauna of the country in a systematic fashion. Any newcomer with an intelligent interest in the subject was likely to be accepted readily.

Nuttall went to work in a local print shop to support himself, but he collected plants on his Sundays off. He soon made acquaintances among the Philadelphia natural-history crowd, including Dr. Benjamin Smith Barton, a physician who five years earlier had been among those who briefed Meriwether Lewis before his departure for the West. In addition to that distinction, Barton was a professor at the University of Pennsylvania medical school, a lecturer in botany, President of the Linnaean Society and Vice President of the American Philosophical Society. He was also, it seems, a bit unscrupulous. He appears to have been almost pathologically ambitious for fame but uninterested in the hard, tedious work by which men earn real reputations. Barton tried to solve his dilemma by becoming a kind of scientific Fagin, engaging dedicated young naturalists without reputation to do his collecting and classification for him. Having just lost one such apprentice, he apparently sized up Nuttall as an ideal replacement. The English boy was obviously talented and enthusiastic. Better yet, he was totally inexperienced in scientific infighting and hence could pose no real threat to his employer. As Barton commented to a friend, Nuttall was delightfully "innocent."

In the winter of 1810 Barton proposed that Nuttall undertake an incredible wilderness journey for the glory of American science and Benjamin Smith Barton. He suggested that the young man travel, alone, through the Appalachians into the Great Lakes country to Lake Winnipeg in what is now the Canadian province of Manitoba—a distance of more than 1,200 miles from Philadelphia. Then he was to move up the Saskatchewan River, swing south to the Missouri system, and return through Illinois, Indiana, Kentucky and Virginia to Philadelphia. While Nuttall was making this stupendous tour through territory that was mostly roadless and unmapped, he was to collect "animals, vegetables, minerals, Indian curiosities, etc.," which he would periodically ship back to Barton. (How he was to ship them out of a howling wilderness was unclear.) He was also to keep a daily journal that would become Barton's exclusive property, and he was not to communicate with anyone about scientific matters without Barton's express consent. In return Barton would outfit Nuttall and pay him the somewhat less than princely wage of eight dollars per month during an anticipated trek of two years.

Barton seems to have had a rather clear if cynical notion of exactly what he was asking of the young Eng-

Nuttall's dogwood, which was found near the Columbia, appeared in his *North America Sylva*.

Cherry-sized fruit adorns the river crab apple in this rendering from Nuttall's tome on American trees.

Finding this tree flowering in Monterey, Nuttall dubbed it the California horse chestnut.

lishman. "I have no doubt," wrote the good doctor to a Washington acquaintance, "should his life be spared, that he will add much to our knowledge of geography [and] the natural history . . . of all countries through which he is directed to pass." All things considered it was an excellent speculative venture for Barton. He was risking only the minuscule sum of $200 or so, not to mention the life of a young immigrant without connections or reputation.

Perhaps only an eager, 24-year-old, 19th Century apprentice naturalist could have considered such a proposition a splendid deal for himself, or for that matter would have considered it at all. However, Thomas Nuttall was such a man, and he instantly agreed to Barton's terms. So far as the dangers and hardships of this wilderness journey were concerned, Nuttall knew nothing of them, and if he had, probably would not have changed his plans, so obsessed was he with studying the natural history of the West.

Innocence sometimes has a way of providing a better defense against the world than sophistication. At any rate, that is how matters worked out in the Barton-Nuttall case. Almost as soon as he departed from Philadelphia in April 1810, Nuttall seems to have gone his own way, not troubling himself excessively with Barton's complicated routing instructions. He never got to Canada, although he did make it as far as Mackinac Island in northern Michigan. But he executed his orders to collect and observe far beyond the letter of his contract with Barton. Once he reached the wilderness Nuttall began behaving like a kitten in a catnip patch —ecstatic, almost hypnotized as he moved from one natural wonder to the next. In this fashion he traveled across half the continent for almost two years, collecting countless specimens, accumulating masses of information, starting the work that ultimately would win him the title of father of Western botany. The recognition that the naïve genius was to achieve was almost exactly what was so avidly desired by Benjamin Barton, now

ironically best remembered as an acquaintance of men like Nuttall.

Nuttall started out from Philadelphia with a single trunk that, in addition to his clothes, contained five blank notebooks, a steel pen, a thermometer, one German botany book, a pair of scales and four quires of paper for pressing plants. Despite this scanty gear, he proved himself to be a field man par excellence. At Pittsburgh he turned north, and during the summer collected along the shores of Lakes Erie and Huron. Then he crossed Lake Michigan by boat and proceeded through Wisconsin to the Mississippi. Early on, he contracted fever, and thereafter was laid up periodically with the sweats and shakes.

Nuttall arrived in St. Louis in September of 1810, having been promised a ride farther west the following spring with Wilson Price Hunt, field leader of John Jacob Astor's Oregon-bound party of trappers and traders *(pages 58-59)*. By a peculiar coincidence there was another Englishman and naturalist in St. Louis that winter. John Bradbury, then in his forties, had been sent to America to collect plants for the Liverpool Botanic Gardens. Bradbury, too, had been promised a passage up the Missouri with the Astorians, and while waiting for the Astorians' final departure, he and Nuttall found each other compatible company in St. Louis.

When the time came to move upriver in March, the two men started out on foot, botanizing along the river's banks, rather than waste precious collecting opportunities sitting on Hunt's keelboat. One morning they said howdy to the 77-year-old Daniel Boone, who had tottered back to his Missouri farm after trapping 60 beavers during the spring season. A day or so later they met that archetypal mountain man, John Colter, who was all afire to go west with the Astorians but could not undertake the trip because of the strong objections of his new bride.

Nuttall and Bradbury continued upriver, walking, observing, collecting whenever they could, riding on a keelboat when they had to. It must have been an ex-

The musselshell below, which is commonly found in Western waters, was drawn in two views by Mrs. Thomas Say to illustrate her husband's scholarly opus, *American Conchology*, published in the 1830s.

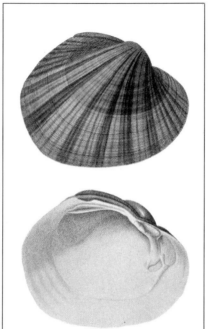

traordinary experience for the two of them. In terms of natural history, their journey might be likened to the first voyage of Columbus. Meriwether Lewis had collected specimens and taken natural-history notes when he had the chance, but he was an amateur with many other things on his mind. Nuttall and Bradbury were the first professional naturalists to get into the Far West. In every place they looked there were new and marvelous phenomena that no one before them had been able to understand and appreciate as they could.

On one of the keelboats was a young journalist named Henry Brackenridge, who was also riding upriver for a distance under the protection of the fur men. In a later account of the trip Brackenridge made a revealing mention of Nuttall. He noted that the Englishman was engaged in botanical pursuits, "to which he appears singularly devoted, and which seem to engross every thought, to the total disregard of his own personal safety, and sometimes to the inconvenience of the party he accompanies. To the ignorant Canadian boatmen, who are unable to appreciate the science, he affords a subject of merriment; *le fou* is the name by which he is commonly known. He is a young man of genius, and very considerable acquirements, but is too much devoted to his favorite pursuit, and seems to think that no other study deserves the attention of a man of sense." After this critique, Brackenridge offered an affectionate apology: "I hope, should this meet his eye, it will give no offence; for these things often constituted a subject of merriment to us both."

The Canadian keelboat hands might call Nuttall the Crazy One, and other frontiersmen would similarly regard other naturalists; but considering what different breeds of men they were, Western traders, trappers and soldiers seemed surprisingly willing to have naturalists accompany them, and treated them with a respect tinged with awe. Although the interests of the scientists were incomprehensible to the frontiersmen, the manner in which they pursued those interests was impressive even to those who found hardship and danger.

The Indians reacted in like fashion; they were much taken with Nuttall and Bradbury. Not unreasonably the tribesmen assumed that men who casually exposed themselves to risks, appeared so defenseless and were so knowledgeable about living things must be great medicine men. The only real difficulty Nuttall seems to have had with Missouri River Indians was that occasionally a warrior would find the bottles in which the naturalist was preserving specimens and would drink the alcohol. Otherwise the Mandans, Arikaras and even the Sioux treated the naturalists with considerable deference.

At the Arikara villages in what is now South Dakota, Hunt and the Astorians left the river and set off on the long journey overland to the Pacific Coast. Nuttall and Bradbury threw in their lot with another party bound 200 miles farther upriver. This group was led by the crafty fur entrepreneur Manuel Lisa, headed for a post he had built near the Mandan villages. Lisa was delighted to take Nuttall along with him, for in an odd crossing of paths, the two men had met a year and a half earlier, when they had been fellow passengers on a stage jolting across the Pennsylvania mountains. Apparently they struck up an immediate friendship. Perhaps it was the attraction of opposites, the unworldly botanist and the most worldly king of the wild frontier. Also Lisa was a man of intelligence, one of the few frontiersmen of that period who could appreciate Nuttall's intellectual concerns.

At the Mandan villages, Bradbury was greatly bothered by the swarms of mosquitoes that plagued so many frontiersmen, and when the chance came, opted to return to St. Louis on a keelboat. Downriver, the boat was nearly swamped in a sudden storm and driven up against the riverbank, where it was hastily secured to a solitary shrub until the storm abated. Happily, the shrub held firm, and Bradbury seized the opportunity to inspect it. Dutifully, he recorded its botanical name—*Amorpha fruticosa*—in his journal. ◉

127

A personal investigation by the dean of botanists

So great was the harvest of botanical novelties in the West that plant collectors often did not have the time or the expertise to describe and analyze their own finds. The major share of this crucial follow-up work fell to Asa Gray, a renowned plant authority who spent almost all of his career in residence at Harvard. There he studied and catalogued the avalanche of dried specimens that arrived at his laboratory unsolicited. He acquired other material by commissioning botanists to fill in gaps in his knowledge. Charles Wright, a dedicated collector, described the hardships he suffered on Gray's behalf in Texas in 1849 with this ironic comment: "Sleep all night if you can in the rain and walk 12-15 miles next day in the mud and then overhaul a huge package of soaked plants and dry them in the heat of the clouds."

Gray may have had this warning in mind when, 28 years later, at the age of 67, he made his first expedition to the West, outfitting his party with a full supply of waterproof tents (below).

When Asa Gray (kneeling with plant press) visited Colorado in 1877, he brought his wife (light dress) and a retinue of scientists, including Sir Joseph Hooker, president of the Royal Society of London (seated beside Gray).

ASA GRAY'S PLANT-COLLECTING KIT

A vasculum, or plant box, used to gather small specimens

Hand-held and mounted magnifying glasses

Knife and trowel

The simple array of tools that Gray used during his Western trip represents the basic field kit of 19th Century botanists. On this expedition Gray and his associates documented plant distribution by collecting more than 500 specimens.

Nuttall, whose air of detachment extended to bugs and discomforts of all kinds, stayed on in the Mandan villages until the end of summer, engaged in a sustained botanical orgy. On at least one occasion he experienced something akin to the depth rapture that sometimes causes underwater explorers to run unnecessary risks. He set out on a collecting expedition and, moving from one plant to the next, wandered a hundred miles across the plains from Lisa's fort. Having brought no food or supplies along, he finally collapsed from hunger, exhaustion and exposure. Fortunately he was found by an amazed Mandan warrior who tenderly scooped up the unconscious naturalist, fed him, and carried him back to Lisa.

In the fall, Nuttall too caught a ride downstream on a keelboat, carrying hundreds of specimens of plants, birds, mammals, amphibians and snakes. He proceeded past St. Louis to New Orleans. There, in accordance with the terms of his contract, he shipped his journal and specimens to Barton in Philadelphia, keeping duplicates, seeds and a few living plants for himself. Barton somehow thought that he had been cheated, despite the extent of the findings. He had wanted Nuttall to help in classifying them — as well as some specimens from the Lewis and Clark expedition that had not yet been catalogued. Although he apparently never communicated this desire to the young botanist, he was incensed that Nuttall did not return to Philadelphia as their contract had specified. Nuttall, rather pointedly, did not say a public word about his onetime mentor for the rest of his life.

With the War of 1812 between Britain and America imminent, Nuttall sailed to England, where he remained until the war was over, working on his collections, mulling over his Western experiences and discussing them with other scientists. Partly as a result of these discussions, he was elected a member of the Linnean Society of London, an honor accorded only to the most prestigious naturalists. When he again returned to America in 1815, the innocent who had arrived on its shores only seven years earlier was a ranking botanist, a scientist of formidable reputation. Barton undoubtedly writhed at this turnabout.

Nuttall's prestige was further enhanced by a series of collecting trips in the South and Southwest and in 1818 by the publication of his *Genera of North Amer-ican Plants,* a botanical classic. In 1823 he was invited to Harvard as curator of the university's botanical gardens and as a lecturer in natural history. He remained at Harvard for the next decade, mixing botany with mineralogy and ornithology (his *Ornithology of the United States and Canada* was a definitive reference work throughout the 19th Century). During his Harvard years he was known not only as a scientific celebrity, but also as a towering eccentric. He would deal only with faculty members and students whom he judged to be seriously interested in the natural sciences. Living in a Harvard-owned rooming house, he had his meals served through a hole in the kitchen wall, and had a trapdoor installed in a closet ceiling to enable him to move from one part of his quarters to another without being seen by other tenants. Ultimately Nuttall came to regard Cambridge society and even the university itself as a distraction, a waste of his precious time. In 1834, shortly after his salary had been increased, he informed astonished Harvard administrators that he was quitting to cross the continent as a member of an expedition being organized by a Boston merchant, Nathaniel Wyeth.

Nathaniel Wyeth was one of the near-important figures of Western history. Essentially he hoped to revive the earlier, grandly conceived plan of John Jacob Astor to establish a colony on the Columbia River. This community would in part support itself with a fisheries industry and would serve as a shipping point through which Western goods, chiefly furs, could be sent out of the mountains by sea. There was nothing particularly wrong with the plan, except that Wyeth, like Astor, was somewhat ahead of his time. And there was nothing wrong with Wyeth. He was a sensible field leader. However, he was unlucky and a bit too civilized to do business successfully with the irresponsible mountain traders.

In 1832, Wyeth had prudently gone West on a kind of geographical and commercial reconnaissance. He attended the Green River rendezvous of 1833 and there made a contract with the partners of the Rocky Mountain Fur Company to haul in their supplies for the next year's rendezvous. Returning to Boston (where he asked Nuttall and his protégé the physician-ornithologist John Kirk Townsend to accompany him the next spring), he set about organizing

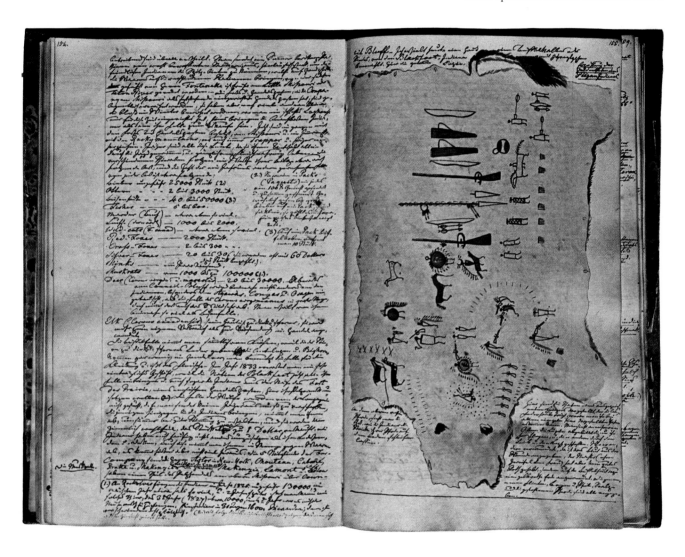

his supply caravan, assuming, as any Boston businessman would, that a contract was a contract. However, when he arrived at the rendezvous, Wyeth found that Billy Sublette, a former Rocky Mountain Fur Company partner and the brother of a remaining partner, had arrived a few days before and already sold supplies to the fur men. Simply and brutally, the trappers told Wyeth what he could do with his contract.

They were, after all, men not overly given to niceties, legal or otherwise. While they were throwing Wyeth's contract in his face, they ran through the usual gamut of rendezvous games, affording Nuttall and Townsend a glimpse of the frontier's chaotic brand of fun. "This being a memorable day," reads Townsend's journal entry for July 4, "the liquor kegs were opened. We, therefore, soon had a renewal of the coarse and brutal scenes of the rendezvous. Some of the bacchanals called for a volley in honor of the day. We who were not 'happy' had to lie flat on the ground to avoid the bullets which were careering through the camp." Despite the prevailing disorder of the occasion, science was not neglected by the two naturalists. "In the little stream," Townsend observed in the same journal entry, "the fish probably average fifteen or sixteen inches in length."

Stuck with a caravan full of supplies and no buyers, Wyeth did what he could to recoup. Taking Nuttall and Townsend with him, he led his expedition to the upper Snake, where he built a post, Fort Hall, and tried to peddle some of the goods to Indians and free-

131

A composite engraving of Karl Bodmer's sketches of the upper Missouri riverbanks celebrates the diversity of sandstone

formations, which his patron, Prince Maximilian, described as looking like "colonnades, pulpits, pipe organs and castles."

133

An eerie arrangement of buffalo and human skulls placed around slender stakes was sketched by Karl Bodmer in a Mandan village on the Missouri River in 1833. Here the Indians shouted petitions to their gods.

An eerie arrangement of buffalo and human skulls placed around slender stakes was sketched by Karl Bodmer in a Mandan village on the Missouri River in 1833. Here the Indians shouted petitions to their gods.

lance trappers. Nuttall and Townsend must have realized that Wyeth was in trouble but it did not seem to disturb or inconvenience them greatly. At about the time Wyeth was in his direst straits, Nuttall was triumphantly discovering a new whippoorwill, *Phalaenoptilus nuttalli*. Townsend, not to be outdone, bagged an undescribed mountain plover, *Eupoda montana*. A few weeks later, while the dispirited Wyeth and his men were constructing Fort Hall, trying to hold off the Blackfeet as they did so, Nuttall found a Western marsh wren, and wrote about it as though he were in a Cambridge garden: "It is a remarkably active and quaint little species, skipping and diving about with great activity after its insect food and their larvae among the rank grass and rushes."

From Fort Hall, the party headed for Oregon, crossing the awful Snake River lava beds—a plain of jagged rocks without water or grass. But in the midst of their nightmarish crossing of this region, Nuttall observed "beautiful pebbles of chalcedony and fine agate." While the rest of the party sweated and cursed among the barren rocks, he blithely noted that "the sweet berries of a hawthorn (*Crataegus sanguinea*) which occurred sporadically from the Rockies westward were welcome food." On September 2, a day from the Columbia River, the naturalist roasted and dined on an owl that Townsend had shot.

Reaching the coast late in the year, Nuttall waded out into the water (and by doing so became the first professional naturalist to make a crossing of the continent). Rather casually he scooped up four new crustaceans and a theretofore undescribed marine bivalve, now known as Nuttall's Cockle.

By this time Nuttall and Townsend between them had several thousand plant specimens and hundreds of preserved birds, amphibians, reptiles, mammals, inver-

tebrates and mineral samples. They began to worry about the effects of the damp, cold Oregon weather on their collections. Ever resourceful when it came to science, they hitched a ride on a schooner to Hawaii, spent the winter in its paradisical climate, then returned for more collecting in Oregon in the spring. Nuttall, who predictably made some excellent finds in Hawaii, returned to those islands again in the winter of 1835. Finally in the spring of 1836 he started home in a leisurely fashion, stopping at Monterey, then exploring the natural history of the coast southward. By mid-April he was in the vicinity of San Diego waiting for the brig *Alert,* on which he was to take passage back to Boston. While biding his time, he made a final haul, picking up on the San Diego strand 21 new shells and 15 new crustaceans.

As it happened there was a former Harvard student of his, Richard Henry Dana, on board the *Alert.*

Dana had shipped on as a seaman, and eventually was to produce his own classic book, *Two Years before the Mast,* in which he commemorated Nuttall.

"I had left him quietly seated in the chair of Botany and Ornithology in Harvard University," Dana wrote, "and the next I saw of him, he was strolling about San Diego beach, in a sailor's pea-jacket, with a wide straw hat, and barefooted, with his trousers rolled up to his knees, picking up stones and shells. . . . The crew called Mr. Nuttall 'Old Curious,' from his zeal for curiosities, and some of them said that he was crazy, and that his friends let him go about and amuse himself in this way. Why else a rich man (sailors call every man rich who does not work with his hands) should leave a Christian country, and come to such a place as California, to pick up shells and stones, they could not understand. One of them, however, who had seen something more of the world ashore, set all

Plate III

On the Missouri, Audubon found a charming pair of white-tailed jack rabbits for his book *Viviparous Quadrupeds of North America.*

Audubon at Green Bank Almost, Happy!! — Sep 5 1826. Drawn by himself.

had traveled "not for his own amusement, but for the benefit of mankind."

Like Nuttall, virtually all of the naturalist-explorers lacked the resources, experience and temperament to organize their own expeditions into the West. Generally they were dependent upon the charity of commercial enterprises like the fur companies and the Boston firm that owned the *Alert*. Some of them, like the brilliant zoologist Thomas Say, managed to hook up with government-sponsored expeditions. Say, between 1819 and 1820, traveled widely on the plains in a reconnaissance party led by Major Stephen Long (*page 162*) and he collected numerous specimens of Western shells and insects.

One naturalist who was by no stretch of the imagination dependent on anyone's charity was Alexander Philip Maximilian, hereditary sovereign of the German principality of Wied-Neuwied. Born in a castle on the Rhine, Prince Max was nonetheless no royal dilettante; he took up arms during the Napoleonic wars and, as a major-general in the Allied army, led a division in the capture of Paris in 1814. After the war ended, he mounted a two-year-long exploring expedition to South America, and spent the ensuing 10 years back in his castle writing two monumental works on Brazil's flora and fauna, as well as compiling a detailed atlas of the country.

He had long dreamed of producing similar works on the American West, and in 1832 he sailed for the United States — with, of course, a suitable entourage. He brought along not only his manservant, David Dreidoppel, but also the Swiss artist Karl Bodmer to make pictorial records of the royal findings. Prince Maximilian once characterized the artist as "an able draughtsman," but he was something more than that and, ironically, the prince is today best known as Bodmer's sponsor. Bodmer had studied in Paris, absorbing a romantic but precise style that would stand him in good stead in the West.

In St. Louis, the prince and his entourage — the aging Toussaint Charbonneau, Sacajawea's husband, was later hired as interpreter — took passage aboard one of the American Fur Company's steamboats for a 2,500-mile journey up the Missouri. While Maximilian made compendious notes, Bodmer painted at a frenzied rate, capturing the wildlife along the river, the

to rights, as he thought; 'Oh, 'vast there! You don't know anything about them craft. I've seen them colleges and know the ropes. They keep all such things for cur'osities and study 'em, and have men a' purpose to go and get 'em. This old chap knows what he's about. He a'n't the child you take him for. He'll carry all these things to the college, and if they are better than any they have had before, he'll be head of the college. Then, by and by, somebody else will go after some more, and if they beat him, he'll have to go again, or else give up his berth. That's the way they do it. This old covey knows the ropes. He has worked a traverse over 'em and come 'way out here where nobody's ever been afore, and where they'll never think of coming.' "

Nuttall arrived in Boston in September to the acclaim of the academic community. A few days after his return he went to the offices of the owners of the *Alert* to pay for his passage. There he was told by the hardheaded Yankee merchantmen that he had been given a free ride home, on the ground that he tawny landscape, the curious Indians watching the strange vessel move upriver.

At Fort McKenzie, the farthest point that he and the prince reached, the painter was able to sketch a fight between Assiniboins, Crees and Piegans — an encounter that the inhabitants of the fort mistook for an attack upon themselves. Maximilian seized his gun, charged it with powder and fired upon an advancing Assiniboin. Unfortunately, he had forgotten that he had already charged the weapon, and the resulting recoil sent the short prince careening backward across the fort until he fetched up stunned on the opposite wall. Nonetheless, he contended that he had shot his Indian, and was miffed when he could not obtain the Assiniboin's skull to take home as a specimen. There was no great loss, however: *Travels in the Interior of North America in the Years 1832-1834,* the two-volume Bodmer-illustrated work that Prince Maximilian eventually produced, became a definitive European reference work on the American wilderness.

The prince had already made a less direct contribution to the natural history of the West — simply by being an inspirational figure. In St. Louis in 1833, he had encountered another European nobleman, William Drummond Stewart. The second son of Sir George Stewart, 17th Lord of Grantully and fifth Baronet of Murthly, he was also a veteran of the Napoleonic wars, having served as a dashing young officer at Waterloo. Stewart's interest in natural history was minimal; he had come West to indulge his taste for big-game hunting. But he was much impressed by Prince Maximilian's tactic of bringing along an artist to record his travels. It occurred to Stewart that whatever a German prince could do, a Scottish patrician could do too, and on a subsequent journey to the American West in 1837 he had his own artist in tow — Alfred Jacob Miller, a Baltimore painter who had received some training in Europe.

Stewart headed straight for the Green River rendezvous, where he proceeded to amuse himself in fine mountain-man fashion. He was accepted as an equal by the trappers because he was a superb shot and a durable, enthusiastic hell-raiser who found Indian girls at least as interesting as buffalo. While Stewart explored every source of fun, blood sport and adventure, Miller labored diligently throughout the summer, making one

of the few firsthand pictorial records of the mountain men and the pristine world that they roamed. In a moody, ethereal style, he memorialized scores of Western scenes: a lake in Wyoming that, alas, no longer bears the name Loch Drummond that William Drummond Stewart bestowed on it but is called New Fork Lake; buffalo hunting in the Wind River range; Stewart surrounded by Indian friends, most of whom — predictably enough — seem to be girls.

In 1843 Stewart came West again for a final fling. He was by this time Sir William, having succeeded to the title on the death of his older brother. As befitted his new status, he mounted an expedition in the grand manner: 10 carts, a two-mule wagon, a New Orleans newspaperman to keep a record of the trip and a Scots naturalist, who collected 350 species of seeds to be germinated on Sir William's holdings. And, perhaps in an effort to match Prince Maximilian's nice historical touch in taking Sacajawea's husband along to serve as interpreter on his trip, Stewart hired as his wagon-driver their son, Baptiste, the boy born on the Lewis and Clark trail.

On this trip, Stewart just missed attaining a further measure of vicarious fame. The great artist-naturalist John James Audubon, anxious to complete his work, *Viviparous Quadrupeds of North America,* felt it necessary to travel west that same year to observe fauna. He and Stewart had mutual acquaintances, and Audubon had long planned to accompany the laird into the West. But when the two met in St. Louis, Audubon, by then 51 years old, became alarmed at stories of life in the wilderness and, instead of going with Stewart to the Rockies, chose to take the same cruise up the Missouri that Maximilian had made 10 years earlier. On this well-traveled route he found several new species of birds as well as some fine material for his book. From specimens collected along the way, Audubon created portraits of such Western animals as the badger and the grizzly bear. At Fort Union, the painter forgot about his art for a moment and became an avid buffalo hunter, although in his diary he expressed sorrow over the slaughter of the great herds by whites and Indians.

Stewart himself soon returned to Scotland and faded from history, spending the rest of his years tending his ancestral estates and sighing over Miller's paintings

Although Audubon's picture of a badger devouring a quail is a vision of ferocity, he made a pet of the animal while out West.

of the glory days in the West. He had had Billy Sublette ship him a few live buffalo for old times' sake, but they did not do well in the highlands. Passing across Stewart's land on her honeymoon, Queen Victoria remarked that she was not much taken with "these strange, hump-backed beasts from America."

Perhaps the most remarkable — and certainly the most extensive — visual record of the wilderness was that of George Catlin. He came earlier to the West and stayed longer than the others. Also he was as much a scientist, ethnologist and anthropologist as he was an artist, being one of the few 19th Century Americans to systematically observe and record the life style of the Western Indian tribes before they entered their precipitous decline. Catlin brought to his work a profoundly unconventional viewpoint. Almost alone among the Western figures of the time, he believed that the culture of the American Indian was admirable — often equal and sometimes superior to that of the white man — and he devoted much of his life to expressing this belief in both his paintings and writings.

Catlin was born in 1796 into a gentle, educated Pennsylvania family. His father was a lawyer and farmer. His mother, a cultured woman, spent long hours reading aloud to her son and telling him stories about her experiences as a seven-year-old captive among the Iroquois Nation after she had been seized during a brief uprising in 1778.

The boy loved the outdoors. "The early part of my life," he wrote, "was whiled away . . . with books reluctantly held in one hand, and a rifle or fishing pole firmly and affectionately grasped in the other." He also carried drawing materials and enjoyed sketching and painting. The mundane necessity to earn a living forced him to give up his avocation for a time. At 21 he went to law school, joined the bar and practiced halfheartedly for three years in Wilkes-Barre. But in 1823 he chucked his legal career and went to Philadelphia to study art. A year later he was admitted to the Pennsylvania Academy of Fine Arts and almost immediately became a popular, well-paid portraitist, traveling along the East Coast painting likenesses of the gentry. However, this quick and easy success apparently did not satisfy Catlin. Perhaps influenced by his mother's stories about her childhood captivity, he was fascinated by Indians, and he began to seek out, sketch and paint

surviving members of the shattered Eastern tribes.

By 1830 the fascination had become a passion, and Catlin went West looking for wild Indians. In St. Louis he met a man who could provide powerful assistance for his project. This was William Clark, the surviving co-leader of the first transcontinental expedition. Now 60 years old, Clark was a general, and the unofficial elder statesman of the West. Perhaps as important, he was also the Superintendent of Indian Affairs. The old explorer took an immediate liking to the young artist, gave him his enthusiastic support and became the nearest thing to a patron Catlin was to have. Clark was, after all, one of the first to have seen the Indians in their natural state, and perhaps he perceived in Catlin some of his own youthful eagerness to discover and comprehend the alien wonders of the West.

One of the most practical things Clark did for Catlin was to introduce him to St. Louis society and recommend him as a noted Eastern artist. On the strength of this introduction, Catlin received a number of commissions to paint portraits of leading St. Louis citizens (including Clark himself); the fees would finance his forthcoming trip into the wilderness. During that summer, Clark also took the artist with him to several negotiating and ceremonial sessions with Indians, whom Catlin studied and painted. In the spring of 1831, again with Clark's support, Catlin went up the Platte with a military reconnaissance party. During the spring of 1832 he secured passage on the maiden voyage of the *Yellowstone,* the steamboat put into service that year by the American Fur Company to serve the firm's Missouri posts.

He spent a year on the journey and produced more than a hundred paintings of the Blackfoot, Crow, Sioux, Mandan and other tribes. In these paintings, his style began to undergo a marked metamorphosis. His portraits had been facile but formal — almost neutral in their treatment of character. But his Indian studies took on a raw directness that the portraits lacked. It was as if, in painting primitives, he deliberately changed his style to that of a primitive. Yet at the same time all of his best work is notable for its detail, the loving care given to a bear-claw necklace, the drape of a robe, a dog in the background, a design on a tipi. Some critics later felt that the Indians in his pictures were overly noble (John James Audubon, duplicating his route a decade later, remarked that Catlin's Indians resembled none he saw). But the details of Catlin costumes and backgrounds were almost always scrupulously portrayed.

The realism was of course in keeping with Catlin's temperament and plan. He came West not to sketch pretty scenes and exotic faces, but to collect and record facts. He jammed not only his paintings but his notebooks with specific, detailed information on how the tribesmen lived, what they ate and wore and thought about, how they played, worshipped and spoke. In addition, he bought, bartered for and collected quantities of Indian goods and artifacts.

One small but instructive example serves to illustrate Catlin's approach. Unlike most whites, Catlin had enough respect for the Indians to learn their proper names, and his captions and notes are therefore sprinkled with the sonorous, dignified, phonetical versions of the names of the men with whom he lived: *Man-to-tchee-ga* (The Little Bear), *Shon-ka* (The Dog), *Tah-teck-a-da-hair* (The Steep Wind).

It seems probable that only such a sensitive, admiring, genuinely interested man as Catlin could have accomplished what he did among the tribes at that time. In 1832 the Indian nations Catlin portrayed were still strong, independent and dangerous; had they been so minded, they could have gobbled up not only a wandering artist but very likely all of the whites on the upper Missouri. Furthermore, Catlin's work — creating faithful likenesses of them with paint and brushes —was absolutely foreign to the tribesmen; it had overtones of magic. Often it was a very near thing whether Catlin would be able to quiet the suspicions of the Indians, who were both intrigued and a little frightened by his strange medicine. In a Sioux village, for example, Catlin got into terrible trouble when he painted a profile of one warrior. When it was finished, an onlooker twitted the model, saying that the white medicine man had now made him a half-faced man. The gibe touched off a bloody shoot-out. The subject of the portrait was killed, and the entire tribe, in an uproar, began to focus their anger on Catlin. Some white traders interceded and gained the artist enough time to make his escape.

Such unpredictable outbursts of violence did not shake Catlin's feeling for the West or his admiration for its indigenous inhabitants. After he returned to St. Louis, he spent eight more years painting Western and Southern Indians and studying their culture. At the conclusion of these researches he was able to write: "I have visited forty-eight different tribes, the great part of which I found speaking different languages, and containing in all 400,000 souls. I have brought home safe, and in good order, 310 portraits in oil, all painted in their native dress, and in their own wigwams; and also 200 other paintings in oil, containing views of their villages — their wigwams — their games and religious ceremonies — their dances — their ball plays — their buffalo hunting and other amusements (containing in all over 3000 full length figures); and the landscapes of the country they live in, as well as a very extensive and curious collection of their costumes and all their other manufactures from the size of a wigwam down to the size of a quill or rattle."

But this impressive catalogue does not measure the full significance of his work. He touched upon a deeper dimension of his art when he wrote this tribute to the tribes on another occasion: "I love a people who have always made me welcome to the best they had . . . who are honest without laws . . . who have no poor house . . . who never take the name of God in vain . . . who worship God without a bible and I believe that God loves them also . . . who are free of religious animosities . . . who never raised a hand against me or stolen my property . . . who never fought a battle with white men except on their own ground . . . and oh! how I love a people who don't live for the love of money."

A great many white men saw the Western tribesmen before George Catlin visited them. However, with his artist's eye and sympathetic mind, Catlin was one of the very first to see the full scope of their pride and splendor. And for some of these Plains peoples, he was among the last to observe them. By 1837 the Mandans, one of the most powerful and advanced of the river tribes, were almost entirely obliterated by the white man's smallpox. Shortly thereafter the brutal Indian wars began in earnest, and in this long, grinding conflict the remaining tribes were to be progressively altered, their ethnic and cultural integrity ultimately destroyed. But, at least in the phantom form of lines and pigments, George Catlin preserved their dying world.

The Author painting a Chief, at the base of the Rocky Mountains.

G. Catlin.

In a wry self-portrait, Catlin recorded the wonder of Mandan tribesmen watching the likeness of Chief Mah-to-toh-pa appear on canvas.

An artistic tribute to a vanishing people

In 1832, after witnessing a gruesome rite of self-torture conducted by the Mandan tribe, George Catlin wrote, "Thank God, it is over, that I have seen it, and am able to tell it to the world." Telling the world about Western Indians was the mission and the obsession of artist Catlin's life. After some casual painting of Indians on reservations in the East while earning his living as a society portraitist, Catlin left his family to spend 10 years studying the alien ways of the Plains tribes. His observations were published in a two-volume work, *Illustrations of the Manners, Customs, and Condition of the North American Indians*. Despite its ponderous title, Catlin's book was highly readable, combining evocative prose with vivid, richly detailed engravings, some of which are reproduced on these and the following pages.

Although Catlin was not the first artist to visit the Western tribes, he had a unique respect and affection for Indian culture that allowed him to interpret it on its own terms. In return, the Indians warmed to this free spirit who roamed across their land working with furious intensity (during one 86-day trip on the upper Missouri, Catlin produced 135 paintings while traveling an average of 18 miles a day). His efforts to win the Indians' trust gained him access to many of their secret rites and sanctuaries, including a sacred quarry in Minnesota where tribes obtained stone for pipe bowls. No white man had ever been permitted to visit the site before.

This engraving of Mah-to-toh-pa includes battle scenes and symbols of valor on his robe.

Scalping was not always fatal, as Catlin showed in a droll sketch of a scalped man removing his derby *(below, at right)*. Once scalps had been stretched on hoops, they were hung from weapons, horses and tipis.

On a page of his field notebook Catlin portrayed festive Mandan warriors at an archery contest, and the glum deliberations of a war party returning home following a costly raid against neighboring Arikaras.

Mandan Indians

page 141 *Game of the Arrow* 60

page 153 63

Foot-War Party in Council

In this engraving of Teton Sioux articles,
Catlin showed a shield and quiver of arrows, tobacco pouches *(top, right)* made
from animal skins, and musical instruments
—drums, rattles and whistles *(bottom)*.

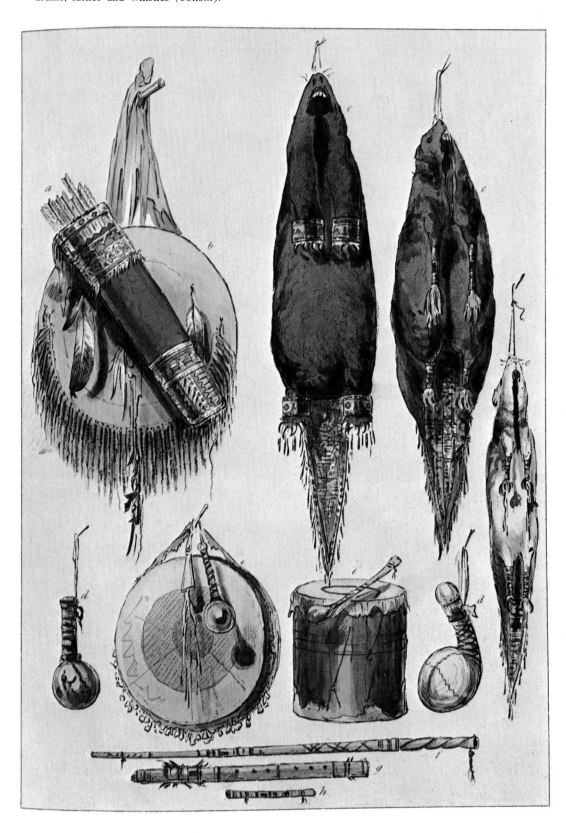

Artifacts vital to mobility were canoes and snowshoes. Catlin praised the Chippewa canoe as a "most beautiful and light" boat. His sketch at bottom shows hunters on snowshoes killing buffalo mired in drifts.

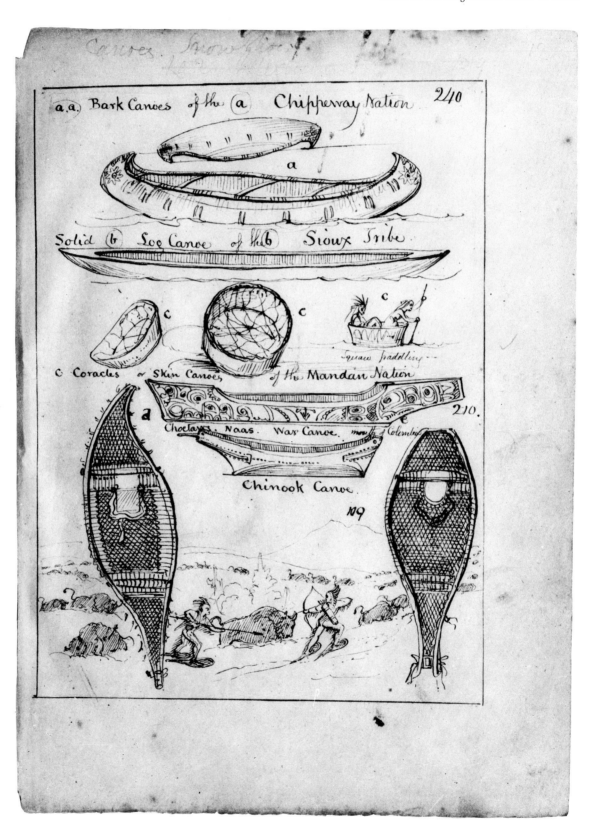

a.a.) Bark Canoes of the (a) Chippeway Nation 240

Solid (b) Log Canoe of the (b) Sioux Tribe.

c Coracles or Skin Canoes, of the Mandan Nation

Squaw paddling

Choo{lay} Naas War Canoe. mouth Columbia

Chinook Canoe.

210.

109

Dancing and shuffling toward his patient, this Blackfoot medicine man, clothed in a bearhide robe in Catlin's portrait, clutches a magic spear and a rattle. Dead birds, frogs and snakes adorn his bizarre attire.

Catlin made this composite sketch of six Indian dances in his notebook. The Sauks and Foxes *(top, right)* and the Sioux *(bottom, left)* both held begging dances—at which visitors were asked for a handout.

Dances of the North American Indians
(Chippeways)

237 Dog *(Sioux)* 243 Snow Shoes 293 Beggars Dance *(Sacs & Foxes)*

103 Begging Dance *(Sioux)* 75. Great Spirit *(Minatarees)* 104 Scalp *(Sioux)*

5 | A realm for the taking

Spectacular and inviting, this portrayal of the Wind River range of the Rocky Mountains is a fitting symbol of a new phase of exploration. Beginning in the late 1830s, the West was mapped and analyzed by the Army Corps of Topographical Engineers, whose goal was to promote westward expansion. The best known of all the engineers, John Charles Frémont, scaled the snow-crowned peak in the background. By describing such experiences as glorious adventures, he helped create a new image of the West as an exciting, rewarding and, above all, attainable land.

Albert Bierstadt's painting of the Rockies blends majestic wilderness with pastoral Shoshonis in the foreground.

A scramble for the summit with the Great Pathfinder

By the late 1830s the fur trade was in decline. Beaver was scarce after three decades of trapping, and prices for the few pelts that were taken fell sharply because of a worldwide depression and changes in fashion ("Hell's full of high silk hats," said disgruntled trappers when the demand for beaver hats began to fade). Yet interest in the West did not decline. In fact, the 1840s ushered in a period in which the nation was preoccupied with the trans-Mississippi region as never before. Americans were starting to look at the West in a new way—not just as a region where men could skim off a fortune in peltry if they were willing to risk life and limb every day; and not as an arena of innumerable natural marvels that could sate the appetite of the most ambitious scientist or artist. Now they began to view it as a potential home for the common man, a place where he could carve out a farm, start a business, raise a family.

The drive to occupy and develop the West became a powerful political movement, generally known as expansionism. In time, expansionist ideas gave rise to a loose creed called Manifest Destiny.

At the heart of Manifest Destiny was the notion that the North American continent, from one shining sea to the other, should belong to citizens of the United States. Not only did Americans want and need Western lands but, according to Manifest Destiny, getting those lands was in keeping with the purposes of some higher power—Nature, History or God. National expansion took on something of the nature of a crusade, a holy war that was waged by powerful politicians with the enthusiastic support of much of the electorate.

Thomas Hart Benton, the senior Senator from Missouri and one of the principal exponents of Manifest Destiny, summed it all up in a single high-flown sentence: "In a few years time, the Rocky Mountains will be passed, and the 'children of Adam' will have completed the circumambulation of the globe by marching to the west until they arrive at the Pacific Ocean."

To realize this grandiose vision the expansionists needed some practical instrument to encourage and assist the westward movement. They found their instrument in the United States Army. The period between 1812 and 1840 had been dull and unchallenging for the Army, and its trans-Mississippi activities had been minimal during the mountain-man period. But by 1840 many officers and men were looking to the West as the place where glory, promotions and national reputations might be won. A number of ranking military officers were expansionist by temperament, and the special circumstances of the 1840s made expansionism particularly attractive to the military.

Perhaps the most inspired of all the steps taken toward the fulfillment of the Army's ambitions was the creation of the Corps of Topographical Engineers in 1838. This remarkable organization was ostensibly a group of surveyors and mapmakers at the service of the infantry and cavalry. Actually, the Corps was to become a body of military explorers that would lead both the Army and the people as a whole across the continent to the shores of the Pacific.

Although at full complement it numbered only 36 officers, the Topographical Corps played a disproportionately large role in Western reconnaissance during the 19th Century. Its officers were regarded—and regarded themselves—as the intellectual elite of the military; they were scientists as much as they were engineers. Nearly all of them were men of exceptional vigor and intelligence: to gain an appointment to the Topographical

A stagily posed John Frémont plants a flag atop what he took to be the Rockies' highest peak, in this engraving of an episode from the explorer's first expedition in 1842.

155

Corps, they had to graduate near the top of their West Point class—although a few individuals got into the Corps on the strength of political influence alone.

From the 1840s to the 1860s, the Topographical Corps took on many assignments. Some were strictly military, such as providing tactical maps for field commanders trying to find and fight Indians. Other tasks included making surveys for the transcontinental railroad that would be built after the Civil War, and mapping out postal and wagon-train routes across the West. And even while the men of the Corps published atlases and volumes of geographical lore to help make the West accessible to settlers, they secured territorial gains made at the expense of other nations. One topographic expedition marked out the 49th-parallel boundary between Oregon and Canada. Another, led by the brilliant Major William Emory, established the southwestern border with Mexico—reaping a wealth of scientific knowledge in the process *(pages 174-181)*.

William Emory may have been the most versatile and accomplished of the Topographical Engineers. But the most famous, by all odds, was John Charles Frémont. Between 1842 and 1854 he made five expeditions into the West, a record that earned him the popular nickname of the "Pathfinder." The designation galled many of his contemporaries, for Frémont actually found few new paths himself and sometimes needed help to stay on paths that other men had already established. Yet he became a living symbol for the expansionist-Manifest Destiny movement. For, while Frémont was sometimes a slipshod explorer, he was such a glamorous, persuasive, appealing figure that he aroused the westering impulse of the American people as no other man ever did before or after him. Simply as a promoter, John Charles Frémont was a man of immense influence in the development of the West.

He was born an illegitimate child in Savannah in 1813. His mother, Anne Whiting, was the daughter of a prominent Virginian; at 17 she had married John Pryor, a Richmond businessman, but in 1811, without benefit of divorce, she ran off with a handsome, penniless French refugee named Charles Fremon. Their son took his natural father's name, later adding the terminal "t" and the accent on the "e."

The family wandered through the South, teaching school, giving dancing lessons, keeping boardinghouses.

Their affair had rocked polite Southern society, and the scandal followed wherever they went. In 1818 when Charles Fremon died, his widow settled more or less permanently in Charleston, South Carolina. There, as a precocious 16-year-old, John Charles Frémont entered Charleston College, where he distinguished himself as an outstanding student, although one instructor felt that he lacked the seriousness of a true scholar.

In Charleston, Frémont displayed one trait that was to mark all of his later career. Perhaps because of his wandering boyhood and the taint of illegitimacy, he yearned to associate with men of great means and power. He was, to put it simply, a social climber, and a very adept one. While still in his teens he found his first important patron, Joel Poinsett. Wealthy, a world traveler and a distinguished diplomat and statesman, Poinsett was a leading citizen not only of Charleston but of the American republic as well. Moreover, he was especially interested in exploration and natural history. After serving as the first American minister to Mexico from 1825 to 1829, he returned home with a valuable collection of tropical plants, one of which, the poinsettia, was named for him. He took a great liking to Frémont and in 1836 obtained for him his first surveying assignment, with an Army party working in the southern Appalachians.

Poinsett later became Secretary of War under President Martin Van Buren, and in 1838 helped organize the Army Corps of Topographical Engineers. In this position he worked to secure his Charleston protégé a second lieutenant's commission. Even before the commission was approved, Poinsett saw to it that Frémont was assigned as a civilian to the new Corps's first major Western project, an expedition into the country between the upper Mississippi and Missouri Rivers. The party was commanded by Joseph Nicollet, like Frémont's father a French émigré, and perhaps the most competent and thorough topographer in America at that time. The map that resulted from Nicollet's mission was based on 90,000 instrument readings and 326 astronomical determinations of location.

Frémont later remarked that his two years with Nicollet were his "Yale College and Harvard." Certainly, Nicollet taught him his trade. The French scientist showed Frémont how to take astronomical and barometric readings; the technique of making systematic botanical, mineralogical and meteorological observations; and the art of sketching an accurate field map.

Returning to Washington in 1839 after two seasons in the field, Frémont and Nicollet made their quarters with the Swiss scientist Ferdinand Hassler, then the head of the United States Coast Survey. With Nicollet, Frémont turned to the long tedious work of transcribing and collating the records of the survey. Both Nicollet and Hassler thought highly of the young lieutenant's competence and energy, and came to depend heavily upon him.

But on his own time Frémont sought more lively company than that of these two middle-aged men. Young and good-looking, he possessed fine Southern manners and was already showing great promise in his career. To these winning virtues there was added an aura of Byronic mystery stemming from the family scandal in his background. Inevitably, Frémont cut a considerable swath through Washington's high society. In the course of his social rounds he fell in love with a 15-year-old girl named Jessie Benton, a beauty who had already received two proposals of marriage—and who was the daughter of none other than Thomas Hart Benton, the senior Senator from Missouri.

Jessie Benton was one of the most extraordinary women of the 19th Century. Lovely, intelligent, courageous, she was to contribute importantly to Frémont's triumphs and would stand by him loyally in his disasters. But in terms of Western history the character —and the power—of the father was of even more significance than that of the daughter. As the leading expansionist of the day, Thomas Hart Benton was one of the makers and shakers of the Senate, a shrewd, manipulative politician and a powerful orator. His character was less than pleasant. He had a terrible temper, was stiff-necked and self-righteous and possessed a colossal ego. On one occasion Benton informed the Senate, in dead earnest, that in the remote areas of the republic small boys eagerly awaited news of his political triumphs and that such news inspired American youth to careers in public service.

Benton violently opposed the romance between his daughter and the promising but penniless Frémont. But Jessie was as willful as her father. She and Frémont were secretly married in October 1841, and during the following month they broke the news to her father

—who was, predictably, furious. During the confrontation, Frémont stammered and blushed while Benton, bombastic at the best of times, thundered: "Get out of the house, and never cross my door again! Jessie shall stay here!" At this point Jessie intervened with a speech that would have done credit to any 19th Century melodrama. Grasping her husband's arm and gazing into his eyes, she spoke the Biblical words of Ruth: "Whither thou goest, I will go; and where thou lodgest, I will lodge." The Senator was silenced, and soon afterward Frémont came to live with his in-laws.

Thomas Hart Benton was above all else a politician, a practitioner of the art of the possible. With the marriage a *fait accompli,* he cooled down, accepted his son-in-law and almost immediately set out to make use of him. In spite of Frémont's poverty and family history, he had the makings of an excellent political asset. The younger man already had some reputation as a Western topographer and could be an ideal instrument to advance the expansionist policies of his father-in-law. Not long after Jessie and John Frémont eloped, Senator Benton and some of his like-minded colleagues pushed through Congress an appropriation of some $30,000 to be used for a survey of the Oregon Trail. Nicollet was supposed to lead the topographic party, but the Frenchman had been exhausted by his work in the Missouri country and his health took a serious turn for the worse that fall. By some hard political bargaining, Senator Benton succeeded in having his new son-in-law named to head the Oregon survey.

Frémont's instructions were specific. He was to proceed from Fort Leavenworth on the Missouri River, to the central Rockies, making cartographic and other observations as he went. In the Rockies he was to pay particular attention to the topography of the South Pass, already recognized as the gateway to Oregon. Then he was to return and draw up a full report.

It seemed to be a routine topographic assignment. Americans had been traveling back and forth between St. Louis and the central Rockies for 35 years; the need now was not to explore the country, but simply to describe it accurately and exhaustively. However, Frémont also had a second, unofficial mission—a mission that Senator Benton and his political faction considered at least as important as the technical job of mapmaking. Not only was Frémont to prepare maps and describe

The prophet of Manifest Destiny

The nation's leading advocate of expansionism and a formidable rhetorician on the subject was Senator Thomas Hart Benton of Missouri. But he had a good deal of help in his cause. The man who coined the phrase that became the movement's slogan was a New York City journalist named John L. O'Sullivan. In July 1845, in an editorial calling for the annexation of Texas by the United States, O'Sullivan referred to the American people's "manifest destiny to overspread the continent allotted by Providence for the free development of our yearly multiplying millions." His message fell on ready ears. Expansionist sentiment was already widespread in the country and its partisans needed just such a sonorous battle cry as "manifest destiny."

Reasons for expansionism's wide appeal abounded, one of them being a population boom, caused mainly by a sudden swell in immigration. Nevertheless, a selling campaign for expansionism was needed, for a number of Senator Benton's Congressional colleagues failed to see the wisdom of the movement. Some legislators objected that the government would overreach itself in trying to maintain control over remote areas. Others pointed out the difficulty of assimilating peoples of an alien Spanish culture if the Southwest were acquired. And there was also the risk of aggravating the already divisive question of slavery: abolitionists argued that expansion into the Southwest would extend slavery, while Southerners, wary of being ringed by free states, strongly opposed the idea of bringing

Thomas Hart Benton in the late 1840s

Western territories into the Union.

To allay these fears the expansionists sought to present their cause as a divinely ordained mission. Just as the Puritans in 1630 were destined to establish a model republic in the wilderness, so now other Americans must carry the benefits of that republic—democratic government, economic progress and individual freedom—to every corner of the continent.

Expansion, they asserted, did not require aggressive action by the U.S. government. Texas furnished the best example of how the process would work. From the 1820s on, Americans had pushed into that Mexican province until, by 1836, they formed a majority. At that point, yearning for the sort of rule they had known in the East, they revolted against the Mexican government, won their independence and began clamoring for ad-

mission into the United States. Nine years later they were invited in, thus adding 267,000 square miles of territory to the nation.

When some foreign observers suggested that the acquisition of Texas had been achieved by a covert sort of aggression, the exponents of Manifest Destiny lapsed into high-flown philosophizing about the proper use of land. The Mexicans, it was alleged, lacked the industrious energies of American frontiersmen. The implication of this notion was clear. Said the *New York Morning News* in an editorial: "Public sentiment with us repudiates possession without use, and this sentiment is gradually acquiring the force of established public law."

In addition to spreading the virtues of democracy and American dynamism, the crusade of Manifest Destiny held out the promise of a larger share of world trade for the United States. As far back as 1819 Thomas Hart Benton—then a 37-year-old St. Louis newspaperman—had urged the establishment of an overland trade route to the Pacific Coast, whence goods could be shipped to Asia. This overland trail, he wrote, would cut 20,000 miles off the sea route around Cape Horn. But Benton also viewed westward expansion as a means for bringing about profound social change. After he was elected to the Senate in 1820, he urged poor farmers and workmen in the East to start a new life as freeholders in the West. After they had successfully settled in the backlands and on the far fringes of the continent, Benton argued, these yeomen could develop a confident new culture, free from what he regarded as America's hangdog dependence on European customs.

Despite his penchant for bombastic oratory, Benton often took moderate stands. One such occasion was the 1845-1846 Congressional debates over how much of the disputed Oregon territory the U.S. should claim. When some zealous expansionists insisted that the land up to Alaska's southern boundary belonged to the United States and that we should fight for it, Benton backed the compromise that finally was agreed upon —giving Britain control north of the 49th parallel. Benton also would have preferred a compromise solution to the U.S.-Mexico quarrel over the Southwest, but the hawks had their way this time and full-scale war broke out.

At the end of the Mexican War, with the acquisition of California and its natural boundary of the Pacific Ocean, the fervor of the expansionist movement waned. Like many a man who has outlived his cause, Benton's political career went into eclipse. In 1850 he lost his Senate seat to a proslavery candidate. In 1856, a lonely widower suffering from cancer, he ran for governor of Missouri. He was resoundingly defeated, but after his death a year and a half later, the city of St. Louis erected a bronze statue of him —looking toward the West.

An 1872 painting depicts a buxom spirit of Manifest Destiny, stringing telegraph wire as she goes, moving west with the settlers.

the land, he was also supposed to make Western travel and the West itself appear as attractive as possible to Americans living east of the Mississippi.

The expansionists who stood for Manifest Destiny knew that their semimystical program could prevail only when Americans settled permanently in the Far West, even in those regions that were claimed or clearly possessed by other nations. At the time, Oregon was jointly held by the United States and Britain, and California and the Southwest were owned outright by Mexico. The mountain men had represented an important first step toward American settlement of the West, but a handful of nomadic trappers, themselves often regarded as white savages, was not enough. There had to be farmers, ranchers, miners, storekeepers, preachers, towns — in short, a sizable American community, preferably with strong ties to the East. No matter what political party was in power, a community of this kind would force the government to spend money on such Western public works as roads and forts, and to protect American interests there by diplomacy or conquest. This was, at least, how Benton and the other Manifest Destiny men reasoned.

Frémont himself was an expansionist. As a member of the Benton household he undoubtedly had Manifest Destiny politics for breakfast, dinner and supper. Hence, he welcomed his assignment to map and promote the world beyond the Mississippi. And he achieved both of these objectives, though with varying success. His topographical survey was adequate, his promotion of the West positively brilliant.

The Frémont party set off across the plains in mid-June and returned in mid-October. Altogether, that may well have been the best summer of John Frémont's life. He was 29 years old, and in command of his first expedition. The weather was beautiful, danger and hardship were negligible, and there were no difficult decisions to make. In his own exhilarated words, he was caught up in "the true Greek joy in existence — in the gladness of living."

Traveling with Frémont as he crossed the Western plains for the first time were two men who were to contribute conspicuously to his expeditions. The first was Kit Carson, whom Frémont had met on a Missouri River steamboat and hired as a guide. Carson was only 33 that year, but he was a bona fide mountain man,

having become a beaver trapper in his teens. Quiet, competent and level-headed, he had been befriended and instructed by some of the most famous of the older mountaineers — the Sublettes, Jim Bridger, Tom Fitzpatrick and Joe Walker. By the time Frémont met him, Kit Carson knew his business well. He had fought his Indians, endured his winters and wandered through the West from Mexico to the Pacific Northwest, and his application for the job of guide reflected a lusty frontiersman's confidence: "I told Colonel Frémont," he later recalled, "that I had been some time in the mountains and thought I could guide him to any point he would wish to go."

The two men took an immediate liking to each other and the friendship was to last throughout their lives. From the first, Frémont not only valued Carson as a guide but also found him a thoroughly romantic figure — and a figure who could be used. He was to publicize Carson furiously as a kind of Hawkeye of the West. For his part, Carson seems to have been impressed by Frémont's Eastern sophistication and his good connections. Moreover, while Carson was as skillful a frontiersman as anyone, he was not a natural leader of men. Throughout his career, he served more aggressive individuals as a steady second-in-command, an able technical consultant. Perhaps only such an unambitious man could have gotten on as well and for as long as Carson did with the fiercely ambitious Frémont.

The second of Frémont's valuable assistants was Charles Preuss, a tall, blond, red-faced German topographer whom Frémont hired in Washington on the recommendation of Ferdinand Hassler. Preuss was a first-rate technician. Although during the 1842 expedition Frémont made many topographic observations himself, Preuss spared him a great deal of the routine drudgery. In his subsequent expeditions Frémont concerned himself less and less with topographic science, leaving that area increasingly to the hard-working and meticulous German. In his reports and memoirs Frémont gave full credit to Charles Preuss for his contributions, praised him as a loyal subordinate and described him as a devoted friend.

Preuss's opinion of his boss was different. During his travels with Frémont, the German topographer kept a private journal in the form of a continuing letter to his wife, Gertrud. And while Frémont may have thought of Preuss as a kind of admiring, scientific Man Friday, this journal shows that Preuss was actually a gloomy, embittered man, constantly exasperated by what he considered Frémont's posturing and by his romantic and unscientific attitudes. Even in a very early note, the third entry of his first diary, dated June 6, 1842, Preuss wrote, "Annoyed by that childish Frémont."

With Carson guiding the way over the well-traveled prairie, Preuss attending to many of the scientific details and Frémont reveling in the glory of command, the party reached central Colorado in mid-July. They then ascended the Sweetwater Valley and came eventually to the South Pass. Though Carson had previously described it to him, Frémont was disappointed in the wide, gently sloping pass, which is in fact a sandy saddle, only about 7,550 feet high and capable of accommodating a number of wagon trains. Perhaps already composing his public report in his mind, Frémont seems to have expected something much more dramatic — something perhaps along the lines of a tortuous gorge. He was so unimpressed by what he found that, when he arrived at the summit of the pass, he did not even bother to take observations of its latitude and longitude.

A few days later, having entered the Wind River range, Frémont decided to climb what he arbitrarily decided was the highest peak in the Rockies. The peak he selected, which now bears his name, is 13,785 feet high — lower than Gannett Peak, only five miles away, and lower in fact than some 55 other mountains in nearby Colorado, each exceeding 14,000 feet. But Frémont was convinced that he had picked the loftiest of all, and on August 13 the climbers set out.

The climb was to have a dramatic impact on Frémont's career and upon the public imagination; but the ascent itself, as recalled by dour Charles Preuss, was more comic than heroic. "The leader, Carson," Preuss wrote, "walked too fast. This caused some exchange of words. Frémont got excited, as usual, and designated a young chap to take the lead — he could not serve as a guide, of course. Frémont developed a headache, and as a result we stopped soon afterwards, about eleven o'clock. He decided to climb the peak the next morning, with renewed strength and cooler blood."

At dawn on the 14th the party once again attempted to reach the summit. "The hike was disagreeable all around," commented Preuss. "No supper, no breakfast, little or no sleep — who can enjoy climbing a mountain under these circumstances? Moreover, all the men, with perhaps two exceptions, would have much preferred to stay in camp. What possible interest do these fellows have in such an undertaking?"

The party soon began to straggle, and Preuss found himself alone in soft snow 1,000 feet below the summit. Finally a man came along saying that Frémont was again feeling peckish and had retired to camp. Preuss could not find the path to the top, so he made his readings in the snow field and returned to camp. Later he wrote, "I could not keep from remarking that in such an undertaking some preparations for sleeping, eating, and drinking would not be altogether amiss and might indeed be conducive to better success.

"But what about the mountain? I did not wish to suggest anything. It finally looked as if Frémont would be satisfied with the altitude I had established and would add five or six hundred feet in order to fix the assumed highest point.

"Before we lay down to sleep, he arranged with Kit that the latter should return with some of the people to

"The Great American Desert"

Stephen H. Long

Twenty years before Frémont produced his effusive descriptions of the West, another Army explorer, Major Stephen H. Long, published a different sort of conclusion about the Great Plains: "In regard to this extensive section of the country, I do not hesitate in giving the opinion, that it is almost wholly unfit for cultivation, and of course, uninhabitable by a people depending upon agriculture for their subsistence."

Long was attempting to find the headwaters of the Arkansas, Platte and Red Rivers. His expedition was characterized by a series of misjudgments and minor disasters. He got confused about the rivers: he never found the source of the Arkansas and mistook the Canadian for the Red River. He lost most of his scientific records when three deserters ran off with them. And he succeeded in branding the Plains with a discouraging and largely misleading name. On the official map of his expedition thousands of square miles were labeled "Great Desert."

This view was echoed by virtually every traveler on the Plains for the next generation, with the notable exception of Frémont. In *Astoria,* an account of the Western fur trade written in 1836, Washington Irving described the vast region between the Mississippi and the Rocky Mountains as: "undulating and treeless plains, and desolate sandy wastes, wearisome to the eye from their extent and monotony."

Major Long felt the arid Plains were a blessing in disguise, explaining that they would "serve as a barrier to prevent too great an extension of our population westward." Such an idea was anathema to the expansion-minded Frémont. He minimized the region's shortcomings and instead emphasized the presence of rich, arable soil, sparkling streams and lush grasses. "Everywhere," he exulted, "the rose is met with and reminds us of cultivated gardens and civilization."

the mules and that we should follow with five animals that had been brought up and eat breakfast there. I did not learn anything about this arrangement. When we awoke early in the morning, Kit and several others had already left. 'Well Mr. Preuss,' said Frémont, 'I hope we shall, after all, empty a glass on top of the mountain.' We had taken along some brandy expressly for this purpose as well as an American flag."

Finally, on the morning of the 15th, Frémont and his five companions waded through the soft snow and scaled the peak. "The highest rock was so small that only one after the other could stand on it," reported Preuss. "Pistols were fired, the flag unfurled and we shouted 'Hurrah' several times."

The only other eyewitness account of the climb, published by Frémont, varies considerably in both tone and detail from that of Preuss. Frémont described a perilous ascent through the ice and snow and told how he himself worked his way across a vertical precipice, clinging to crevices. Then, "I sprang upon the summit and another step would have precipitated me into an immense snow field five hundred feet below. To the edge of this field was a sheer icy precipice; and then, with a gradual fall, the field sloped off for about a mile until it struck the foot of another lower ridge."

Frémont and his men enjoyed the view for a few minutes, then walked down the mountain and started back east. On the return trip the only true crisis of the expedition occurred. At the Platte River, which was then in flood, Frémont divided the party. He had decided to send the larger group overland, while he, Preuss and five others shot the rapids, using a collapsible rubber boat that had been carried all the way from the East in anticipation of an opportunity to survey this very river. Shortly after launching, the boat entered a narrow canyon filled with foaming waves. It capsized, and many scientific records were lost or soaked.

In comparison with the great calamities of Western exploration it was a minor incident (though it might have been a more tragic one if Frémont's luck had not been very good). However, it was a portent of things to come. There was little reason to shoot those rapids other than Frémont's compulsion to enhance his image as a bold adventurer. And though things turned out relatively well on the Platte, on later occasions the same flaw of character was to have far more serious consequences for Frémont and for those who followed him.

On this occasion, having added a good white-water adventure story to go with his mountain-climbing tales, Frémont continued east without further incident. He arrived in Washington late in October, only a few days before Jessie presented him with their first child, a daughter. Scarcely was Jessie out of her childbed when she and her husband began to work feverishly on his report, with Jessie doing much of the writing while Frémont dictated. Their division of labor was explained by Jessie in this way: "The horseback life, the sleep in the open air, had unfitted Mr. Frémont for the indoor work of writing—and second lieutenants cannot indulge in secretaries. After a series of hemorrhages from the nose and head had convinced him that he must give up trying to write his report, I was let to try and thus slid into my most happy life-work."

Finished late that winter, the 207-page report thus assembled by the husband-wife team had all the ingredients of a promotional masterpiece. In addition to descriptions of scenery, Indians and wild animals, it offered directions on where to find campsites, grass, food and water; it also mentioned the supplies an emigrant would need and the places where he might find them. This factual information was served up in a sauce of rich, evocative prose. The dramatic climax of the book turned out to be the account of the ascent of Fremont Peak. After describing his own heroics, Frémont reared back and dictated a truly inspired paragraph:

"Here, on the summit, where the stillness was absolute, unbroken by any sound, and thus the solitude complete, we thought ourselves beyond the region of animated life; but while we were sitting on the rock, a solitary bee *(bromus, the bumble bee)* came winging his flight from the eastern valley, and lit on the knee of one of the men. It was a strange place, the icy rock and the highest peak of the Rocky Mountains, for a lover of warm sunshine and flowers; and we pleased ourselves with the idea that he was the first of his species to cross the mountain barrier, a solitary pioneer to foretell the advance of civilization."

The Frémont report was presented to Congress in March of 1843 and so dazzled the legislators that they ordered the printing and distribution of 10,000 copies. It was an immediate sensation among the press and public, spreading the notion into the far corners of the republic that going west was both an exciting and an easy thing to do and that the West was a pleasant and profitable place in which to settle. Perhaps the best sense of the impact of Frémont's book has been provided by the poet Joaquin Miller, who was later to become no mean Western promoter himself.

Miller was first exposed to Frémont's report when his father read it aloud to him at their Indiana farm, stirring in the poet-to-be an exhilarating vision of Frémont's men scaling "the savage battlements of the Rocky Mountains, flags in the air, Frémont at the head, waving his sword, his horse neighing wildly in the mountain wind, with unknown and unnamed empires on every hand. It touched my heart when he told me how a weary little brown bee tried to make its way from a valley of flowers far below across a spur of snow, where he sat resting for a moment with his men; how the bee rested on his knee till it was strong enough to go on to another field of flowers beyond the snow; and how he waited a bit for it to go at its will. I was no longer a boy. Now I began to be inflamed with a love for action, adventure, glory, and great deeds away out yonder under the path of the setting sun."

E ven while taking bows for his first expedition Frémont was planning a second journey for the Corps of Topographical Engineers, this one also under Benton's sponsorship. It was to be an extension of his first trip. Once again he was to proceed to the South Pass, but this time he would continue on to the Oregon Territory. There he was supposed to complete the work of an earlier military explorer, Naval Lieutenant Charles Wilkes who, during 1841 and 1842, had made a study of the Northwest Coast harbors and part of the interior. Wilkes had set a formidable precedent. His data on the natural resources and the Indians of the region filled 16 volumes. But, lacking the political clout of Frémont, he won no honors commensurate with his accomplishments. Frémont would do better.

By May of 1844 Frémont was in St. Louis, gathering equipment for the journey. One article he selected was quite extraordinary—a carriage-mounted brass howitzer that fired 12-pound cannonballs. When Frémont's superiors in Washington got word that the supposedly peaceful scientific party would take a cannon along, they were appalled, fearing that the reckless Frémont

At the base of the Sierra, Frémont's half-starved party made a welcome stop at trout-filled Pyramid Lake. To the left of the tipi in which they kept their gear is a howitzer that Frémont insisted on bringing along.

might well create an international incident, if not outright war with Mexico or Britain. The chief of the Topographical Corps immediately composed a letter instructing Frémont to abandon the gun or return to Washington to explain exactly why he needed it.

The letter was delivered to Jessie Frémont, who was supposed to forward it. This missive and Jessie's response to it became part of the making of the Frémont myth. As it happened, the letter from Washington arrived too late for Jessie to send it on in time; it remained in her hands and Frémont set off for the West without ever knowing of it. But in memoirs written years after the event, both Jessie and her husband gave a very different account of their actions. According to them, Jessie opened the letter, read the ominous orders within, and, instead of forwarding it to her husband, sent another letter to him by special messenger, urging him to head West immediately. "Only trust me and GO," she wrote—or said she wrote. Ever trustful of his wife's instincts, Frémont set off at dawn the next morning and was soon beyond the reach of his superiors. And thus the Frémonts' little story ends—a complete fiction as it happens, but a wonderfully effective one, suggesting their devotion to higher causes.

Later, Frémont argued that he brought the artillery piece along to frighten potentially hostile Indians. It is also likely that he simply enjoyed the image of himself leading his horsemen across the continent with a cannon trundling in his wake—and he knew that it would make good copy. For whatever reason, he took the howitzer across some 3,000 miles of prairie, desert and mountain, much to the disgust of the men who had to do the dragging. Charles Preuss probably expressed the common opinion in the ranks when, in his journal, he exclaimed, "If we had only left that ridiculous thing at home." Preuss also revealed that Frémont used the cannon to get meat, lobbing shots into buffalo herds with murderous effect. Frémont himself never mentioned this rather ignoble function of his cherished howitzer.

Since Kit Carson would not join the party until it reached Colorado, Frémont hired another guide in St. Louis, the veteran mountain man Broken Hand Fitzpatrick, a former Rocky Mountain Fur Company partner. It must have been easy work for Fitzpatrick,

since the Frémont party generally followed the beaten wagon road westward. For a time they traveled alongside one of the emigrant trains on the trail that summer, a group of some 50 men, women and children who, at Fort Bridger, hired as a guide none other than Joe Walker. Walker led the emigrants' wagons southwestward toward Walker Pass, which he had discovered back in 1834. The emigrants crossed the Sierra in December and Joe Walker thus added another achievement to a record already chock-full of achievement: he became the first man to bring wagons successfully across the continent into California.

Meanwhile, Frémont continued on toward Oregon. On September 6 the party caught sight of the Great Salt Lake, "stretching in still and solitary grandeur," Frémont wrote, "far beyond the limits of our vision." Apparently assuming that the region was unexplored — although mountain men knew it well — Frémont added: "I am doubtful if the followers of Balboa felt more enthusiasm when from the heights of the Andes, they saw for the first time the great Western Ocean." Looking at the system of rivers and creeks that drain into the lake, he pronounced the area a "bucolic region."

From there, the party followed the Snake and Columbia Rivers to Oregon and on November 8 finally arrived at Fort Vancouver, across the Columbia River from the present site of Portland, Oregon. At this point Frémont's orders from the Topographical Corps called for him to turn around and take his party back east over the Oregon Trail. Instead, he led his men toward California. The decision violated his orders. As it turned out, he would make further decisions that would lead him to cross the Sierra in the dead of winter and invade Mexican territory with a military detachment.

Since there were so many good reasons for not taking this route, why did Frémont do it? It is likely that he set off across the mountains for much the same reason that he had climbed Fremont Peak, run the rapids on the Platte River and hauled a cannon to Oregon. It seemed to him a dashing, romantic thing to do. It suited his image of himself, and it would enhance his public stature when he told the story in the East.

Leaving the Columbia in late November the party turned south, came to the Sierra and followed the range

165

more or less along the present border between Nevada and California. It was a dreadful trip, marked by the predictable cold, hunger and eating of horses. These difficulties of the Pathfinder and his men were compounded by the fact that they were often lost. "We are having a day of rest today," wrote Preuss on January 26, ruefully adding: "We still do not know where we really are." (They were probably somewhere near the present site of Bridgeport, California.)

Eleven days later Preuss described the situation of the floundering group in some detail: "For two days now we have been camping on the slope of the mountain crest. Snow prevents us from moving on. The horses are down below to scratch up a little grass. Today the 'field marshal' marched out with a party on snowshoes to open a way to the summit, about ten miles distant, it appears. Tomorrow we shall probably know whether it is possible to get through. The men had to work terribly hard to drag the baggage up the steep mountain; the beasts are too weak for it. Two of them rolled down the snow about two hundred feet. No longer any salt in camp. This is awful." It was so awful, in fact, that Frémont was forced to abandon his beloved cannon in a deep snowdrift. "We left it," he wrote, in one of the many moving passages of his report on the expedition, "to the great sorrow of the whole party, who were grieved to part with a companion which had made the whole distance from St. Louis."

Eventually, the party got out of the mountains, owing mainly to the common sense of Carson and Fitzpatrick — and to good luck with the weather. An average blizzard would probably have killed many of Frémont's weakened men, but the winter of 1844 was mild for the Sierra. On March 6 the expedition reached Sutter's Fort, the settlement established on the Sacramento River in 1839 by the pioneer John Sutter. They rested there for three weeks, bought supplies, horses and mules, then went south down the San Joaquin Valley. At the Mojave River they turned east, more or less backtracking Jed Smith's old trail to California (page 90).

Like Smith before them, they had Indian trouble — one man was bushwhacked by the Diggers, and the entire party was harassed by the Utes — but they were extricated from their difficulties by the ubiquitous Joe Walker, who turned up unexpectedly at Mountain Meadows in Utah. Wrote Frémont of the meeting:

"We had the gratification to be joined by the famous hunter and trapper, Mr. Joseph Walker, who now became our guide. He had left California with the great caravan and perceiving, from the signs along the trail, that there was a party of whites ahead, which he judged to be mine, he detached himself from the caravan, with eight men (Americans) and ran the gauntlet of desert robbers, killing two, and succeeded in overtaking us. Nothing but his great knowledge of the country, great courage and presence of mind and good rifles, could have brought him safe from such a perilous enterprise." Joe Walker guided the expedition across the Rockies to Bent's Fort in southeastern Colorado. Both Walker and Kit Carson remained there, believing — correctly on this occasion — that Frémont was capable of finding his way home across the prairie.

In August, when Frémont returned to Washington, he and Jessie once again set to work at their writing. The second installment of his adventures was even more detailed than the first, but it also included several errors of fact. Frémont reported, for example, that the freshwater Utah Lake and the Great Salt Lake were one and the same body of water, an absurdity that almost any mountain man — or, for that matter, any logician — could have corrected. Furthermore, Frémont touted north-central Utah as a garden spot, fertile and well watered. This judgment contributed to the subsequent migration of the Mormons to the area and was largely responsible for the low opinion that Brigham Young, struggling with sagebrush and drought, formed of Frémont's veracity and intelligence. Years later, Young was to provoke a national controversy by describing Frémont's "bucolic" spot near Great Salt Lake as a desert, and by ridiculing Frémont's assertion that, as Young paraphrased it, "the south end of the lake was fresh and the north salt."

Despite such flaws, the second report provided a comprehensive account of a vast area of the West, including the Oregon Trail and parts of California and the Great Basin; another 10,000 copies were snapped up by a public eager for good news from the West. With an immense popular reputation as a Western expert, Frémont set out on a third expedition in the summer of 1845. This time he planned to reconnoiter the forbidding Great Basin country and the dangerous passes through the Sierra to California. He met Joe Walker

in Missouri and picked up Kit Carson at Bent's Fort.

From there the group traveled up the Arkansas River, across the Continental Divide, over the plateaus of western Colorado and eastern Utah and down into the Great Basin. After pausing to survey the shores of the Great Salt Lake and collect specimens of flora and fauna, the party of 60 men struck off across the desert toward the Sierra. Frémont was at pains to see the bleak region in the best possible light. He later recounted how the slopes of one mountain that rose above the arid plain "made a good camping ground, for the November nights were cool and newly-fallen snow already marked out the higher ridges of the mountains. With grass abundant, and pine wood and cedars to keep up the night fires, we were well provided for."

The cozy spot also provided a fillip of mystery and adventure calculated to delight Frémont's Eastern read-

ers. "We had made our supper on antelope and were lying around the fire, and the men taking their great comfort in smoking. A good supper and a pipe make for them a comfortable ending no matter how hard the day has been. Carson, who was lying on his back with his pipe in his mouth, suddenly exclaimed, 'Good God! look there!' In the blaze of the fire, peering over her skinny, crooked hands, which shaded her eyes from the glare, was standing an old woman, apparently eighty years of age, nearly naked, her grizzly hair hanging down over her face and shoulders. She had thought it a camp of her people and had already begun to talk and gesticulate, when her open mouth was paralyzed with fright, as she saw the faces of the whites. She turned to escape, but the men brought her around to the fire."

Apparently the aged Indian woman had been abandoned by her people because she had outlived her

167

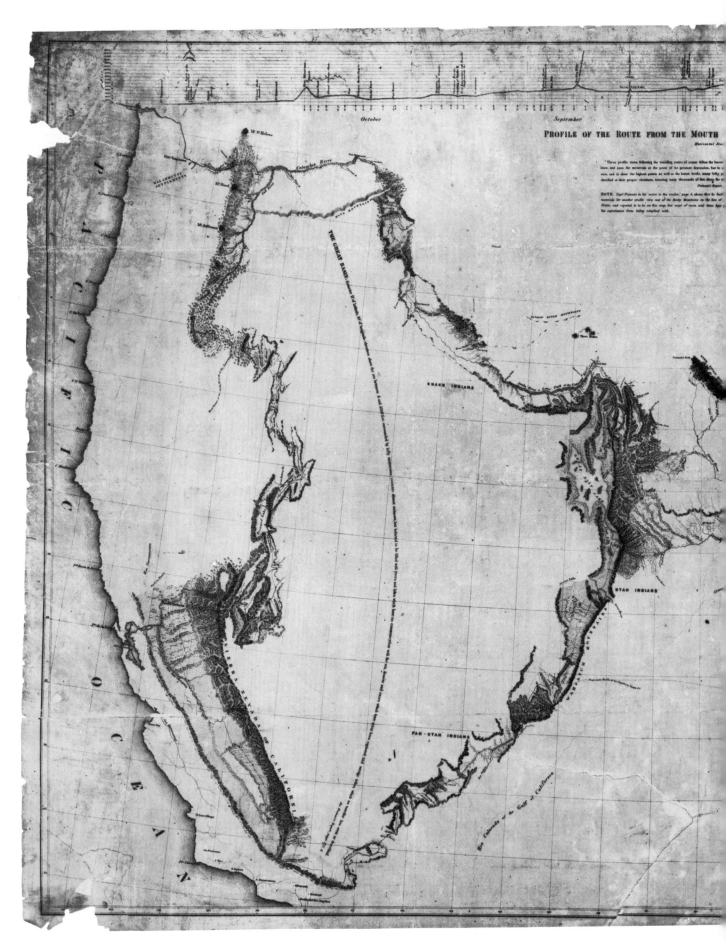

PROFILE OF THE ROUTE FROM THE MOUTH

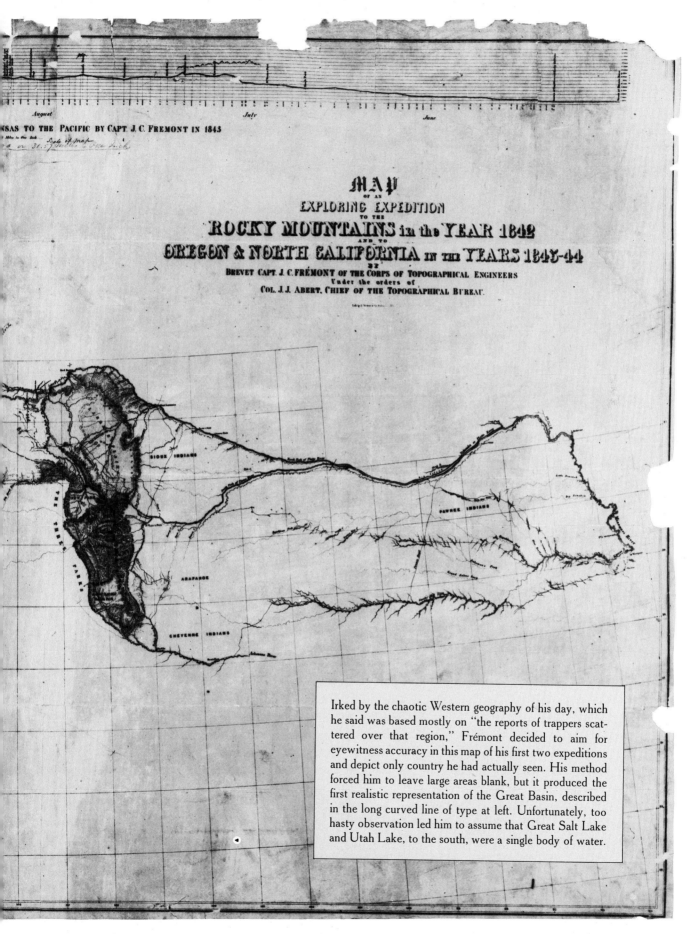

NSAS TO THE PACIFIC BY CAPT. J. C. FREMONT IN 1843

MAP
OF AN
EXPLORING EXPEDITION
TO THE
ROCKY MOUNTAINS in the YEAR 1842
AND TO
OREGON & NORTH CALIFORNIA IN THE YEARS 1843-44
BY
BREVET CAPT. J. C. FRÉMONT OF THE CORPS OF TOPOGRAPHICAL ENGINEERS
Under the orders of
Col. J. J. ABERT, CHIEF OF THE TOPOGRAPHICAL BUREAU.

Irked by the chaotic Western geography of his day, which he said was based mostly on "the reports of trappers scattered over that region," Frémont decided to aim for eyewitness accuracy in this map of his first two expeditions and depict only country he had actually seen. His method forced him to leave large areas blank, but it produced the first realistic representation of the Great Basin, described in the long curved line of type at left. Unfortunately, too hasty observation led him to assume that Great Salt Lake and Utah Lake, to the south, were a single body of water.

In a macabre illustration from Frémont's *Memoirs,* his third expedition, camped in the Great Basin, is startled by the appearance of an old, starving Indian woman. Given meat, she vanished into the night.

usefulness. Frémont gave her a supply of food and expressed the hope that she would survive through the approaching winter, observing, in his usual optimistic fashion, that "nut-pines and cedars extend their branches out to the ground and in one of their thickets, as I have often proved, these make a comfortable shelter against the most violent snow-storms."

The next day the men resumed their journey. At the eastern foot of the Sierra the party divided. Walker led most of the men and stock southward to Walker Pass and into the San Joaquin Valley, a trip that was becoming something of a milk run for him. Frémont, seeking adventure as always, proceeded with Carson and 14 others directly into the mountains. He probably crossed them at what was later to be known as Donner Pass. The passage was made just before the first heavy snows of winter. Only a year later the Donner party, a

group of 80 emigrants, took the same route but were caught by blizzards; half of the men, women and children in the party died and some of the survivors resorted to cannibalism before they were rescued.

Frémont and Walker rejoined forces in February on the ranch of an American settler near San Jose. By now Frémont's relations with the Mexicans were strained. Throughout the United States men like Thomas Benton had been trumpeting the policy of Manifest Destiny, which advocated the taking of California and other Southwestern possessions. In Texas, Mexican officials had had a recent and painful demonstration of how the policy worked. First had come settlers. When there were enough of them they had rebelled against Mexico, taken Texas, and finally joined it to the United States. California, which already harbored a number of Americans, seemed to be another Texas in the making. Naturally enough, the Mexican officials doubted Frémont's story that he was nothing but a harmless surveyor. When Frémont and Walker joined forces, putting some 60 well-armed men under the command of an American Army officer, the Mexicans decided the situation was intolerable and ordered Frémont and his party out of the province.

Frémont reacted belligerently at first. He withdrew his men to Hawk's Peak in the Gabilan Mountains, fortified the summit and unfurled the American flag. From this strongpoint he strafed the Mexicans with rhetoric, daring them to dislodge him. The Mexicans began gathering their forces to take up his challenge. After maintaining his defiant pose for three days, Frémont slipped off Hawk's Peak one night and headed northward, eventually reaching Oregon.

He left California without Joe Walker. Like many of the mountain men, Walker was an expansionist. He was convinced that America must acquire California, and he apparently thought that Hawk's Peak was a fine place to begin the conquest. Furthermore, Walker was incensed by the idea of fleeing from the Mexicans, whose martial prowess he held in low esteem. In a rage, he severed his connection with Frémont. Later on he was to express a blunt opinion of the Pathfinder: "Frémont morally and physically was the most complete coward I ever knew, and if it were not casting an unmerited reproach on the sex I would say that he was more timid than a woman. An explorer! I knew more of the unexplored region 15 years before he set foot on it than he does today."

Leaving California in late April, Frémont cooled his heels in Oregon for a month. Unbeknownst to him, the very day he left California, relations between the United States and Mexico had reached the snapping point. President Polk, an ardent expansionist, had attempted to purchase New Mexico and California, and he was willing to pay as much as $40 million. But just to create the right sort of negotiating attitude on the Mexicans' part, he sent an army under General Zachary Taylor to the Rio Grande—which was in disputed territory. The Mexicans demanded that Taylor withdraw, and when he refused and attempted to blockade the river, they attacked his troops. Polk immediately called upon Congress to declare war, announcing that blood had been spilled "upon American soil." Congress speed-

ily voted its support for the declaration. Now Manifest Destiny would show its teeth.

John Frémont's role in the subsequent conquest of California is still shrouded in mystery and speculation. What is known is that, in Oregon, Frémont received a message from a Marine lieutenant, Archibald Gillespie. Gillespie had been sent from Washington the previous fall with secret instructions for the American consul in Monterey. Whether he had the authority to give orders to Frémont—and indeed, whether he actually gave them—remains a matter of debate. It is a fact, though, that after receiving Gillespie's messenger, Frémont turned back to California with his 60 armed men in what must have seemed to the Mexicans an outright invasion —even though Frémont himself was still unaware that war had been declared.

Soon after Frémont entered California, the so-called Bear Flag revolt, an uprising of American settlers, began in the northern part of the territory. He did not at first take an active part in the insurrection, but he tacitly encouraged it and held his forces as a kind of reserve for the settlers. Enemies and critics of Frémont were later to claim that he bided his time in hopes of taking over the rebellion and becoming the founding father of a new nation, like Sam Houston in the Republic of Texas. Within a few weeks, Frémont did, in fact, assume a position of leadership in the insurrection by organizing both his own men and the Bear Flag rebels into a motley organization known as the California Battalion. The Battalion found little opportunity to do any real fighting (the Mexican forces in California were weak and small, and knew it), but managed to put the northern part of the territory under an American flag.

After Frémont learned that war between the United States and Mexico had broken out, he sent the California Battalion southward. They arrived in the vicinity of Los Angeles just after the area had fallen to the official American invasion force, the Army of the West, commanded by General Stephen Kearny, who had marched overland from Fort Leavenworth. General Kearny's conquest of southern California had been achieved with the aid of forces led by a Naval officer of equal rank, Commodore Robert Stockton. When Mexican resistance ceased, Stockton appointed Frémont the civil governor of California. Whether Stockton had the right to make the appointment is a matter of conjecture. In any case, Kearny did not take either Stockton or Frémont seriously.

General Kearny was a hot-tempered frontier veteran. He saw Frémont as a flighty, lightweight junior officer who was attempting a brazen power grab. Acting quickly to put the upstart in his place, the general issued orders for the disbanding of the California Battalion. Frémont hesitated for a few days, then finally refused to comply. This was just the sort of open defiance that Kearny had hoped to provoke. Frémont was placed under arrest and sent back to Washington for a court-martial on charges of mutiny, insubordination and conduct prejudicial to good order and discipline.

At last the Pathfinder had overreached himself. In the course of the court-martial proceedings, he accused Kearny of perjury and declared that "my acts in California have all been with high motives and a desire for the public service." His defense did not avail. He was found guilty on all charges and faced a dishonorable discharge. President Polk, after studying the record and consulting with his Cabinet, offered to let Frémont remain in the Army, but Frémont wanted no compromise. He submitted his resignation, and it was accepted.

The ins and outs of the court-martial and its decision were hotly debated throughout the nation. Frémont's California activities were irregular, to say the least; but the whole conquest of California was irregular in many respects. Actually, Frémont may have been treated with exceptional harshness for reasons that had little to do with his actions in California. For one thing, Kearny apparently had a strong personal dislike for Frémont. For another, Frémont was caught in the middle of a fierce Army-Navy conflict.

The California affair left some permanent tarnish on Frémont's image as a brave and selfless hero, but it did not end his career by any means. He was to remain a major national figure for many years to come. And, although he never again traveled for the Topographical Corps, he did conduct two more "explorations."

In 1848, an opportunity arose for Frémont to go west again on a mission calculated to restore his prestige. The idea of building a transcontinental railroad was in the air, and the route of the road had become an issue of bitter contention. Prominent in one combine of railroad promoters was Thomas Hart Benton, who backed a route that would run westward from St. Lou-

is, more or less along the 38th parallel. To forward his father-in-law's plans Frémont agreed to lead a private midwinter expedition across the Rockies, reasoning that such a crossing at the worst time of year would prove the practicality of the route.

The expedition reached Bent's Fort on November 16, 1848. There, mountain men tried to dissuade Frémont from continuing into the Rockies on what they considered a fool's mission, but the Pathfinder pushed on. At Pueblo he found the only man who could be talked into serving as a guide, a 62-year-old mountain veteran named Bill Williams. Old Bill must have been one of the very first American trappers to go into the Santa Fe country; there are indications that he may have entered the southern Rockies as early as 1810. Thereafter he traveled back and forth across the West, a companion in adventure and suffering with such men as Jed Smith, Joe Walker, Broken Hand Fitzpatrick and the Sublette brothers.

Williams was not a geographical genius of the order of Walker, but after living in the wilderness almost 40 years he must have learned a thing or two about survival. Soon after the party left Pueblo, he recommended that they turn south and continue on through easier country and milder weather. Frémont ignored the suggestion; as far as he was concerned, the whole point of the mission was to force a way across the worst of the mountains in the worst of weather.

In mid-December Frémont's luck ran out — or, perhaps more accurately, the absurdities of the venture and the weaknesses of his own character caught up with him. On December 16 his party was high in the San Juan Mountains above the headwaters of the Rio Grande. The temperature dropped to 20° below zero. Ten feet of snow lay on the ground, and still more snow, driven by howling winds, was falling. The suffering of the men was excruciating. "Hands, and feet, ears and noses, of some people were frozen," wrote the dour but durable Charles Preuss. "That old fool Bill lay down and wanted to die just at the summit. Many animals perished here."

The day after Christmas Frémont sent a party of four men, including Williams, back toward the New Mexican settlements to organize a rescue party. The remaining 29 men, growing weaker and colder day after terrible day, huddled at the foot of a mountain waiting for relief that did not come. After two weeks Frémont's nerve broke. On January 11, with four of the strongest remaining men, he set out to seek help himself. He left behind him an order "which we scarcely knew how to interpret," wrote Micajah McGehee, one of the abandoned men who survived the ordeal. The order was to the effect that "we must finish packing the baggage and hasten on down as speedily as possible to the mouth of Rabbit River where we would meet relief and that if we wished to see him we must be in a hurry about it, as he was going on to California."

After that it was more or less every man for himself, with Frémont in the lead and rapidly improving his position. A week after leaving the main party he caught up with the group he had sent for aid. One of them, Henry King, whom Frémont had appointed the leader, was dead of exposure and starvation. Williams and the other two were hollow-eyed and emaciated; they had survived by eating their shoes, gun cases and pack straps. (Some members of Frémont's expedition were later to claim that the three men had also eaten parts of King, a charge that was never proved.)

On January 27 Frémont reached Taos. He was in fairly good shape even though he suffered from frostbite and snow blindness, but 10 of his original party had died of cold and hunger in the mountains. In Taos, drinking hot chocolate and resting up, he wrote to Jessie that "the survey has been uninterrupted up to this point and I shall carry it on consecutively." Later he was to say publicly of the railroad-charting expedition: "The result was entirely satisfactory. It convinced me that neither snow of winter nor mountain ranges were obstacles in the way of a road." These incredible statements could only have been made by a man whose perceptions and powers of analysis had been badly eroded, not only by disaster, but also by vanity.

Frémont rode off toward California, following a warm, sunny trail far to the south of the projected railroad route that he was supposed to follow. The next spring Williams and several others went back into the San Juan Mountains to search for notes and other baggage that Frémont had abandoned. As a postscript to the disaster, Williams and his companions disappeared, presumably killed by Ute Indians.

By then Frémont was in California embarked on a new career that promised to be at least as glorious as the best moments of his past. For $3,000 he had bought a 70-square-mile tract of wilderness in the Sierra foothills. The purchase was actually an error; he had instructed an agent to buy no more than a small plot near San Francisco—but the man had somehow misunderstood his orders. Just when Frémont was contemplating legal action to recover the money, gold was discovered on the huge estate, and its value instantly soared into the millions.

Now rich beyond his wildest dreams, Frémont entered politics. In December 1849, the territorial legislature selected him to represent California in the U.S. Senate when it became a state—an event that occurred only 10 months later. The choice was logical enough: Frémont's political connections and known commitment to the building of a transcontinental railroad would make him an excellent advocate for California's interests. He served only 21 working days in the Senate due to time consumed in travel, a recurring illness and the fact that he had the shorter term of California's two Senators. In 1850 another election was held. But this time pro-Southern forces in California successfully rallied against him because he was an outspoken opponent of slavery. After his defeat, he attempted a second railroad survey along the 38th parallel; he lost another man this time, and the route received little serious consideration. Then, in 1856, glory beckoned again. The newly founded Republican Party, looking for a leader who was both famous and progressive in his views, chose Frémont as their first Presidential candidate. He made a surprisingly good run, but suffered another defeat.

Thereafter, disasters followed in unbroken succession. During the Civil War, he served as an impolitic, bungling general who was stripped of his command by Lincoln. Poor business judgment turned his fabulous California estate into a losing proposition, and he finally lapsed into bankruptcy by attempting to promote a railroad between Memphis and San Diego. Toward the end of his life, Jessie Frémont supported the family by turning out a stream of books and articles. In 1890 the Pathfinder died in a dreary Manhattan boardinghouse, pathetically separated in distance, time and spirit from the days when a young hero had ridden across the prairie with Kit Carson at his side, "caught up in the true Greek joy in existence—in the gladness of living."

From the Western notebooks of "Bold Emory"

William Hemsley Emory

If Frémont represented an extreme of glorymongering among Army explorers, William Hemsley Emory exemplified the opposite extreme of dedicated professionalism. With little fanfare, Emory —shown at left as he looked in his mature years as a brigadier general in the Union Army—contributed as much to the understanding of the West as Frémont. His pioneering studies of the Southwest not only earned him a solid reputation in scientific circles but also helped define the United States position toward its territorial gains after the Mexican War.

The scion of a prominent Maryland family, Emory entered West Point with the sponsorship of John C. Calhoun. His classmates there included Jefferson Davis and Henry Clay Jr. who nicknamed the youthful redhead "Bold Emory" for his fiery courage. After graduating, Emory joined the artillery and then transferred to the Army Corps of Topographical Engineers, the elite group of officers charged with surveying and mapping the nation's frontiers.

When war broke out with Mexico in 1846, Emory was put in command of a small topographical detachment that marched with General Stephen Kearny's Army of the West to seize California from the Mexicans. Though he fought heroically in the battle of San Pascual—saving Kearny's life by shielding him from a Mexican lance—Emory's chief contribution was scientific. The *Notes of a Military Reconnaissance,* which he submitted to Congress at war's end, was the first reliable body of information about the Southwest.

One of the problems arising from the war was that no one knew exactly what territory had been won or lost. Between El Paso and San Diego there were only a handful of settlements, and the best available map of the area was grossly inaccurate. Lieutenant Emory's *Notes of a Military Reconnaissance* supplied Congress with an excellent map of the region, and at the same time delved into many aspects of its culture and its natural resources, from Indian hieroglyphics *(below)* to the strange plant forms native to the Southwestern desert. So when Congress appointed a commission to undertake a comprehensive survey of the border area, Emory was the logical choice to command the detachment of Army topographers. He spent a major part of the next six years helping to establish the line across the Southwest that had represented the last unresolved boundary of the United States.

Emory discovered these Indian pictographs on a mound of stones in present-day Arizona.

This exotic assortment of cacti, sketched by an assistant, illustrated Emory's *Notes of a Military Reconnaissance.*

Although Emory was assigned to the Mexican Boundary Survey Commission in 1849 with the rank of brevet major and the ringing title of "Chief Astronomer and Commander of the Escort," the actual work of surveying a border between the United States and Mexico could not begin until the diplomats had decided where the line should run. While the American and Mexican boundary commissioners negotiated, Emory's teams surveyed the California and Texas ends of the border, living in bivouacs like the one shown below. The heat was intense, Indians harassed the surveying parties, and many of the men deserted.

To make matters even worse, the inept head of the U.S. Boundary Commission, John Bartlett, ceded to the Mexicans land south of the Gila River that included the only feasible right of way for a future transcontinental railroad to southern California. Enraged, Emory protested to his powerful Washington friends; his opinion helped persuade Congress to buy back the vital land in 1853 for $10,000,000—in the Gadsden Purchase, named for the U.S. envoy to Mexico. Emory was also given Bartlett's job.

With the last uncertainties behind him, he and his men rushed the work to completion. Erecting markers and putting up flagpoles, the surveyors, by October 1855, had finished laying out the entire 1,500-mile border from the Gulf of Mexico to the Pacific Ocean.

The tents of one of Emory's encampments are laid out with a surveyor's precision on a valley floor ringed with barren desert mesas.

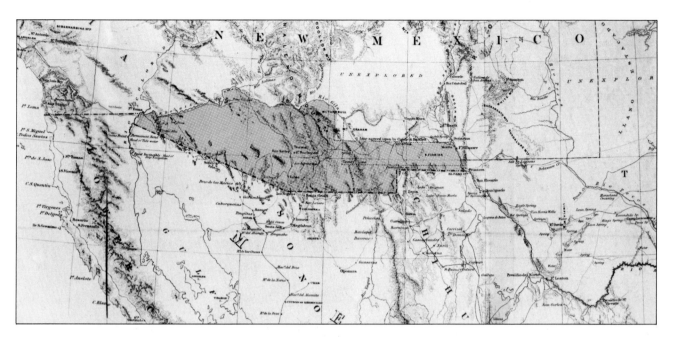

To mark the border, Emory's surveyors sometimes built stone pyramids, but often simply raised a U.S. flag like the one on the far ridge.

Even while Emory was carrying out his primary job of surveying the United States-Mexican border, he directed a group of civilian scientists in assembling an encyclopedic description of the Southwest. Published in three volumes between 1856 and 1859, the *Report of the United States and Mexican Boundary Survey* contained a master map and sections on topography, geology, zoology and botany. It also included Emory's general description of the land, in which he judged the arid region to be largely unsuitable for farming, although he felt that it might well "be settled by a mining and pastoral or wine-making population."

For the cause of science the Southwest was a bonanza. Emory's men collected 2,648 species of plants and numerous mammals, birds, fish and reptiles that lived in this region. The animal specimens were later dissected and rendered in drawings such as those at right and on the following pages—in depictions that, for sheer anatomical detail, outshone even the celebrated studies of John James Audubon.

The *Report's* accumulated findings set a formidable precedent for all future exploration. Reviewing the botanical section, Asa Gray of Harvard University wrote that it deserved to be "ranked as the most important publication of the kind that has ever appeared."

The *Report's* sketch of a Western diamondback rattlesnake

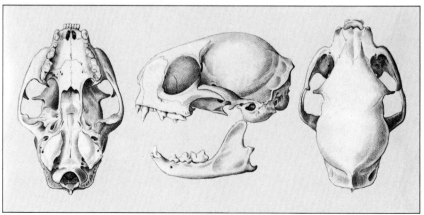

Bottom, side and top views of the skull of a wildcat

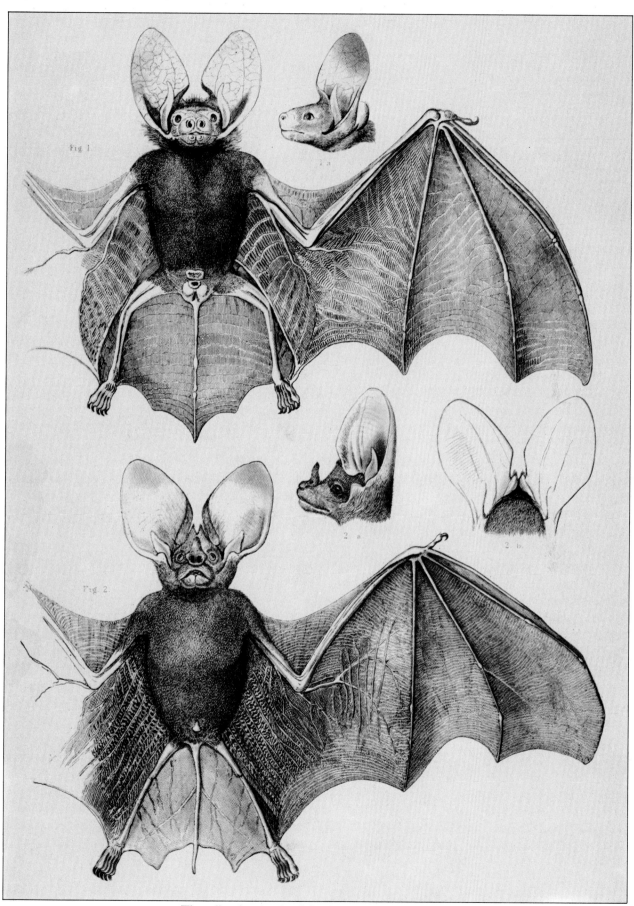

The yellow bat *(top)* and the California leaf-nosed bat

This poisonous beaded lizard was set on its tail in order to fit it life size onto the page in Emory's report.

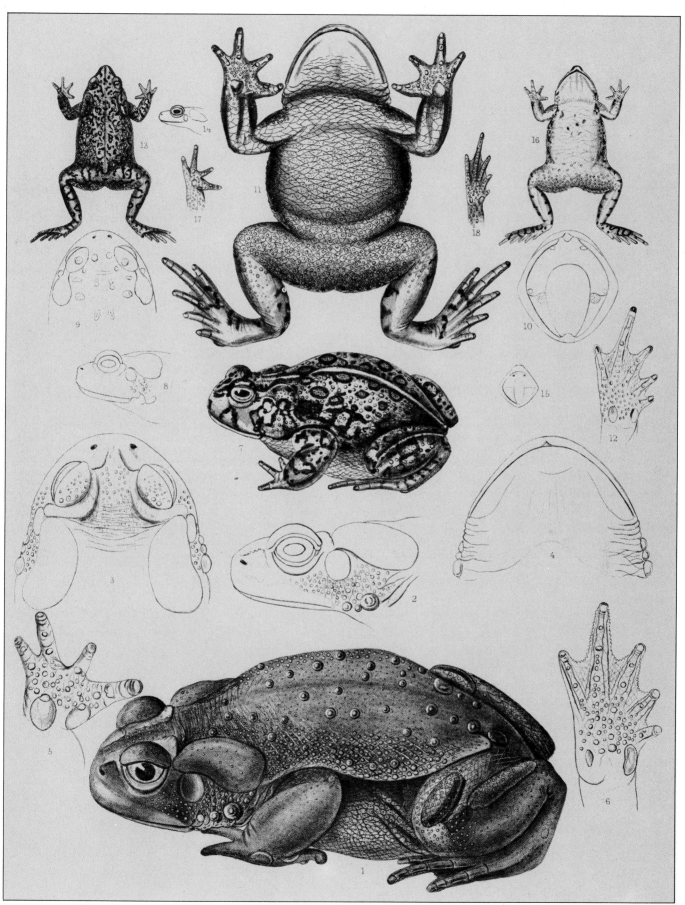

These three species of toads native to the Southwest were added to the scientific lists by the Boundary Survey.

6 | Filling in the blank spaces

After the storm of the Civil War had passed, Americans looked West once more, sensing that the hour had finally arrived when the nation would reap the full promise of the West. But if virginal reaches of the plains, the mountains and the deserts were to be used intelligently, a comprehensive inventory of their assets and hazards was needed, in order to "lay before the public such full, accurate and reliable information as will bring from the older states the capital, skill, and enterprise necessary to develop the great natural resources."

These words belong to Ferdinand Vandiveer Hayden, who—along with Clarence King, John Wesley Powell and the Army's Lieutenant George Wheeler—led teams of scientists, cartographers and photographers into the trans-Mississippi lands. Their undertakings, known collectively as the "Great Surveys," laid the foundation for all future development of the West and, by 1879, brought to completion the work initiated by Lewis and Clark.

The Hayden expedition, 32 men strong, enters Yellowstone valley in 1871.

Before embarking from Green River, Wyoming, in May of 1871, members of John Wesley Powell's second expedition through the Grand Canyon rest at their campground. On this trip the Powell Survey charted the last unknown river in the United States—to be named the Escalante.

185

During a rare moment of calm in their 1871 ascent of the Colorado, Lieutenant George Wheeler's surveying party, including an Indian guide *(at the bow)*, rests at the riverbank. The men rowed and dragged their boats 260 miles against the current to the lower reaches of the Grand Canyon.

The wild places defined with transit and camera

Threescore years after the Corps of Discovery took the measure of the continent, most of the Western American wilderness had been seen and traversed by white men. The passes through the mountains were known, and well-beaten trails ran through them. Towns that would become cities were acquiring the dignity of names. Some had grown and already died, the first ghost towns. The rails were being laid inexorably westward.

But mysteries and dangers enough remained. It was still possible for a greenhorn or reckless wanderer to lose his horse or his scalp to an Apache or Paiute. And while the contour and the extent of the land were known and increasingly traveled, there was still much to be learned about precisely what it contained and how its resources could best be used.

Prior to the Civil War, the Army, through its elite Corps of Topographical Engineers, had exercised a virtual monopoly over the business of codifying the West's assets and liabilities. However, the Army was mainly concerned with establishing the borders of the American dominion and the best routes for the movement of men and goods within those borders. The greatest beneficiaries of exploration by the Topographical Engineers were the railroads. Between 1853 and the eve of the war in 1860, four great railroad surveys to the Pacific were performed, and all of the findings gleaned from these and other missions of the Topographic Corps were consolidated on a single map, drawn to a scale of 1:3,000,000 by Lieutenant Gouverneur K. Warren. This monumental work encompassed the entire trans-Mississippi region to the Pacific and gave the nation the first dependable geographic portrait of the West.

Once the war was finished, the task of filling in the small gaps in Lieutenant Warren's map and completing the inventory of the West's physical contents fell largely upon civilian shoulders. The next decade and a half became known to history as the period of the "Great Surveys." The period was dominated by four exceptional men, each of whom led a major surveying operation. Three, Ferdinand Vandiveer Hayden, Clarence King and John Wesley Powell were civilian scientists. The fourth, the implement of the Army's last fling at Western exploration, was a topographic officer, Lieutenant George Montague Wheeler.

Among them, these men prowled most of the territory that would one day comprise eight big Western states—Nebraska, Colorado, Wyoming, Utah, Nevada, California, Arizona and New Mexico—and they penetrated the fringes of Montana, Idaho and Oregon as well. When they and their colleagues finished their work around 1879, precious little about the West remained to any man's imagination. They analyzed the region's geologic structure and history, measured its mountains (55 "fourteeners"—peaks above 14,000 feet—in Colorado alone), shot the rapids of its rivers, located and assayed its mineral deposits, catalogued its flora and fauna, staked out its arable sections, delineated its deserts, and studied how best to make use of the land while preserving it from waste and despoliation.

Hayden, the eldest of the Great Surveyors, was not only the first in the field, but stayed in it the longest. By the formality of a college degree (Albany Medical School, 1853), Hayden was a physician; by the more ardently pursued courses of his education at Oberlin and Albany, a geologist and paleontologist; by both his career and the generally grateful acknowledgment of history, a scientist-explorer; by natural bent, an insatiable tourist. Considering his latter passion, it was fitting that

Using a theodolite, the topographer's indispensable tool, members of the Hayden Survey take bearings of nearby peaks from the summit of Sultan Mountain in Colorado.

In a Wyoming meadow, cook "Potato John" *(far left),* whose nickname commemorates a vain attempt to boil spuds at 12,000 feet, serves lunch to Ferdinand Hayden *(hatless at center)* and his team.

Hayden personally lobbied through Congress and to signature by President Grant on March 1, 1872, the bill creating Yellowstone National Park, only eight months after he first laid eyes on Mammoth Hot Springs and described their wonders in his journal.

"The beholder," Hayden noted, "stands amazed at nature's handiwork, a snowy white ground, with every variety of shade, of scarlet, green and yellow, as brilliant as the brightness of our aniline dyes." The hot pools of the springs he found "so perfectly transparent that one could look down into the beautiful ultramarine depth to the bottom of the basin," and he "enjoyed the luxury of bathing in these most elegantly carved natural bathing pools."

Hayden had a way of being granted primacy in discovery even when he did not in so many words assert it

—though he frequently implied and scarcely ever denied it. Thus he is usually given credit for the discovery of the springs, although, in all probability, they are part and parcel of the "Hell" that John Colter, the great precursor of the mountain men, described 64 years before Hayden got there.

When Hayden came into the valley of the Yellowstone River in the summer of 1871, he was already a seasoned explorer. He had been roaming along the littoral of the Missouri River ever since 1853 when, instead of hanging out a shingle as a newly ordained doctor of medicine, he had yielded to his heart's real temptation and joined a fossil-collecting expedition. In the years leading up to the Civil War, Hayden—slight of stature, energetic, jumpy and garrulous—became a familiar figure on the Western frontier. Indians of the region, observing his habits with amazement, coined a devilishly accurate name for him: Man-Who-Picks-Up-Stones-Running. Some of his white professional associates were less kind; one especially biting comment by a colleague described his as a "grasshopper mind."

During the early stages of his career, he was a kind of semiprofessional scientist, skimpily financed by such organizations as the Smithsonian Institution and the St. Louis Academy of Sciences, but happy to do without luxuries. After enduring the Civil War as a post surgeon—the only medicine he ever practiced—he got back to the frontier as quickly as he could. He was still short of cash, but now bore some official cachet as a surveyor for the new state of Nebraska. One of his instructions was to find all the state's "deposits of ores, coals, clays, marls, peat and such other mineral substances." There was not much to find, but he did turn up iron ore deposits adjacent to lignite (brown coal) beds along the Union Pacific right of way near Laramie. The double-barreled discovery inspired in him a vision of an incipient steel industry, and he predicted that conjunction of the two minerals "would exert the same kind of influence over the progress of the great West that Pennsylvania exerts over all the contiguous states."

This report was typical of Hayden's perennial optimism. The West never had a more enthusiastic booster, although sober post-mortem study of his work disclosed that some of his scientific conclusions were superficial or ill considered. Occasionally he was downright wrong. In 1869, without bothering to question its validity, he lent his growing prestige to a theory—articulated by the Reverend Cyrus Thomas of his party—that "rain follows the plow." At the end of an unprecedented cycle of rainy seasons, Thomas, who was a botanist and anthropologist as well as a clergyman, boldly predicted the end of all droughts in the West's arid lands.

"It is a common expression among the Mexicans," he wrote, "that the Americans bring rain with them. As the population increases, the amount of moisture will increase. This is the plan which nature herself has pointed out. The perpetual snows of the great central axis are the sources of the various streams which rush down upon the margin of these plains, but chiefly sink in their effort to cross it. Let the population gather around the points where these burst from the mountains and as it increases pushing out on the plains eastward, I believe the supply of water will accompany it."

Some pioneers were lured westward by this bizarre idea, and land speculators happily endorsed it. But the dream was shattered soon enough when the dry years inevitably came in their turn.

By 1870, Hayden's renown had so increased that Congress, hitherto niggardly in granting funds to support his work, appropriated $25,000 to finance the Hayden Survey of the Western territories for the Department of the Interior. In his new affluence, Hayden made one of his most significant contributions to the technique of exploration. He had already been accustomed to surrounding himself with all the scientific entourage that his meager money but rich persuasiveness would allow. In his train came botanists, zoologists, ornithologists, agronomists, topographical sketchers, painters, anthropologists and paleontologists. Now on his way west again, he stopped off in Omaha and hired William Henry Jackson, a 27-year-old studio photographer, as a member of his party.

The tactic of bringing the eye of the camera to bear on the West would be used by the other leaders of the Great Surveys. For the first time, the land would be depicted with undeniable accuracy. After the work of men like Jackson and Timothy O'Sullivan—another gifted photographer who worked for Clarence King and Lieutenant George Wheeler—the West, with all its splendors and pitfalls, was a very real, almost palpable place to the public at large, and doubts about the veracity of earlier explorers were effectively removed (or, in some cases, verified).

In the era of the Great Surveys the state of the photographic art had progressed very little beyond the techniques employed by Mathew Brady in photographing the Civil War. The cameras of the day exposed images on sensitized wet-glass plates that had to be kept moist until developed. The standard camera took plates 6½ by 8½ inches, which proved far too meager for the majestic scenes that Jackson wanted to photograph—and the craft of enlarging had yet to be perfected. In these straits, Jackson developed into one of the hardest physical workers of his profession. By his second season in the field, he was using a camera that would accept 11-by-14 plates, and before he was through he was toting an outsized one that took 20-by-24 pictures. He also

Encountering this eerie smoking cone at the edge of Yellowstone Lake in Wyoming, Hayden's party called it Fish Pot because they found they could cook trout in the hot spring bubbling inside the crater.

"Most accommodating," was the way survey leader Hayden described Old Faithful. "As we were leaving, the grand old geyser which stands sentinel at the head of the valley gave us a magnificent parting display."

devised a camera that took 360° panoramic views.

To lug his bulky equipment across the West, Jackson needed several mules, one of which he named Gimlet. This particular animal proved to be a terrible liability. Recounting the fate of one set of dramatic images of mountain landscapes in central Colorado, Jackson wrote that the "evil mule slipped his pack and broke many of my exposed plates. The Doctor [Hayden] himself was the first to notice. He found plates along the trail and galloped to learn the cause. By that time Gimlet had scattered most of his load. All my 11 by 14s were irreparably shattered. I have never been so distressed in my life."

Perhaps Jackson's most trying experience coincided with his greatest professional thrill, photographing the fabled Mountain of the Holy Cross. For years tales had been told of a great mountain somewhere beyond Denver that bore on its eastern face a gigantic, perfectly delineated cross etched in perpetual snow. The cross was said to vanish if one attempted to approach it. To the Hayden party, particularly Jackson, the Holy Cross was a tantalizing legend. Indeed, the photographer half-feared it was a myth, for he could find no one who had actually seen the cross.

Then, late in summer, as the party was winding through the mountains of central Colorado, the rumored cross abruptly materialized. Jackson, in the vanguard, was the first to see it. Later he vividly recalled the moment: "Suddenly, as I clambered over a vast mass of jagged rocks, I discovered the great shining cross dead before me, tilted against the mountainside." He wasted no time admiring the miracle. "I quickly devoured the

A sinuous wonder of Yellowstone, this rock formation of the Grotto Geyser was created by mineral deposits from innumerable eruptions.

Triumphs of the intrepid photographers

On a hot day in July 1870, Ferdinand Hayden walked into William Henry Jackson's photography studio in Omaha, looked at his portfolio of photographs and declared flatly, "This is what I need." A week later Jackson was on his way to the Rocky Mountains with the survey.

What Hayden needed and Jackson could provide was an unimpeachable visual record of the Western terrain. Earlier explorers had described the West in words, sketches and paintings; but now the camera was the ultimate weapon with which to silence all skeptics. Even more important, it could show Congress what Hayden's Surveys were accomplishing—and thereby gain further funding.

Although Jackson won the greatest renown, a number of other cameramen also provided records of the Great Surveys. Timothy O'Sullivan, a Civil War protégé of Mathew Brady, joined King's Fortieth Parallel Survey in 1867, and later worked with Wheeler. And John Wesley Powell hired several photographers, including E. O. Beaman and a self-taught ex-boatman named Jack Hillers.

These photographers had to endure all the hardships and hazards of the expeditions plus the additional problems of their trade. The chief difficulty was the sheer unwieldiness of their equipment. In addition to bulky wet-plate cameras, they needed an assemblage of chemicals, fragile glass negatives, tripods and light-proof tents in which to prepare their emulsions. To transport the 300-odd pounds of gear, an old Army ambulance served on level ground, but in the mountains everything had to be toted by mules.

The actual act of taking a picture was anything but spontaneous. After unpacking and setting up the equipment at each site, the photographer generally needed at least 45 minutes

High in the Rockies, Jackson and his assistant stand next to their tentlike "dark box."

to prepare a plate, make the exposure and develop it. But the process could take much longer. When photographing the 132-foot Tower Falls in the Yellowstone canyon from the bottom, Jackson had to climb down the steep sides of the gorge with his camera; then he scrambled up again, prepared a plate and rushed down again; as soon as he took the exposure, he wrapped the plate in a wet towel to keep it from drying, and climbed back up to develop it. In a whole day's work he shot only five exposures.

Despite the hard work and the complexity of their craft, the photographers of the Great Surveys scored some stunning triumphs. Using a magnesium flash, O'Sullivan took the first mine photographs in history, hundreds of feet below Virginia City, Nevada, in the Comstock Lode. Hillers' images of the Paiute Indians were among the first records of the Smithsonian's Bureau of Ethnology. And Jackson's work helped to create a national legacy. In 1872 when a reluctant Congress was debating whether or not to make Yellowstone the country's first national park, the supporters of the proposal gave each Congressman a folio of Jackson's photographs of the region's numerous marvels. The bill was quickly and unanimously passed.

hefty sandwich I had. No art was ever any better because the artist was hungry at his work." However, clouds swirled in and blocked sight of the vision before he could set up a camera. Jackson spent that night on the mountainside, foodless and blanketless. At dawn, he rushed to his vantage point with his camera, but again he was thwarted. Sunrise on the peak was still so cold that no ice had yet melted to furnish the water he needed to prepare a plate. By the time the day warmed enough to yield a little ice water, lengthening shadows were just about to obscure the cross. Stuck between two natural crises, he managed to make eight hasty exposures. They turned out to be among the finest pictures of Jackson's long career.

Having proved that the legendary mountain did indeed exist, the party proceeded to discover why the cross was said to vanish when anyone drew near. The solution was somewhat anticlimactic: it turned out that another, lower peak blotted out the cross when the approach was made from a certain angle.

In the Rockies, the Hayden party decided to challenge another towering peak, the Grand Teton in Wyoming. Rearing to a height of 13,766 feet, this sheer pinnacle, along with two slightly lesser fellows, had been given their improbable name, *Les Grandes Tetones* (the Great Breasts), because they had reminded some lonesome, sex-starved French-Canadian trapper of the smooth contours of a woman's body. The name stuck, although Hayden himself suggested renaming the cragged group more realistically as the Shark's Teeth, and several of his party, soft-soaping the boss, tried to rechristen the ruling giant as Mount Hayden.

At the end of July 1872 Hayden's right-hand man, James Stevenson, undertook to lead 13 men to the summit between sunup and sunset. For mountaineering equipment each man had an alpine staff and a bacon sandwich. The expedition struck Jackson as sensible under the circumstances, and he wrote, "Since they had no way of knowing that it would later be regarded as one of the truly difficult peaks of North America, they simply went ahead and climbed it. That, in my mind, is the way to climb a mountain."

Whether they did climb it in fact remains a matter of doubt. Stevenson afterward claimed they succeeded, and in support of this claim one of his men described a man-made rock enclosure at the summit, which they theorized was the ruin of some aboriginal religious shrine. No subsequent climber has ever seen any such work of man atop the Grand Teton.

Up until 1878, Hayden returned to his beloved West year after year. During off-seasons, he wrote prolifically and published a long series of monographs and reports. Despite some nagging questions about his professional competence and judgment, his work contributed greatly to knowledge of the trans-Mississippi lands and, even more, mightily stimulated the nation's curiosity about the West. The railroad promoters were particularly grateful for his ringing endorsement of the West as an excellent place to invest private and governmental funds. Wrote the chief geologist for the Union Pacific Railroad: "I regard your work as the most beneficial to science, and adaptable to the wants of the miner and explorer, as well as to the capitalist who seeks investment, of any yet presented to the American people."

For his surveys, Hayden had staked out a vast north-to-south franchise, reaching up to Yellowstone country and beyond, and down to the cliff dwellings of Colorado and the mountains of the Southwest. The next of the Great Surveyors — Clarence King — worked in a 100-mile-wide band running west-to-east from the California Sierra to the border of Nebraska.

King was born into impoverished aristocracy in Newport, Rhode Island, in 1842, and he developed into a lifelong snob. Explaining himself to a scientific colleague, he once wrote, "I wish it could be intimated in my life and engraved on my tombstone that I am to the last fibre aristocratic in belief, that I think that the only fine thing to do with the masses is to govern and educate them into some semblance of their social superiors."

Although his choice of career thereafter threw him much into the company of the masses — mule skinners, Indians, frontier Army privates — King's social preferences remained unmistakable. He picked his close friends from among the wealthy, the intellectuals and the nation's most prominent citizens. A few made use of him, but mainly he used them to singular advantage.

King's widowed mother was a doting parent and, though always short of funds, saw to it that he got the best education to be had and that his whims were indulged. By the time he was seven he had a whim for picking up pretty rocks. Consequently, having been prepared at the Endowed Grammar School in Hartford,

On August 24, 1873, William Henry Jackson took the first photographs of Colorado's Mountain of the Holy Cross. According to legend, during the 18th Century a pair of wandering Spanish monks named it for the 1,000-foot-long cross of permanent snow lying in crevices on the peak.

Connecticut, he went on to the Sheffield Scientific School at Yale, where he was exposed to the ideas of Charles Darwin and James Dwight Dana, giants in the emerging natural sciences.

Strong, handsome and a witty raconteur, King renewed an incongruous friendship at Sheffield with a frail and sickly fellow student he had known during childhood, James Terry Gardner, who shared his scientific interests. The pattern of their lives coalesced in the summer of 1863, not long after their graduation from Yale. Most of their fellow graduates proceeded directly from the campus to the battlefields of the Civil War. But such a prospect did not appeal to these two young men, for the summer of '63 was marked by some of the bloodiest fighting of the war: Vicksburg fell after a siege that cost 19,000 casualties, and Gettysburg wrought its awful carnage. On the basis of Gardner's fragile health and the clear inadvisability of going off to that kind of war, King and Gardner persuaded their families to let them seek their fortunes in distant California.

On a river steamer out of Sacramento, King fell in with an official of the California Geological Survey, while Gardner went on to San Francisco and found work with the Topographical Engineers. In 1864, after less than a year with the Engineers, Gardner rejoined his friend as a topographer on the California Survey. Thus, both men were quickly cast in lifetime roles as collaborating explorers and scientists.

On a Sierra mountaintop, King had a breathtaking idea that was to crystallize formally as the United States Geological Exploration of the Fortieth Parallel. His basic plan was simple: a survey from the Pacific to the Great Plains to facilitate the final punching through of the transcontinental railroads. He went to Washington to seek governmental backing for the plan and, though he was still a stripling of 25, he was armed, as always thereafter, with the recommendations of powerful and influential men.

He got the job from Secretary of War Edwin Stanton. "Now, Mister King," Stanton said, "the sooner you get out of Washington, the better—you are too young a man to be seen about town with this appointment in your pocket—there are four major generals who want your place."

King's orders were more comprehensive than his original notion. They directed him "to examine and de-scribe the geological structure, geographical condition and natural resources of a belt of country extending from the 120th meridian eastward to the 105th meridian, along the 40th parallel of latitude with sufficient expansion north and south to include the line of the 'Central' and 'Union Pacific' railroads. It should examine all rock formations, mountain ranges, detrital plains, coal deposits, soils, minerals, ores, saline and alkaline deposits, collect material for a topographical map of the regions traversed, conduct barometric and thermometric observations, make collections in botany and zoology illustrating the occurrence and distribution of plants and animals."

The orders, in short, amounted to an unlimited franchise to explore—a franchise that Clarence King was prepared to make full use of. When he assembled his scientific associates for the survey, King characteristically recruited men of his own kind, the elite of Eastern colleges. After a farewell dinner at Yale, where the group was extolled as "the best equipped by training of any that had thus far entered the field of American geology," King and his party sailed for Panama. They crossed the isthmus by train and took ship northward again to San Francisco.

King established his base camp at Sacramento, preliminary to assaulting Donner Pass and then the Nevada deserts, along a desolate route that Mark Twain later described as a road so littered with the bones of oxen and horses that "we could have walked the forty miles and set our feet on a bone at every step."

Soon the mule drivers and camp workers arrived, followed by the expedition's assigned military escort, a platoon of 20 tough troopers. The soldiers were bristling with arms—including pistols in their boot tops—but many of them were too drunk to draw a bead. The self-assured young explorer quickly seized an occasion to establish the proper degree of respect among this motley crew. When a disgruntled private deserted, King went after him personally.

"I chased him one hundred miles," wrote King, who had a gift for unbridled hyperbole, "across the desert and through the mountain ranges of northern Nevada, trailing him like a bloodhound. I captured him in a hand to hand struggle by which I nearly lost my life, and only saved myself by dodging his shot and cramming my pistol in his ear in the nick of time. The fact of his capture

forever reduced the soldiers and the working men of the survey to obedience."

Pressing into the Nevada wasteland, the party received a swift education in the hazards of the wilderness. They struggled through enervating heat and finally into the Humboldt Sink. During the previous months this swampy region had been so ravaged by floods that now it was a stinking miasma of rotting tule, with hordes of mosquitoes so dense they snuffed the flame of candles. One by one the men fell sick of a strange fever —the "mountain ail" they called it—until King, sick himself, had to sound retreat to an ascending canyon in the west Humboldt Mountains, where the air was sweet and the men slowly recovered.

As his own strength returned, King took a small party into the mountains between Salt Valley and the Carson Sink. There, on a day of wind-driven squalls, he set up a theodolite on the summit of Job's Peak and prepared to take observations of the elevation. The wind was herding a thunderhead in their direction, and King began to notice that the theodolite was chattering on its tripod, the rocks around him were singing, his beard tickled and the hair on his head was standing straight up. Tending to be impatient of interruption when he worked, he dismissed these odd phenomena and bent to adjust his instrument. At that moment a bolt of lightning struck; the phenomena he had noticed had been caused by that single thunderhead drifting toward him, bearing within it the energies of a full-scale electrical storm. The wrecked theodolite was tossed 20 feet and King was left stunned and prostrate.

"I was staggered and my brain and nerves severely shocked," King later wrote in his account of the incident. "My right side and arm turned brown."

But narrow escapes seemed part of Clarence King's life style. Altogether, during the course of the Fortieth Parallel Survey, he was to spend six full years in the field, and in every one of those years he not only added to scientific knowledge but also had some hair-raising adventures of his own. When nature or lightning or runaway troopers failed to provide peril, he created it himself. Retiring toward winter quarters at the end of one season, King saw a big grizzly and trailed it until it went to ground in a cave so restricted that the beast scraped off some of its fur getting in. Whereupon the youthful explorer, in an act of certifiable idiocy, got

At Pyramid Lake in northwestern Nevada, Clarence King's Survey investigated these strange domes, which were formed as the water in the landlocked lake evaporated, leaving calcium carbonate deposits behind.

down on all fours and, shoving his rifle ahead of him, crawled in after the beast. Within the cave, unaware that his chances of escaping this situation with his life were practically nil, he waited until he could locate the bear by the gleam of its eyes. They were nose to nose when King fired. Simultaneously a muscular sergeant outside seized King's protruding ankles and hauled him out, doing his face some of the damage the bear had not had the presence of mind to inflict before it died.

With this kind of daredevil exploit as well as impressive scientific accomplishments to show for his efforts, King's fame burgeoned, and Congress gladly extended his original two-year commission. Returning to the wastelands each successive season, he and his men learned to endure fierce extremes of natural conditions and physical hardship — heat so searing that men sought shelter in the slender shade of a camp flagpole, blizzards so sudden that the party sometimes despaired of finding its way out of the mountains. On occasions when supplies dwindled down to nothingness, the men learned to appreciate the blue flesh of mules that had died of famine. King became adept at improvising his way out of difficulties. Striving for an early start one season, before summer had reasonably reduced the snows in mountain passes, King learned the stratagem of traveling only at night, when a solid crust covered the snow, for in warmer daylight the mules broke through and became stranded in 30-foot drifts.

Although he was a volcanologist by scientific preference, King broke into quite another geological specialty when, in 1870, he made the only unique discovery of his career. Guided by a local postmaster, he scaled the 14,162-foot rim of Mount Shasta's crater and, gazing down from this noble elevation, saw the courses of three active ice glaciers. Later, he smugly described his find as "somewhat startling when we consider that Whitney, Brewer, Dana and Frémont, all visited the Peak without observing them; and that Whitney, Dana and Agassiz have all published statements that no true glaciers exist in the United States." The men thus singled out and lightly dismissed by King were all his superiors in achievement or reputation. Josiah Whitney was the head of the California Survey and William Brewer was his second-in-command; James Dana had been King's teacher at Yale; the naturalist Louis Agassiz was perhaps the most famous American

scientist of the day and John Frémont was certainly its most famous trailblazer.

Between his periods of rawhiding through the wilderness, King returned to San Francisco and enjoyed reminding himself that he was "to the last fibre aristocratic." In the city, he would turn himself out in clawhammer coat, gold watch chain across the vest, and doeskin trousers with stripes down the side; then, twirling a cane in devilish fashion, he would repair to the Union Club to socialize with his peers.

At about this time King, a gifted spinner of campfire tales, decided to try his hand at literature by extracting adventure stories from his field notes. He began by writing up an article about the falls of the Snake River and giving it to a friend, the writer and editor Bret Harte — who promptly published the piece in the October 1869 issue of his periodical Overland Monthly. King, chronically short of funds, was pleased to get a check for $25. Thus encouraged, the explorer turned to the composition of a series of semifactual articles about his Western travels for the Atlantic Monthly, whose editors received them enthusiastically and described them as "gems." When the explorer's colorful literary style began to get the better of his professional conservatism, Harte twitted him by inscribing one of his own works "To Clarence King, author of Geology of the fortieth parallel and other works of fiction."

On a visit to San Francisco in the spring of 1872, King became aware that his supposedly comprehensive survey of resources along the 40th parallel was being threatened with a credibility gap of professionally disastrous proportions. Not only that Western metropolis, but also centers of finance as distant as New York, London and Amsterdam, were seething with reports of a fabulous find of diamonds, rubies, sapphires and garnets somewhere in the Rocky Mountains. This gemstone bonanza — if it existed — was said to lie somewhere within the craggy precincts that King had been meticulously combing for five years. If all this were true, it followed that he had been unforgivably remiss at his own trade; like any other rock, a diamond falls among the legitimate concerns of a practicing geologist.

King learned that the report had had its origin some months previously when a roughhewn, taciturn pair of prospectors, Philip Arnold and John Slack, had appeared out of a fog one early morning, pounded on the

door of a San Francisco bank and presented a leather pouch for safe deposit. When a clerk wanted to know what the pouch contained, Arnold and Slack, with a show of reluctance, spilled out its glittering contents and identified them as uncut diamonds. Then the miners vanished back into the fog.

There could be no stopping what their appearance had set off. The prominent banker William C. Ralston took the lead in organizing the New York & San Francisco Mining & Commercial Company, and before long had enlisted as eager shareholders such financial heavyweights as Baron Ferdinand Rothschild of London and Charles Tiffany of New York. Ralston had a heady vision of the future; he could foresee a time when San Francisco would supplant Amsterdam as the world center of diamond cutting.

The California diamond project moved rapidly forward, especially after Arnold and Slack permitted them-

selves to be found and were cut into the company as shareholders. Soon afterward they allowed themselves to be bought out for a mere $300,000 each; they were not greedy, they said. The sample gems were submitted for appraisal to Henry Janin, a reputable mining expert, and to Tiffany; both pronounced them genuine and immensely valuable.

Before getting their payoff Arnold and Slack were urged to offer some additional proof that their diamond field actually existed, for they claimed sole knowledge of its location. Eventually, they agreed to conduct Janin to the field — but they led him there blindfolded all the way. Janin returned completely convinced. However, he still had no knowledge of the location other than the fact that its immediate surroundings, as he reported them, consisted of a desert plateau distinguished only by "a conical but flat topped mountain" and a nearby stand of pines. The only other facts he had to report were that he had traveled 36 hours aboard a train and two more days aboard a pack mule and that, most persuasively, he now possessed another sack of gems he had personally thumbed out of the gravel.

With their professional reputations now in hazard, King, James Terry Gardner and King's chief geologist, Samuel Franklin Emmons, sifted through their combined knowledge of mountain terrain in an effort to figure out where the diamond field might lie. They succeeded admirably. King and his party set off, by train and horseback, for a mesa about 15 miles southeast of the conjunction of Wyoming, Utah and Colorado. Arriving as skeptics, they soon became converts as, down on hands and knees, they began plucking diamonds and rubies out of the glittering quartz gravel with their bare, frozen fingers.

The suspension of disbelief did not last long. No scientist, so far as they knew, had ever recorded precious gems in this sort of deposit before. Even more suspicious was the location of one unusually fine stone, found lying in the open atop a boulder, where any rainstorm would have washed it away; furthermore, rubies were turning up only at the bottom of holes in anthills where either provident ants had buried them or somebody had poked them in with a stick.

The diamond boom collapsed amid much embarrassment for Tiffany and Henry Janin, and new admiration for the abilities of Clarence King. The original source of the gems was eventually traced. Apparently, the two frontier confidence men, Arnold and Slack, had journeyed to Amsterdam and bought $25,000 worth of flawed rejects from that city's gem merchants. Both Janin and Tiffany, with considerable discomfiture, had to offer the lame explanation that they had been fooled because they were unaccustomed to dealing with diamonds in the raw.

Despite his personal flamboyance and his lapses into hyperbolic semijournalism, King finished his work with an impregnable reputation for having accomplished scientific work of immense value to his country. When his survey was completed he published his masterwork, *Systematic Geology,* a brilliant, speculative thesis exploring the origins and significance of the geologic formations he had examined. King hoped that the work would survive "either as a permanent contribution to knowledge or as a stepping stone worthy to be built into the great stairway of science." It has done both.

In producing *Systematic Geology* and editing the reports of his colleagues, King settled down to the sobriety proper to the profession. "The day has passed in geological science," he wrote, "when it is either decent or tolerable to rush into print with undigested field operations." The process of turning out the expedition's seven volumes and an atlas—during which King grew bald, portly and broke—took until 1880, but earned an impressive accolade. "Mr. King's graceful pen never showed itself to better advantage," declared the *American Journal of Science.* A year earlier, when Congress consolidated all Western exploration in the office of the United States Geological Survey, Clarence King was appointed the first director of the agency. His successor would be John Wesley Powell.

All of the Great Surveyors were fame-hungry, proud men—but none more so than Powell, the last of the postwar triumvirate of civilian explorers. He came of humble origins, born in New York State's Genesee Valley in 1834, the son of a parttime Wesleyan preacher, farmer and occasional tailor. By his teens, the family was more or less settled on a half-cleared Wisconsin farm. Powell might well have lived out his days behind a plow, except that during the family's stop-and-go journey westward he had, in Ohio, attracted the attention of a learned Calvinist farmer who stimulated his interest in education, particularly natural history. When he was 18 and his contemporaries were slopping hogs and getting married, John Wesley wangled an appointment to a country schoolhouse as a selfinstructed teacher. To keep ahead of his students, some of whom were older than he, Powell studied harder than they did and exhausted the library of a modestly intellectual family with whom he boarded.

He joined the Union Army early in 1861 and obtained a commission as a lieutenant and military engineer and subsequently won promotion to captain of artillery. As the Battle of Shiloh began, Powell raised his right arm in signaling his battery to open fire. A Minié ball hit his elbow; his arm was amputated two days later. But Powell stayed in the service throughout the war and left the Army as a major. Renewing his studies after the war, he managed to get appointed as professor of geology at Illinois Wesleyan University

John Wesley Powell, shown with a Paiute chief, Tau-gu, was a lifelong friend of Indians and learned several of their languages. In 1879 he founded the Bureau of Ethnology, for the study of Indian culture.

and curator of the Illinois Natural History Society.

But Powell found that he was more interested in learning than in teaching. In the spring of 1867, like Ferdinand Vandiveer Hayden and Clarence King that same season, the one-armed veteran was in Washington hunting money to go exploring in the West. He got none, but the War Department came through with some castoff wagons, livestock and camp equipment; the Smithsonian Institution added some surveyor's instruments. Powell was also able to raise a little money from an Illinois college. With his wife and a party of friends and students, he set out for Colorado.

His choice of companions was typical of the Powell method and earned him a great deal of criticism later; he was an unregenerate believer in nepotism. He took along his brother even though he knew that Walter Henry Powell had never recovered from a spell of insanity brought on by a scarifying experience as a Confederate prisoner of war. The Colorado River and its hardships left Walter permanently deranged.

In the summer of 1868, Powell and his men decided to climb a peak discovered earlier by Major Ste-

phen Long but never scaled by white men. He had already formed a shrewd guess at what the view would reveal—a navigable water passage toward the Pacific, the very fundament of the exploratory ambitions of John Wesley Powell. Reaching the mountaintop was a difficult task, in which the climbers were balked one night by an impassable precipice, and another by losing their way behind intervening ridges. Finally they found a way up the south face and surmounted a last capstone of granite, their "life depending upon a grasp of the fingers in a crevice that would hardly admit them," as one member of the party, William Byers, wrote.

From the summit, Powell saw exactly what he had planned to see: the interlocking, deep-cleft valleys of the numerous rivers of the Colorado watershed—the Virgin, Yampa, Green, Grand and Paria Rivers—all converging on the Colorado. Instantly, he made up his mind to return to the region and conquer this final section of unmapped wilderness.

That winter he hustled more donations and in Chicago ordered the construction of four boats—three load carriers stoutly built of oak, double-ribbed and fitted with watertight compartments, and a lighter vessel of pine for command and exploration. In this fleet, he proposed to navigate through whatever hazards the rivers could offer, from the cradle of the Rocky Mountains to the Pacific Ocean.

Other surveyors had already been on the Colorado River—both upstream and down—beginning 12 years before Powell got there, and only about 150 miles of the great watershed could properly be described as unexplored by 1869. But Powell envisioned himself as the conqueror of the mighty waterway, and history recognizes him as such.

His encounters with the river and its tributaries furnished toil and adventure enough for any man. The party lost one of the heavy boats within the first two weeks when it broached against the rocks in a hellish sluiceway that the party named the Canyon of Lodore. The wreck cost them a third of their food and spare clothing. Clothing was a never-ending problem, for it was always wet. They solved it, in a way, by going without. "Major Powell said he was dressed when he had his life preserver on," one of the men later observed, and added a rueful comment on his own predicament. "I had a pair of buckskin breeches. They

Surveying New Mexico during his first expedition, Powell's party visited this Zuñi Indian village, whose rooftops sprout chimneys and the poles of ladders giving access to rooms below. The ruins of an even older settlement of these agricultural Indians lay atop the mesa rising in the distance.

were so wet all the time that they kept stretching and I kept cutting off the lower ends till I had nothing left but the waist band. I cut holes in my shirt tail and tied the loose ends around my legs."

Powell, who could not resist exploring the cliffs at every campsite in the gorges, soon had occasion to be grateful that the party had not all reverted to total nakedness. The major got stuck high up on the face of a precipice and could make no progress, up, down or sideways. As he held on by the fingertips of his single arm, his muscles began to quake and his grip was failing fast when a fellow climber above him stripped off his one garment—long johns. He lowered this lifesaving device and hoisted his commander to safety.

Three months into the river, reduced to meager rations of soggy flour and rancid bacon, the Powell party ran into "the worst rapid seen yet," as one man wrote in a waterlogged diary. "The water dashes against the left bank and then is thrown furiously back against the right. The billows are huge and I fear our boats could not ride them. The spectacle is appalling. We have only subsistence for five days and have been trying for half a day to get around this one rapid while there are three others in sight below. There is discontent in camp tonight and I fear some of the party will take to the mountains but hope not." On the very next day, as it turned out, three of the men decided they had had enough and scaled the cliffs.

After passing through a series of thundering rapids, the remainder of the party reached the Colorado's confluence with the Virgin River. There, Powell called it quits for the season. Making his way to a Mormon settlement not far away across the mesa, he started back for Washington to raise money for another go at it.

Up on dry land, he learned that the three men who left him at the rapids had encountered a war party of Shivwit Indians and been killed. For Powell, this turned out to be something of a boon, for news of the murders reached Salt Lake City and stirred much interest in the expedition. The project had earlier received a somewhat similar boost when a strange frontier character named John Risdon, later jailed for a horse theft, had unaccountably spread a rumor that the entire party had been drowned and swept away by the river. Recognizing a good opportunity for headlines when he saw it, Powell embarked on a lecture tour calculated

Although he neglected to take a photographer on his first Grand Canyon expedition, Powell brought one on the second trip in 1872, reaping this vision of the awesome quarter-mile-deep Inner Gorge.

to increase his renown along with that of the river.

By the time he launched his next voyage, his money troubles were over, largely because of the publicity he had so astutely courted. Between 1870 and 1873 Congress appropriated $44,000 to finance his continued study of the river. By this time, his conception of the deportment befitting command of a scientific expedition had undergone some alteration. He no longer shot rapids as drenched and unclad as his crew. Instead, he adopted as his command post an armchair lashed to the center deck of the lead boat. There, above the flying spume, he gave his orders and signals or, when the waters were placid, sat enthroned above his men and read aloud to them soothing passages from *The Lady of the Lake* by Sir Walter Scott.

Powell's fame was always associated with his adventure on the river, but his real accomplishments were more solid than that. He had an original and discerning mind, best demonstrated in his major work of observation, the *Report on the Lands of the Arid Region of the United States*. Along with technical information, the report provided a brilliant essay on the ecological problems of the West. Powell argued that the large arid regions of the West could not support a dense population; he believed that an attempt to impose the small-farm pattern of the East on the arid lands would lead to disaster for the settlers, disruption of a fragile environment and spoliation of the land itself. In short, Powell urged an environmental approach to public land policies in the West: the nature of the land, not the nature of man, should dictate the way it was used.

After his adventures in the West, Powell succeeded Clarence King as Director of the United States Geological Survey and held the post for 14 years. He established the bureau as the principal agency for mapping and studying the American land and assaying its resources, a function that it still performs.

Of the four Great Surveys, that of the Army's Lieutenant Wheeler exerted the least impact upon the nation's physical development. This shortfall in useful result came about despite the fact that Wheeler covered far more territory than all his rivals together. He crossed and recrossed 175,000 square miles from the Mexican border to Oregon, from the Sierras to eastern Colorado.

The only really original accomplishment of Wheeler's decade of work from 1869 to 1879 was the re-sult of an act of God—an excruciating toothache that befell one of his aides, a certain Lieutenant William L. Marshall. In late November, 1873, while the surveying party was holed up for the winter in the San Juan Mountains, Marshall's jaw became so swollen that he was forced to live on gruel, which he sipped through his clenched teeth. The nearest dentist was in Denver, a long 300 miles away through the only known route, the Cochetopa Pass. But in his agony Marshall determined to find a shorter route to the city. The stricken man dimly recalled a depression in the mountains that he had noted, not very attentively, earlier in the season. Now he took a single companion and headed for the neglected mountain notch. He had, it turned out, followed a sound hunch, for that avenue today is known as Marshall Pass and it cuts fully 125 miles off the route to Denver.

By all rights, Lieutenant Wheeler's painstaking expeditions should have achieved much more than they did. As the embodiment of the Army's last hopes to retain a major role in the exploration of the West, he could and did requisition the very best in men and equipment. His labors were planned on the grandest possible scale: he was supposed to spend 15 years mapping out more than a million and a half square miles of Western lands. And his attitude toward the job seemed constructively unselfish; in 1871 he wrote, "the day of the path-finder has sensibly ended," suggesting that personal glory was not his goal.

Although Wheeler applied himself seriously to the vast surveying task that the Army had set for him, he spent much of his time reexploring portions of the Colorado plateau and the Grand Canyon region, in an effort to meet the competition of Hayden, King and Powell. This proved to be a costly error, for Wheeler soon found that he had picked the wrong men to tangle with. The three civilians openly regarded him as a trespasser in their private arenas of exploration. Strong-willed men all, they set out to destroy the officer's career. In 1873, Hayden announced to Wheeler's geologist, "You can tell Wheeler that if he stirs a finger or attempts to interfere with me or my survey in any way I will utterly crush him—as I have enough congressional influence to do so and will bring it to bear." Powell declared that Wheeler's maps were worthless (in fact, they were perfectly adequate), and Clarence

Another explorer of the Grand Canyon was
Lieutenant George Wheeler *(foreground),*
who traveled upriver into its gloomy battlements after this respite on the Colorado.

Gathering a diversity of data, Lieutenant Wheeler's survey party measured and photographed an inscription by a Spanish officer who in 1726 had carved his name and his mission into a bluff in New Mexico.

Lieutenant Wheeler's surveyors surmount the adobe ruins of Indian homes, built centuries earlier within the natural fortress of a cave situated 60 feet above the floor of Canyon de Chelly, in northern Arizona.

King's colleague James Terry Gardner said that Wheeler had "marched around and looked into but did not enter great regions as large as Connecticut and Rhode Island put together." In the end, the civilians induced Congress to order a cessation of mapmaking in the West by the Army in 1879. But by this time the Great Surveys were completed.

They had cost the United States taxpayer something over a million and a half dollars, divided thus: Hayden had spent $690,000; King, $387,000; Powell, $259,000; Wheeler, $550,000. In spite of the idiosyncrasies of the leaders, and their several kinds of flair for self-aggrandizement, the taxpayers' money was probably never better spent. When these four men were through, every nook and cranny of the West was known, and its commercial assets — as well as its liabilities — were fully recognized.

These final explorers of the West were the legatees of all who had gone before them, from Meriwether Lewis and William Clark onward. The progenitors of their profession were, of course, long vanished from the scene before the era of the Great Surveys. Lewis died untimely at 35 in 1809, while en route to Washington to edit the journals of the Corps of Discovery. In Tennessee, on a desolate stretch of the Natchez Trace, he had stopped for the night at a cabin in a lonely clearing. During the night two pistol shots rang out from his room, and in the morning his hostess, Mrs. Robert Grinder, found him dying. The first reports indicated that Lewis, who had been suffering spells of depression, had killed himself; later it was discovered that there

was only 25 cents on his body, and the rumor spread that he had been a victim of robbery and murder. Whatever the truth may be, Meriwether Lewis' end was ghastly, for with gaping wounds in his chest and head he fought death off through most of a night and into the next day. His last words were: "I am no coward, but I am so strong. It is so hard to die."

His old companion William Clark had a very different end, expiring peacefully in 1838. That year Hayden was nine, Powell four; and it would be another four years before King and Lieutenant Wheeler were born. At his death, full of honors, William Clark was U.S. Superintendent of Indian Affairs, a respected negotiator with the red brother, and his staunch friend.

A few durable men, who had been striplings on the frontier or just a-borning when Lewis and Clark went up the wide Missouri, were still around and active when the Great Surveyors were within a couple of years of completing the final roundup of Western knowledge. As late as 1865, the former mountain man Jim Bridger was showing General Grenville M. Dodge's surveyors how to punch the Union Pacific through the mountains to the coast. In his ripening years, Bridger formed a taste for written literature, although he could not read the stuff himself. From time to time he found ways to satisfy this hunger. It came on him, for example, in the winter of 1862-1863 at Fort Laramie where he was in the service of Captain J. Lee Humfreville. To pass the tedium of winter nights, the captain took to reading *Hiawatha* aloud to his guide.

"Bridger became very much interested and asked which was the best book that had ever been written," Humfreville noted. "I told him that Shakespeare's was supposed to be the greatest book. Thereupon he made a journey to the main road and lay in wait for a wagon train, and sought a copy from some emigrants, paying for it with a yoke of cattle. He hired a German boy at $40 a month to read to him. Bridger took great interest in reading, listening most attentively for hours at a time. It was amusing to hear Bridger quote Shakespeare. He could give quotation after quotation. Sometimes he seasoned them with a broad oath."

Two of Bridger's oldest friends among the mountain men were also still active in the West. Kit Carson had become an Indian fighter and an officer in the U.S. Army; he eventually died, famous and honored, in

1868. And Joe Walker, that indomitable composition of human rawhide, who had been six years old when the Lewis and Clark expedition headed west, continued to turn up everywhere.

After leaving Frémont in 1846, Walker had gone back into the horse trade, driving herds of horses eastward from California and selling them to the Army of the West. He also reconnoitered the country of the Colorado and Virgin Rivers, and in 1850 led a party to the Zuñi Indian villages in that region. In 1853 he testified before a California legislative committee, recommending his own Walker Pass as the prime candidate for a railway passage through the Sierra. The legislators did not adopt the route, but the pass continued to be a major artery for emigrant wagon trains.

In 1859 Walker was back in the field again as an Army scout, leagued with Kit Carson against the Indians. The military men he guided were amazed at his ability to sense the lay of the land ahead. Without previously having seen the line of march, he seemed always able to sketch what lay over the horizon, to smell out good grass and potable water.

As the '60s began, something seemed to set Walker thinking about the Southwest, particularly the rough country between the Gila and the Colorado Rivers, which he considered the last big "unexplored region in the territory of the Republic." He showed up in southern Colorado in the summer of 1862 with a party of gold prospectors, pledged to lead them through that virgin wilderness. Walker and the prospectors headed south through Raton Pass, entering New Mexico in October. There they were joined by a 24-year-old prospector named Daniel Conner, who later wrote a lively account of Walker's last adventures.

By then, the veteran was 64 years old but, except for failing eyesight, he was still a remarkably fit man. Conner gives the impression that the members of the party were awe-struck and admiring, well aware that they were traveling in the charge of one of the legendary heroes of the Old West.

Near Santa Fe, the party was briefly caught up in the hysteria of the Civil War. An officious cavalryman in the command of General James Carleton, leader of the Union forces in those parts, "came up to within twenty paces in 'big' style and informed Capt. Walker that his men would have to take the oath of allegiance

to the United States before they would be permitted to proceed further." To Conner's intense relief—for he had been run out of Colorado for his Confederate sympathies—Walker coolly refused to heed the upstart. "I have known Carleton for many years and have had many games of euchre with him," Walker advised the soldier, "but had I known he was not coming I should not have waited nearly a week for a pass, simply because I can take these men and pass anywhere in this wilderness without fear or favor. I only waited here to be courteous to my old friend." So saying, he rode on.

Near what became Deming, New Mexico, the party ran low on water, but Walker was undismayed. He told the men he had passed that way many years before and recollected the whereabouts of a good spring to the southwest. After two more dry days, Conner wrote, there was "much anxiety felt, if not expressed, as to our old Captain's doubtful guess at the true position of a spring after the expiration of thirty years." But on the third day, they came to the foot of a parched, unpromising mountain, and Walker told Conner and four others to begin climbing; near the summit they would find the spring, facing a large flat stone. He warned them, too, to keep an eye peeled for Apaches; water was scarce in this dry country and all manner of men came to it. To their astonishment, the thirsty men found the spring exactly as Walker had described it and got down on their bellies and drank deeply.

Walker's warning about Indians was soon verified in grisly fashion. A little farther on, the party glimpsed a wisp of smoke and then found "three white men who had been crazy enough to attempt a passage alone to California. They were hanging by their ankles all in a row to a horizontal piñon limb. Their hands were tied behind them and their heads hung to within a foot of the ground and a little fire had been built directly under each head. The skin and hair was burned off their skulls, giving them a ghastly appearance as they swung there perfectly naked."

In the spring of 1863, Joe Walker produced his last mystical feat of divination. As he had found beaver, mountain passes, wagon and rail routes, he now led the prospectors to gold. He turned north from the present site of Wickenburg, Arizona, through what came to be called Horse Thief Basin, and finally to the confluence of the Hassayampa River and Lynx Creek. The gold was there, and it panned out at a rich $4.80 the pan. Quite possibly, Walker had known of its presence much earlier but had not been moved by it. He shared the views of Jim Bridger who had said, "They found gold everywhere in this country in those days, but thought it unworthy of their notice to mine for it, as beaver (then worth $8 the pound) was the best paying gold they wanted to mine for in the creeks and rivers."

Others did care, though, and Lynx Creek was soon booming. That summer, the miners acclaimed Walker the first president of their settlement. It was the first public office he had been offered since he had been elected sheriff of Independence back in 1827. Joe declined; apparently his body and spirit were not yet resigned to sedentary occupations.

But the toll of time could not be staved off forever. In 1867 he had his last adventure when the Lynx Creek settlement ran out of food. Though nearly blind by then, he started off for a trading post, La Paz, nearly 200 miles away, taking Daniel Conner with him. It was in Joe Walker's cards that there had to be one more hairbreadth escape from violent death. It came when a pair of Mexican outlaws jumped Conner unawares. Though he was unable to see clearly, all of Walker's instincts and reflexes were fully operative. He drew and fired, driving the bandits off. The fact that he had gotten into the mess in the first place, however, seemed to convince Walker that his powers had declined and soon, depressed, he left Arizona to spend his last years on a nephew's ranch in Contra Costa County, California.

Conner expressed the West's farewell to Joe Walker. "This was the kindest man I ever knew," he wrote, "considering the desperate chances which he had been constantly taking for thirty years amongst the savages, burning deserts, and bleak snows. Brave, truthful, he was as kindly as a child, yet occasionally he was even austere. I was but a boy and he kept me out of dangerous places without letting me know it or even how it was done." The West paid an enduring tribute to him in place names — Walker Pass, Walker Lake, Walker River, Walker Trail, Walker Mining District, all of them his gifts to other men.

In the summer of 1876, gone entirely blind, Walker looked back through his memories and summed them up for a California reporter. Not surprisingly the emphasis

was upon the frontiersman's first necessity — survival.

"How about Sioux Indians? They are numerous and in numbers only they are very formidable, for I have always considered them inferior to many other tribes. I have fought better Indians than the Sioux with odds five to one against me and the position of their own choosing. And I still wear my hair."

Joe Walker's spirit quit at last on October 27, 1876. He was just short of 78 years old when he died and was buried at Martinez, California, under an epitaph that included these lines:

BORN IN ROAN CO. TENN.
DEC. 13, 1798.
EMIGRATED TO MO. 1819.
TO NEW MEXICO, 1820.
ROCKY MOUNTAINS, 1832.
CALIFORNIA, 1833.
CAMPED AT YOSEMITE,
NOV. 13, 1833.

The epitaph scarcely did justice to the scope of this extraordinary man's life. He had seen the West in all of its incarnations. When Walker first headed out beyond the Mississippi, the West was still a land of mystery, a blank place on the maps. As a mountain man and explorer, he helped fill in that blank space; as a believer in Manifest Destiny he had fought to make the Far West part of the United States, and as an emigrant guide he had brought settlers to the shores of the Pacific. During the climactic decades of the Western saga, he was at one time or another an Indian fighter, an Army scout, a gold seeker and even a cattleman — for he ran his own successful spread in Monterey County during the 1850s and lived to see the day when millions of steers pastured on the Great Plains.

Joe Walker survived Kit Carson by eight years; Jim Bridger would survive Walker by less than five, dying peacefully on a Missouri farm on July 17, 1881.

They were the last of the first. Within their lifetimes, the West was discovered, mapped to its farthest corners, and inventoried almost to the last rock, spring and patch of grass. After three quarters of a century, there was no need for their like to come again. It was all found and laid ready for the generations ahead to make use of, if they could summon up some part of the wisdom and courage that had made it all possible.

New perspective on the big country

By the end of the 1870s, the last veil was stripped from the face of the West. In place of the tantalizing and sometimes scarcely credible tales of the early trailblazers, and the very personal views of painters, stood the voluminous scientific reports of the Great Surveys, as well as a growing body of actual photographs. But if the mystery of the West had faded, its awesome proportions remained to impress many a traveler and settler who ventured there.

No one was more impressed than the photographers who came West with the postwar surveyors. To emphasize the scale of the terrain, they used a vintage trick of landscape painters by often including human figures in their images. Thus composed, their pictures of harsh alkali flats, fantastic rock formations and tumultuous waterfalls —shown here and on the following pages—provide an admission of human insignificance in this vast land. But the photographs also serve as a manifesto, declaring that man has come to confront—and to explore—the unknown.

Men and wagons, including O'Sullivan's rolling darkroom, are dwarfed by the Nevada desert.

In central Colorado, William Henry Jackson photographed these massive towers sculpted by wind-blown sand.

221

A member of the Powell expedition of 1871 peers into a defile sliced through solid rock by a tributary stream of the Escalante River.

Devil's Anvil makes a kingly roost for two of Wheeler's men 3,000 feet above the mighty Colorado in this portrait of the Grand Canyon.

O'Sullivan recorded the Snake River's Shoshone Falls and described the scene as "one of nature's greatest spectacles."

Jackson posed an assistant under the spout of Teapot Rock, a bizarre butte near the Green River in Wyoming.

Two of King's men, one a mere speck on the alkali flat *(center right)* in Little Soda Lake, explore the Nevada desert.

Chapter I: excerpts from *Journals of Lewis and Clark,* Bernard DeVoto, ed., copyright 1953 by Bernard DeVoto. Reprinted by permission of Houghton Mifflin Company. Chapter II: 56,57 — Beaver quote courtesy The Hudson's Bay Records Society, London; 68,69 — Sage quotes from *This Reckless Breed of Men,* by Robert Glass Cleland, Alfred A. Knopf, Inc., 1952, pp. 20-21, 33-34; 72 — Gregg quote from *This Reckless Breed of Men,* by Robert Glass Cleland, Alfred A. Knopf, Inc., p. 47; 72,74,77 — Zenas Leonard quotes from *Adventures of Zenas Leonard Fur Trader,* edited by John C. Ewers, new edition copyright 1959 by the University of Oklahoma Press. Chapter III: 91,101, 106,110-111 — excerpts from *Adventures of Zenas Leonard Fur Trader,* edited by John C. Ewers, new edition copyright 1959 by the University of Oklahoma Press. Chapter IV: 127 — Brackenridge quote from *Early Western Travels, 1748-1846,* 32 vols., edited by R. G. Thwaites, The Arthur H. Clark Company, 1904-1907, Vol. VI, p. 102; 135,138 — Dana quotes from *Thomas Nuttall, Naturalist,* by Jeannette E. Graustein, Harvard University Press, 1967, pp. 316-317; 143 — Catlin quotes from *Exploration and Empire,* by William H. Goetzmann, Alfred A. Knopf, Inc., 1971, p. 188, and *George Catlin and the Old Frontier,* by Harold McCracken, The Dial Press, 1959, p. 14.

Chapter V: 161,162,164,166,172 — Charles Preuss quotes from *Exploring With Frémont: The Private Diaries of Charles Preuss, Cartographer for John C. Frémont on His First, Second, and Fourth Expeditions to the Far West,* by Charles Preuss, translated and edited by Erwin G. and Elisabeth K. Gudde. Copyright 1958 by the University of Oklahoma Press. Chapter VI: particularly useful source for the Great Surveys was *Great Surveys of the American West,* by Richard A. Bartlett. Copyright 1962 by the University of Oklahoma Press: quotations reprinted by permission of the publisher; 192,197 — Jackson quotes from *Time Exposure: The Autobiography of William Henry Jackson,* by William Jackson, Cooper Square Publishers, Inc.,1970, pp. 215,217,218; 212 — Hayden quote from *Exploration and Empire,* by William H. Goetzmann, Alfred A. Knopf, Inc., 1971, p. 479; 214 — Humfreville quote from *The Mountain Men and the Fur Trade of the Far West,* LeRoy Hafen, ed., Vol. 6, The Arthur H. Clark Company, 1968, p. 99; 216,217 — quotes from *Joseph Reddeford Walker and the Arizona Adventure,* by Daniel Ellis Conner, the University of Oklahoma Press, 1956, pp. 13,27,28,200,201; 217 — Walker quote from *The West Wind: The Life Story of Joseph Reddeford Walker,* by Douglas Watson, Johnck and Seeger, Printers, 1934, p. 107.

The sources for the illustrations in this book are shown below. Credits from left to right are separated by semicolons, from top to bottom by dashes.

Cover: Herb Orth for LIFE, *The Trapper,* Charles Deas, courtesy Yale University Art Gallery, The Mabel Brady Garvan Collection. 2 — Courtesy Missouri Historical Society. 6,7 — *The Chasm of the Colorado, Thomas Moran* — courtesy U.S. Department of the Interior. 8,9 — *Buffaloes Crossing the Yellowstone,* Charles Wimar — courtesy Washington University Gallery of Art, St. Louis. 10,11 — *Wasatch Mountains, Wind River Country, Wyoming,* Albert Bierstadt, New Britain Museum of American Art, John B. Talcott Fund. 12,13 — Paulus Leeser, courtesy Rare Book Division, The New York Public Library, Astor, Lenox and Tilden Foundations. 14 — Courtesy The Kirby Collection of Historical Paintings, Lafayette College, Easton, Pennsylvania. 16 — Courtesy The Huntington Library, San Marino, California. 17 — Map by Rafael D. Palacios. 20 — Paulus Leeser, courtesy Prints Division, The New York Public Library, Astor, Lenox and Tilden Foundations. 21 — Courtesy Rare Book Division, The New York Public Library, Astor, Lenox and Tilden Foundations. 22,23 — Courtesy Scala, owned by Dienst voor's-Rijks Verspreide Kunstvoorwerpen on loan to the Frans Hals Museum, Haarlem. 25 — Detail of portrait, courtesy The National Gallery of Canada, Ottawa, photo by Wellard — map by Rafael D. Palacios. 27 — Courtesy Independence National Historical Park Collection, Philadelphia. 28 through 32 — Rare Book Division, The New York Public Library, Astor, Lenox and Tilden Foundations. 34,35,36 — Henry B. Beville, courtesy Library of Congress. 37 — Courtesy Missouri Historical Society. 38 — Courtesy The Botany Department of The Academy of Natural Sciences of Philadelphia — courtesy Missouri Hist. Soc.; courtesy The Academy of Natural Sciences of Philadelphia. 39 — Courtesy The Academy of Natural Sciences of Philadelphia. 40 — Dan Bernstein, from Rapho Guillumette, courtesy the Museum of Comparative Zoology, Harvard Univ., Cambridge — courtesy the American Philosophical Society Library. 41 — Courtesy The Academy of Natural Sciences of Philadelphia. 42,43 — Courtesy Missouri Historical Society; The Peabody Museum, Harvard University, Cambridge, courtesy American Heritage Publishing Co.; Hillel Berger, courtesy The Peabody Museum, Harvard University, Cambridge. 44 — Courtesy Oregon Historical Society — courtesy The New-York Historical Society. 45 — Courtesy The Henry Francis du Pont Winterthur Museum. 46,47 — Alfred Jacob Miller, courtesy Northern Natural Gas Company Collection, Joslyn Art Museum, Omaha, Nebraska. 48,49 — Arthur Tait, *American Frontier Life,* courtesy Yale University Art Gallery, Whitney Collection of Sporting Art. 50,51 — Courtesy The Bancroft Library, University of California at Berkeley. 52 — Reproduced with the permission of The Hudson's Bay Company. 54 — Peter Rindisbacher, courtesy The Public Archives of Canada. 55,56, 57 — Reproduced with the permission of The Hudson's Bay Company. 58 — Courtesy Oregon Historical Society. 59 — Paulus Leeser, courtesy American History Division, The New York Public Library, Astor, Lenox and Tilden Foundations. 62 — Paulus Leeser, courtesy Art and Architecture Division, The New York Public Library, Astor, Lenox and Tilden Foundations; courtesy The New York Public Library, Astor, Lenox and Tilden Foundations. 63 — Paulus Leeser, courtesy Art and Architecture Division, The New York Public Library, Astor, Lenox and Tilden Foundations. 64 — Courtesy Missouri Historical Society. 65 — Courtesy Western History Department, Denver Public Library. 66, 67 — George Caleb Bingham, from the collection of The Detroit Institute of Arts, gift of Dexter M. Ferry. 70 — Courtesy The Bancroft Library, University of California at Berkeley — Frank Lerner, courtesy General Research and Humanities Division, The New York Public Library, Astor, Lenox and Tilden Foundations. 71 — Frank Lerner, courtesy General Research and Humanities Division, The New York Public Library, Astor, Lenox and Tilden Foundations. 73 — Paulus Leeser, courtesy American History Division, The New York Public Library, Astor, Lenox and Tilden Foundations. 74 — Courtesy Lower Fort Garry National Historic Park — Gerald R. Brimacombe, courtesy Lower Fort Garry National Historic Park. 75 — Herb Orth for LIFE, from *Wilderness Kingdom: The Journals and Paintings of Nicholas Point, S.J.* Translated by Joseph P. Donnelly, S.J. Copyright (c) 1967 by Loyola University Press, Chicago. Reproduced by permission of Holt, Rinehart and Winston, Inc. 76 — Map by Rafael D. Palacios. 78,79 — Alfred Jacob Miller, courtesy Northern Natural Gas Company Collection, Joslyn Art Museum, Omaha, Nebraska. 80 — Courtesy Library, The State Historical Society of Colorado. 81 — Courtesy American Heritage Publishing Company. 82 — Courtesy The Kansas State Historical Society, Topeka. 83 — Courtesy Photographic Collections — Museum of New Mexico. 84 — Courtesy Oregon Historical Society. 85 — Courtesy State Historical Society of Missouri. 86 — Courtesy State Historical Society of Wisconsin. 87 — Courtesy Oregon Historical Society. 88,89 — *Captain Walker and His Squaw,* Alfred Jacob Miller, courtesy Northern Natural Gas Company Collection, Joslyn Art Museum, Omaha, Nebraska. 90 — Richard Henry, courtesy Map Division, Library of Congress. 91 — *Joe Walker,* Alfred Jacob Miller, courtesy Joslyn Art Museum, Omaha, Nebraska. 92,93 — Paulus Leeser, *Green River,* Alfred Jacob Miller, courtesy The Walters Art Gallery, Baltimore. 95 — Courtesy Western History Department, Denver Public Library. 96 — Courtesy The Kansas State Historical Society, Topeka. 98,99 — Copied by Lee Boltin. 102 — Courtesy Independence National Historical Park Collection, Philadelphia — courtesy The Bancroft Library, University of California at Berkeley. 103 — From Records of the Office of the Chief of Engineers, National Archives Building, Washington, D.C. — map by Rafael D. Palacios. 104,105 — Courtesy Rare Book Division, The New York Public Library, Astor, Lenox and Tilden Foundations. 107 — Rich Clarkson, courtesy Newspaper Collection, Missouri Historical Society. 108,109 — *Yosemite Winter Scene,* Albert Bierstadt, courtesy University Art Museum, Berkeley, gift of Henry D. Bacon. 112,113 — Courtesy The Peabody Museum, Harvard University, Cambridge. 114,115 — *Horse Race,* Erneste Narjot, courtesy Oakland Art Museum, Oakland, California. 115 — *Lassoing a Bear,* James Walker, courtesy Denver Art Museum. 116,117 — *Fandango,* Charles Nahl, courtesy E. B. Crocker Art Gallery, Sacramento, California. 118,119 — Karl Bodmer, Paulus Leeser, courtesy Rare Books Division, The New York Public Library, Astor, Lenox and Tilden Foundations. 120,121 — John James Audubon, courtesy The New-York Historical Society, New York City. 122 — Courtesy Biohistorisch Instituut, Utrecht, Netherlands. 123 through 126 — Paulus Leeser, courtesy General Research and Humanities Division, The New York Public Library, Astor, Lenox and Tilden Foundations. 127 — Lee Boltin, this picture has been reprinted from a book in the collection of The American Museum of Natural History Library. 128,129 — Ivan Massar from Black Star, photographs and reproductions with permission of the Director, Gray Herbarium of Harvard University; Dan Bernstein, from Rapho Guillumette, photographs and reproductions with permission of the Director, Gray Herbarium of Harvard University. 131 — Courtesy Northern Natural Gas Company Collection, Joslyn Art Museum, Omaha, Neb. 132 through 135 — Karl Bodmer, Paulus Leeser, courtesy Rare Book Division, The New York Public Library, Astor, Lenox and Tilden Foundations. 136,137 — John James Audubon, Paulus Leeser, courtesy Stuart Collection, Rare Book Division, The New York Public Library, Astor, Lenox and Tilden Foundations. 138 — John James Audubon, courtesy Private Collection. 140,141 — John James Audubon, Paulus Leeser, courtesy Stuart Collection, Rare Book Division, The New York Public Library, Astor, Lenox and Tilden Foundations. 144 — George Catlin, Paulus Leeser, courtesy Rare Book Division, The New York Public Library, Astor, Lenox and Tilden Foundations. 145 — George Catlin, courtesy Rare Book Division, The New York Public Library, Astor, Lenox and Tilden Foundations. 146 — George Catlin, Paulus Leeser, Rare Book Division, The New York Public Library, Astor, Lenox and Tilden Foundations. 147 — George Catlin, courtesy Thomas Gilcrease Institute of American History and Art. 148 — George Catlin, Paulus Leeser, courtesy Rare Book Division, The New York Public Library, Astor, Lenox and Tilden Foundations. 149 — George Catlin, courtesy Thomas Gilcrease Institute of American History and Art. 150 — George Catlin, Paulus Leeser, courtesy Rare Book Division, The New York Public Library, Astor, Lenox and Tilden Foundations. 151 — George Catlin, courtesy Thomas Gilcrease Institute of American History and Art. 152,153 — *The Rocky Mountains,* Albert Bierstadt, courtesy The Metropolitan Museum of Art, Rogers Fund, 1907. 154 — Culver Pictures. 158 — Courtesy Chicago Historical Society. 159 — *Manifest Destiny,* John Gast, courtesy H. T. Peters Jr. Collection. 160 — *Jessie Benton Frémont,* T. Buchanan Read, J. R. Eyerman, courtesy of Southwest Museum, Los Angeles, California. 162 — Courtesy Independence National Historical Park Collection, Philadelphia. 164,165 — Paulus Leeser, courtesy American History Division, The New York Public Library, Astor, Lenox and Tilden Foundations. 167 — Camera Lucida drawing, Joseph Drayton, courtesy Rare Book Division, The New York Public Library, Astor, Lenox and Tilden Foundations. 168,169 — Office of the Chief of Engineers, National Archives Building, Washington, D.C. 170 — The Bettmann Archive. 174 — Courtesy U.S. Military Academy Archive — Paulus Leeser, courtesy American History Division, The New York Public Library, Astor, Lenox and Tilden Foundations. 175 — Paulus Leeser, courtesy American History Division, The New York Public Library, Astor, Lenox and Tilden Foundations. 176 through 181 — Paulus Leeser, courtesy Economic and Public Affairs Division, The New York Public Library, Astor, Lenox and Tilden Foundations. 182,183 — William H. Jackson, courtesy Collection International Museum of Photography at George Eastman House. Photographs on pages 184 through 188,190, 192,193,194,195,196 — Courtesy National Archives: 184,185 — E. O. Beaman. 186,187 — Timothy O'Sullivan. 188,190,192,193, 194,195,196 — William H. Jackson. Photographs on pages 198 through 201 — Courtesy Collection International Museum of Photography at George Eastman House: 198,199 — William H. Jackson. 201 — Timothy O'Sullivan. 202,203 — Timothy O'Sullivan, courtesy National Archives. 205 — Timothy O'Sullivan, from the James D. Horan Civil War and Western Americana Collection. 207 — John K. Hillers, courtesy United States Geological Survey. 208,209 — John K. Hillers, courtesy Western History Department, Denver Public Library. 210,211 — John K. Hillers, courtesy National Archives. 213 — Timothy O'Sullivan, courtesy Library of Congress. 214,215 — Timothy O'Sullivan, courtesy Collection International Museum of Photography at George Eastman House. Photographs on pages 218 through 221 — Courtesy Collection International Museum of Photography at George Eastman House: 218,219 — Timothy O'Sullivan. 220,221 — William H. Jackson. 222 — John K. Hillers, courtesy United States Geological Survey. 223 — William Bell, courtesy Library of Congress. 224,225 — Timothy O'Sullivan, from the James D. Horan Civil War and Western Americana Collection. 226, 227 — William H. Jackson, courtesy National Archives. 228,229 — Timothy O'Sullivan, courtesy Collection International Museum of Photography at George Eastman House.

Alter, J. Cecil, *James Bridger, Trapper, Frontiersman, Scout and Guide: A Historical Narrative.* Shepard Book Company, 1925.

American Heritage, Editors, *The American Heritage History of the Great West.* American Heritage Publishing Co., Inc., 1965.

Audubon, John J., *Audubon: Watercolors and Drawings,* Edward H. Dwight, ed. The Pierpont Morgan Library, 1965.

Bannon, John Francis, ed., *The Greatest Real Estate Deal in History: The Louisiana Purchase—1803.* Saint Louis University, 1953.

Bartlett, Richard A., *Great Surveys of the American West.* University of Oklahoma Press, 1962.

Billington, Ray Allen:

The Far Western Frontier 1830-1860. Harper & Row Publishers, Inc., 1956.

Westward Expansion: A History of the American Frontier. The Macmillan Company, 1967.

Carson, Kit, *Kit Carson's Autobiography.* University of Nebraska Press, 1966.

Catlin, George, *Letters and Notes on the Manners, Customs and Conditions of the North American Indians,* Vols. I and II. Dover Publications, Inc., 1973.

Chambers, William Nisbet, *Senator from the Old West: Thomas Hart Benton.* Russell & Russell, 1970.

Chittenden, Hiram Martin:

The American Fur Trade of the Far West, 3 vols. F. P. Harper, 1902.

Yellowstone National Park. University of Oklahoma Press, 1971.

Cleland, Robert Glass, *This Reckless Breed of Men: The Trappers & Fur Traders of the Southwest.* Alfred A. Knopf, Inc., 1950.

Coats, Alice, *The Plant Hunters.* McGraw-Hill Book Company, 1970.

Conner, Daniel Ellis, *Joseph Reddeford Walker and the Arizona Adventure.* University of Oklahoma Press, 1956.

Cutright, Paul Russell, *Lewis & Clark: Pioneering Naturalists.* University of Illinois Press, 1969.

Dale, Harrison Clifford, *Ashley-Smith Explorations and the Discovery of a Central Route to the Pacific, 1822-1829.* The Arthur H. Clark Co., 1941.

Darrah, William Culp, *Powell of the Colorado.* Princeton University Press, 1969.

DeVoto, Bernard:

Across the Wide Missouri. Houghton Mifflin Company, 1947.

The Course of Empire. Houghton Mifflin Company, 1962.

The Journals of Lewis & Clark. Houghton Mifflin Company, 1953.

Dillon, Richard H.:

Meriwether Lewis. G. P. Putnam's Sons, 1968.

"Stephen Long's Great American Desert." *Montana Magazine of Western History,* Summer 1968.

Duffus, Robert L., *The Santa Fe Trail.* Tudor Publishing Company, 1930.

Dupree, A. Hunter, *Asa Gray.* Harvard University Press, 1959.

Emory, William H., *Lieutenant Emory Reports: A Reprint of Lt. W. H. Emory's Notes of a Military Reconnaissance,* Calvin Ross, ed. University of New Mexico Press, 1951.

Felton, Harold W., *Jim Beckwourth, Negro Mountain Man.* Dodd, Mead & Co., 1970.

Ford, Alice, ed., *Audubon's Animals: The Quadrupeds of North America.* The Studio Publications, Inc., in association with Thomas Y. Crowell Company, 1951.

Franchère, Gabriel, *Adventure at Astoria, 1810-1814.* University of Oklahoma Press, 1967.

Frémont, John Charles:

Memoirs of My Life. Belford, Clarke & Co., 1887.

Report of the Exploring Expedition to the Rocky Mountains. University Microfilms, subsidiary of Xerox Corp., 1966.

Gass, Patrick, *Journals of the Lewis & Clark Expedition.* Ross & Haines, Inc., 1958.

Goetzmann, William H.:

Army Exploration in the American West, 1803-1863. Yale University Press, 1965.

Exploration and Empire. Alfred A. Knopf, Inc., 1971.

Graustein, Jeannette E., *Thomas Nuttall, Naturalist: Explorations in America, 1808-1841.* Harvard University Press, 1967.

Gregg, Josiah, *The Commerce of the Prairies,* Max Moorhead, ed. University of Oklahoma Press, 1958.

Hafen, LeRoy, ed., *The Mountain Men and the Fur Trade of the Far West,* Vols. I-IX. The Arthur H. Clark Co., 1965-72.

Hollon, Eugene W.:

The Great American Desert. Oxford University Press, 1966.

The Lost Pathfinder—Zebulon Montgomery Pike. University of Oklahoma Press, 1970.

Horan, James D., *Timothy O'Sullivan: America's Forgotten Photographer.* Doubleday & Company, Inc., 1966.

Hulbert, Archer Butler, ed., *Southwest on the Turquoise Trail: The First Diaries on the Road to Santa Fe.* Overland to the Pacific Series, Vol. II, 1933.

Irving, Washington, *The Adventures of Captain Bonneville, U.S.A. in the Rocky Mountains and the Far West,* Edgeley W. Todd, ed. University of Oklahoma Press, 1961.

Jackson, Clarence S., *Picture Maker of the Old West: William H. Jackson.* Charles Scribner's Sons, 1971.

Jackson, Donald, ed., *Letters of the Lewis and Clark Expedition with Related Documents, 1783-1854.* University of Illinois Press, 1961.

Jackson, Donald, and Mary Lee Spence, eds., *The Expeditions of John Charles Frémont: Travels from 1838-1844 & Map Portfolio,* Vols. I and II. University of Illinois Press, 1970.

Jackson, William, *Time Exposure: The Autobiography of William Henry Jackson.* Cooper Square Publishers, Inc., 1970.

King, Clarence, *Mountaineering in the Sierra Nevada.* University of Nebraska Press, 1970.

Kurz, Rudolph F., *Journal of Rudolph Friederich Kurz,* J. N. Newitt, ed. University of Nebraska Press, 1970.

La Farge, Oliver, and Arthur N. Morgan, *Santa Fe: The Autobiography of a Southwestern Town.* University of Oklahoma Press, 1959.

Larpenteur, Charles, *Forty Years a Fur Trader on the Upper Missouri.* The Lakeside Press, 1933.

Leonard, Zenas, *Adventures of Zenas Leonard Fur Trader,* John C. Ewers, ed. University of Oklahoma Press, 1959.

Lewis, Meriwether, and William Clark, *History of the Expedition Under the Command of Lewis & Clark,* Vols. I-III, Elliott Coues, ed. Dover Publications, Inc., 1965.

McCracken, Harold, *George Catlin and the Old Frontier.* Dial Press, 1959.

McDermott, John Francis:

Audubon in the West. University of Illinois Press, 1970.

Travelers on the Western Frontier. University of Illinois Press, 1970.

McKelvey, Susan Delano, *Botanical Exploration of the Trans-Mississippi West, 1790-1850.* Anthoensen Press, 1955.

Mackenzie, Alexander:

Exploring the Northwest Territory, T. H. MacDonald, ed. University of Oklahoma Press, 1966.

Voyages from Montreal . . . to the Frozen Pacific Oceans in the Year 1789 and 1793, with an Account of the Rise and State of the Fur Trade, 2 vols. The Courier Press, Ltd., 1911.

Malone, Dumas, *Jefferson the President: First Term, 1801-1805.* Little, Brown & Company, 1970.

Meigs, William M., *The Life of Thomas Hart Benton.* Da Capo Press, Inc., 1970.

Merk, Frederick, *Manifest Destiny and Mission in American History.* Alfred A. Knopf, Inc., 1963.

Morgan, Dale L.:

Jedediah Smith and the Opening of the West. University of Nebraska Press, 1964.

ed., *The West of William H. Ashley.* Old West Publishing Company, 1964.

Neuberger, Richard L., "Bloody Trek to Empire," *American Heritage,* Vol. IX, No. 15, August 1958.

Nevins, Allan, *Frémont: Pathmarker of the West,* Vols. I and II. Ungar, Frederick Publishing Company, 1961.

Oregon Writers' Project, *Oregon: End of the Trail.* Binfords & Mort Publishers, 1951.

Phillips, Catherine Coffin, *Jessie Benton Frémont: A Woman who made History.* John Henry Nash, 1935.

Phillips, Paul C., and J. W. Smurr, *The Fur Trade,* 2 vols. University of Oklahoma Press, 1967.

Porter, Mae Reed, and Odessa Davenport, *Scotsman in Buckskin.* Hastings House Publishers, Inc., 1963.

Powell, John Wesley:

The Exploration of the Colorado River and Its Canyons. University of Chicago Press, 1957.

Report on The Lands of the Arid Region of the U.S. Harvard University Press, 1962.

Preuss, Charles, *Exploring with Frémont,* translated and edited by Erwin G. and Elizabeth K. Gudde. University of Oklahoma Press, 1958.

Rittenhouse, Jack D., *The Santa Fe Trail: A Historical Bibliography.* University of New Mexico Press, 1971.

Ross, Marvin C., *The West of Alfred Jacob Miller.* University of Oklahoma Press, 1951.

Russell, Carl P., *Firearms, Traps & Tools of the Mountain Men.* Alfred A. Knopf, Inc., 1967.

Sandoz, Mari, *The Beaver Men.* Hastings House Publishers, 1964.

Sibley, George C., *Road to Santa Fe: The Journal and Diaries of George Champlin Sibley,* Kate L. Gregg, ed. University of New Mexico Press, 1952.

Smith, Henry Nash, *Virgin Land.* Harvard University Press, 1970.

Sprague, Marshall, *A Gallery of Dudes.* Little, Brown & Company, 1967.

Sunder, John E.:

Bill Sublette, Mountain Man. University of Oklahoma Press, 1959.

The Fur Trade on the Upper Missouri, 1840-1865. University of Oklahoma Press, 1965.

Thwaites, Reuben Gold, *Early Western Travels, 1748-1846,* 32 vols. The Arthur H. Clark Co., 1904-1907.

Wallace, Edward S., *The Great Reconnaissance.* Little, Brown & Company, 1955.

Watson, Douglas, *The West Wind: The Life Story of Joseph Reddeford Walker.* Johnck and Seeger, Printers, 1934.

Weber, David J., *The Taos Trappers: The Fur Trade in the Far Southwest.* University of Oklahoma Press, 1971.

Wilkins, Thurman:

Clarence King: A Biography. The Macmillan Company, 1958.

Thomas Moran: Artist of the Mountains. University of Oklahoma Press, 1966.

Winther, Oscar Osburn, *The Old Oregon Country: A History of Frontier Trade, Transportation and Travel.* University of Nebraska Press, 1969.

ACKNOWLEDGMENTS

Michael Bell, Public Archives of Canada, Ottawa; Ruth Brown, The Academy of Natural Sciences, Philadelphia; Nellie C. Carico, U.S. Geological Survey, Washington, D.C.; Mrs. Maud Cole, Rare Book Room, The New York Public Library, New York City; Lee Dolton, Supervisory Park Ranger, El Morro National Monument, Ramah, New Mexico; William Dooley, U.S. Geological Survey, Washington, D.C.; Wilson Duprey, The New-York Historical Society, New York City; Richard Finnegan, M. Knoedler and Company, New York City; Dr. Samuel L. H. Fuller, Invertebrate Zoologist, Limnology Department, The Academy of Natural Sciences, Philadelphia; James Goodrich, State Historical Society of Missouri, Columbia; Gail Guidry, Missouri Historical Society, St. Louis; Archibald Hanna, Curator, Yale University Western Americana Collection, New Haven, Connecticut; Janet Hargett, National Archives, Washington, D.C.; Mrs. Fred Harrington, Librarian, Missouri Historical Society, St. Louis; Milton Kaplan, Library of Congress, Washington, D.C.; Jerry Kearns, Library of Congress, Washington, D.C.; Dennis Longwell, George Eastman House, Rochester, New York; Tom Lovcik, The Museum of Modern Art, New York City; Leona Morris, State Historical Society of Missouri, Columbia; Arthur L. Olivas, Photographic Archivist, Museum of New Mexico, Santa Fe; Martha Pilling, The Academy of Natural Sciences, Philadelphia; Mrs. Mary Rabbitt, U.S. Geological Survey, Washington, D.C.; Emily Rauh, Curator, St. Louis City Art Museum, St. Louis; Paula Richardson, National Anthropological Archives, Smithsonian Institution, Washington, D.C.; Elizabeth Roth, Prints Division, The New York Public Library, New York City; Murphy Smith, Librarian, American Philosophical Society, Philadelphia; Arthur Spencer, Oregon Historical Society, Portland; Mrs. Florence Stadler, Archivist, Missouri Historical Society, St. Louis; George Talbot, Iconography, Wisconsin Historical Society, Madison; Dr. John Barr Tompkins, Curator of Pictorial Collections, The Bancroft Library, University of California, Berkeley; William Treuttner, National Collection of Fine Arts, Washington, D.C.; Donald Tuohy, Curator of Anthropology, Nevada State Museum, Carson City; Paul Vanderbilt, Retired Curator, Wisconsin Historical Society, Madison; Thomas Vaughan, Director, Oregon Historical Society, Portland; Pat Walker, The Museum of Modern Art, New York City; Dr. Richard C. Wood, Director of Pacific Center for Western History Studies, University of the Pacific, Forest Grove, Oregon.